Denali Justice

By Peter A. Galbraith

Published by Peter A. Galbraith 2014

denalijustice@gmail.com

Book cover design and formatting services by BookCoverCafe.com

First Edition 2014

ISBN:
978-0-9906076-0-1 (pbk)
978-0-9906076-1-8 (ebk)

Map illustration by Mary Rostad

Bradford Washburn image: #3236 *Head of Kahiltna Glacier and west face of Mt. McKinley. Alaska: August 1949.*

LICENSOR:
Decaneas Archive
295 Endicott Ave.
Revere, MA 02151

LICENSEE:
Peter A. Galbraith

West Buttress photo: Bradford Washburn image #3236. Head of Kahiltna Glacier and west face of Mt. McKinley, Alaska: August 1949

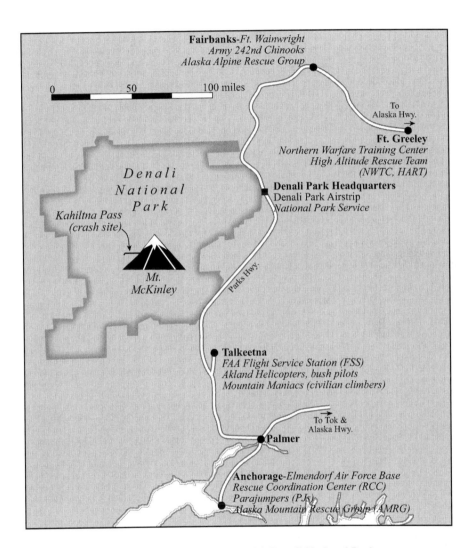

Map of Southcentral Alaska with Denali National Park

Contents

Maps and Photos

Inscription

"I am impressed with the mental stability of Mr. Clouser. I believe many individuals would not have retained their sanity or their ability to function as human beings after living through this."

— U. S. District Court Judge Andrew J. Kleinfeld, oral decision in *Clouser and Scanlon vs. United States of America.*

Dedication

Mike Clouser dedicates this book to Pat Scanlon with the inscription, "To the real hero, who died on the mountain."

The author dedicates this book to Mike Clouser and to Tom Scanlon, brother of Pat Scanlon.

Foreword

This book tells the true story of a December, 1981 airplane crash and rescue on Mt. McKinley in Denali National Park, Alaska. The events were the subject of a civil trial and the story unfolds primarily through sworn testimony at trial. No names have been changed.

At 20,320 feet, Mt. McKinley is the highest peak in North America. Many Alaskans call the mountain by its native name, Denali, which means "the Great One." In 1980, Congress changed the name of Mount McKinley National Park to Denali National Park but left the name of the mountain unchanged. Kahiltna [Kah-hilt-nah] Pass, on the west flank of Mt. McKinley, blends into the mountain at 10,300 feet. The rescue is referred to as the Mt. McKinley rescue or the Kahiltna Pass rescue.

For brevity, clarity, and reading pleasure, many shortcuts are taken with the trial transcript. See *Appendix 1*.

An attorney who participates in a trial is not an ideal narrator. Thanks to childhood exposure to oral storytelling, I believe it is better to tell a compelling story imperfectly than not at all. I express my deep thanks to Mike Clouser and to Tom Scanlon for permitting this story to be told.

Chapter 1

Clouser I

At 11 a.m. on Tuesday, April 7, 1987, Mike Clouser was called as a witness in *Clouser and Scanlon vs. United States of America.* As he slowly walked from counsel table to the witness stand in the federal courthouse in Anchorage, Alaska, his gait reflected the amputations of all of his toes and substantial portions of both feet. When he placed one hand on the Bible and raised the other hand into the air to be sworn as a witness, the amputations of significant portions of all of his fingers were plainly visible.

Clouser would be 37 in June. He was unemployed and lived in Darlington, a town of 800 people in central Indiana. Mike testified that in early December, 1981, he helped a friend, Patrick Scanlon from nearby Clark's Hill, Indiana, drive Pat's pickup truck up the Alaska Highway to Talkeetna [Tal-keet-nah], Alaska.

In Talkeetna, Pat showed Mike photos from two sightseeing flights around Mt. McKinley in the summer of 1981. Mike expressed interest. When they ran into pilot Ed Hommer at the bar of the Fairview Inn on Monday night, Ed proposed a flight for $40 each. "Then the next morning, [Ed] called and said today would be a good day, do you want to go?" They told him yes. The purpose of the flight on Tuesday, December 15, 1981, was "sightseeing, take pictures." Mike had never been in a small plane before. Previous mountain climbing experience? "None whatsoever."

33 color prints, 3" x 5" in size and taken by Clouser on the sightseeing flight, were admitted into evidence. (The judge was provided a set of original color prints; there was no jury.) The first photo showed the loading of the red and white Hudson Air Service Cessna 185, with the other three passengers

standing around. Using a photograph, Mike described how his friend Pat Scanlon was dressed that morning. "He had on a two-piece snowsuit, vapor barrier boots or bunny boots, . . . blue jeans, . . . a flannel shirt, and . . . long johns of some kind." The same photo showed the aircraft's rear seat on the ground with survival gear piled around it, including sleeping bags and a parka.

Standing next to the witness stand (and with the U.S.A.'s attorney, Tara Neda, also standing nearby), I guided Mike through the first roll of film, 24 photographs. These established the weather (blue sky with some high, thin clouds), who was sitting where (Mike was in the right front passenger seat with Pat seated behind him; the third passenger, Dan Hartmann, brother-in-law of the pilot, Ed Hommer, sat in the left rear seat behind the pilot. Hartmann took a few of the photos with Mike's camera.), and the flight path. The judge interrupted to ask how cold it was when the plane took off. Mike asked for his trip diary, Exhibit 101, and answered it was 22 degrees just before takeoff.

As the photos progressed, the aircraft got closer and closer to Mt. McKinley. The last photo on the roll looked up Kahiltna Glacier towards Kahiltna Pass. The plane was flying at a low elevation south to north, up the Glacier, towards Kahiltna Pass on the west flank of Mt. McKinley.

Using a standard 1:50,000 scale Washburn map of Mt. McKinley, I asked Mike to trace the flight route and to locate the crash site. He answered, "Right where that red X is." The judge asked for the map and looked at it for some time.

When the first roll was finished, Mike changed film as fast as he could. The first two photos on the second roll showed the sunlit summit of Mt. McKinley with a lenticular cloud indicating north to south airflow. The third photograph, taken from Mike's right front seat, looked out the pilot's side (left side) and showed a disturbingly low horizon--Kahiltna Pass.

```
Q. Do you know where the aircraft was when you took
   [your last] photographs . . .

A. Approaching the Pass.

Q. What happened then?

A. I woke up and it was dark.
```

Q. Did you receive any warning that the airplane was going to crash?

A. No, I did not.

Q. So you were just sitting there taking pictures and it happened?

A. Right.

Mike had no recollection of the airplane flying through or over Kahiltna Pass. The crash occurred about 1:30 p.m. Mike was knocked out and had "a broken tooth and some cuts and bruises," but was not otherwise injured. Except for extreme frostbite and resulting amputations, Mike had no permanent injuries from the crash.

Q. What do you recall after the crash?

A. When I woke up it was dark and the tail of the plane was downhill, the nose of it pointing uphill. I was outside of the plane slightly uphill ahead . . . of the airplane. How I got there, I'm not really sure, that's just where I woke up. And Ed was out by the left side of the plane. The right wing was tore off and the left wing was sticking about straight up in the air. Most all of the glass was knocked out. One of the doors was tore off. And Dan Hartmann was out on the left side of the airplane. And we tried getting him in a sleeping bag. . . .

[I]t was obvious [Dan] was hurt real bad. He was in intense pain and bleeding. And every time we'd try to move him, it would hurt, and he kept fighting us off.

We finally got him in the sleeping bag, and he was just writhing around and we was afraid he was going to slide down the mountain, so I kicked out some depressions in the snow so we could plant his heels and then also for his rump to help keep him from sliding down. And somewhere along in there, I heard Pat groaning.

Mike went to his friend, Pat Scanlon, who was still inside the wrecked fuselage, and checked him over. The most obvious injury was the right leg, below the knee, where it "just took a turn to the left." Mike squeezed Pat's extremities, one by one. Pat had feeling in his left and right arms and he could feel his right leg above the break. Mike could not remember if he squeezed the left leg.

Q. Did you feel his neck or back?

A. We tried getting a sleeping bag underneath him, and as I did so, I could feel a lump in the small of his back, down in the small of his back –

Q. Do you know that for sure?

A. Not for sure.

Q. And did you think he had a broken neck or a broken back?

A. I suspected it, but I wasn't sure.

Q. What did you do, then, based upon that suspicion?

A. Just tried to get one sleeping bag underneath him and another on top of him.

Q. Did you succeed in getting a sleeping bag underneath him?

A. Yes, I did.

Q. And how about one on top of him?

A. Yes, I did, and rolled up I believe it was the tarp they used for the engine cover to make a pillow to go underneath his head because his head was below the rest of his body and he was real uncomfortable and I didn't feel safe trying to turn him around. . . . [T]he next best thing would be to just elevate his head a bit.

Mike repeated Pat's position. The aircraft tail was downhill, propeller uphill, and Pat was in the fuselage with his head downhill, towards the tail. Mike raised Pat's head a little to level out his body and it seemed to make Pat more comfortable.

All this time Ed was outside with his brother-in-law, Dan Hartmann.
When Clouser finished with Pat, he went to help with Dan.

> Dan was having a lot of pain, and he was
> delirious with pain, and he was thrashing about,
> and he'd unzip the sleeping bag and throw it
> open. Then he got out of those depressions and
> had slid down the hill a little bit, so we took
> the door that had broken off and jammed it down
> into the snow and propped it up against a tail
> wheel to prevent him from sliding down any farther.
> And eventually . . . [h]e got to thrashing around
> again and shortly after that, died.
>
> Q. If you can say, what happened to [the pilot, Ed
> Hommer] when Dan died?
>
> A. He went to pieces.
>
> Q. What do you mean by he went to pieces?
>
> A. He couldn't handle it, obvious. Just crying and
> screaming at him, says, you can't do this to me.
>
> Q. What did Ed do after that?
>
> A. Immediately after that? He just laid there beside
> him for awhile, set there for I don't know how
> long, quite some time.

The next thing Mike remembered was Pat Scanlon calling for him, so he
went back into the plane. Pat had worked his mittens off and said his hands
were cold. Mike put the mittens back on and tried to get Pat bundled up.

> And he wanted to know what had happened, and
> I told him we'd had a crash. He said, well,
> what kind of shape are we in? And I said, it's
> pretty bad. And he wanted to know how bad he was
> hurt. And I told him I suspected he had some
> internal injuries but I wasn't sure. And he
> wanted something to drink. I told him we didn't
> have anything to drink. . . . I'd had a ruptured
> intestine years before and knew that you wasn't
> suppose[d] to drink with that. I explained that

```
     to him. I said, you just need to lay still for
     now, so he tried.
Q.  What happened later Tuesday afternoon or evening?
A.  That cycle went off and on all night, but
     shortly after that was when we heard the
     plane overhead. . . .
```

Mike never saw the plane, but he could tell from the sound that it was big and it was searching for them, flying back and forth.

```
     I asked Ed if there was a flare gun on the
     plane, and he said there should be one in the
     survival kit can. . . . [And I] looked through the
     cans and couldn't find anything, so I took the
     cans to him and pulled items out one by one and
     said, is this a flare? Is this a flare? When I
     was all done, there was no flare.
Q.  Did you ask Ed Hommer to come over to where the
     survival kit was and find a flare?
A.  Yes, I did.
Q.  What was his response?
A.  No.
Q.  He wouldn't do that?
A.  He didn't say no, he just didn't do it.
Q.  So then you took the survival can over to Mr.
     Hommer?
A.  Right.
```

The survival cans were 10 to 12 inches on each side and 12 to 18 inches tall, with a 6 to 8 inch round opening on top. Mike went through all items in both cans and there was no flare. He did find a disposable flashlight. Mike sat on the slope "and leaned back and blinked it at the [big] airplane each time it came over." He could not tell if the airplane saw his light.

The weather Tuesday night was cold with breaks in the clouds, but no big breaks. "A fair amount of wind but it wasn't no blizzard or anything."

Later that night, he heard a second airplane that sounded just like the first and blinked the flashlight at it, too. He never saw the second plane, either.

Q. [W]hat was in the survival cans that were on board?

A. There was a sack of one type of candy – I believe they were called "Chewies." The other one was red and white. And some small, like Hershey Kisses or those little biddy Hershey bars, chocolate. There was a can of dehydrated peaches. A tin of sardines. Several of those little – they call them survival blankets. . . . They come packaged like a small package of tissues would, like four inches by three inches and a half inch thick or so.

THE COURT: Those little aluminum foil things? Look like foil?

THE WITNESS: Right.

    The disposable flashlight. There was a Swiss Army knife. A fish net. Some candles. Some windproof, waterproof matches. I believe three cans of Sterno. There was a pair of snowshoes on the plane, although they were not in those cans.

Mike did not try to light a Sterno can Tuesday night because "with that wing up in the air like that, everything around was soaked with aircraft fuel. I was scared to death of fire. . . ."

The aircraft also carried four sleeping bags and a parka. Mike put on the parka and wore it for the next four days.

Q. What happened to the four sleeping bags?

A. The first one got blew away that very first night.

Q. How did that happen?

A. After Dan Hartmann died, Ed was trying to get in it and he just shook it like that and it filled with wind just like a windsock and off it went. . . . The other two were below and on top of Pat Scanlon.

Q. And then there is a fourth sleeping bag?

A. Dan Hartmann was in one, one got blown away, one underneath Pat and one above Pat.

Q. So Ed Hommer wasn't trying to get in the sleeping bag that Dan Hartmann had been in, he was trying to get into another sleeping bag?

A. Right.

Q. Was there a stove on the aircraft?

A. No, there was not.

Q. A tent?

A. No, there was not.

Q. An ice ax?

A. Not that I remember.

Q. Shovel?

A. No, there was not.

Q. Extra boots?

A. No.

Q. Socks?

A. No.

Q. Any food other than the candy bars and the sardines and peaches you've described?

A. None that I am aware of.

Q. Was there a canteen full of water, or any liquid?

A. No.

Mike was dressed about the same as Pat Scanlon. He wore long johns with thermal underwear, cotton socks with wool socks over them, blue jeans, flannel shirt, two-piece snowmobiling suit, wool sock hat. Unlike Pat, he did not have bunny boots. Mike wore what he called imitation sorrels with a rubber bottom, then leather from the ankles up, with a wool felt liner. He had on a pair of gloves called hot liners. "They were real thin, got metallic thread. A pair of cotton work gloves and a pair of mittens."

Q. What happened Tuesday night and Wednesday morning? Where did you sleep?

A. I tried not to sleep. I stayed outside the plane that night. . . . I stayed out there and sit there and smoked a cigarette and –

Q. Did you have a lighter with you? A cigarette lighter?

A. Yes, I did.

Q. Did you smoke more than one cigarette?

A. No.

Q. Why not?

A. I dropped the lighter and the cigarette trying to light the second one and the lighter and the pack of cigarettes went sliding down the mountain [over the cliff to Peter's Basin].

Q. Anyway, you tried to stay up all night?

A. Yes, I did.

Q. Did you have any conversations with Pat Scanlon or Ed Hommer?

A. I would call out to them at various times through the night to try to keep them awake.

Q. Why were you trying to do that?

A. Because I'd always heard if you get cold like that and you fall asleep there's a good chance you're not going to wake up. To sleep is to die, to quote Jack London.

Tuesday night Pat and Ed were in the plane and Mike was outside. Pat worked his gloves off several times. Mike would rub Pat's hands to warm them and then put the gloves back on. Mike thought it was 5 to 10 below with wind gusts up to 30 mph. It did not snow. As morning approached, the wind "died down a bunch."

Q. What happened Wednesday morning?

> A. Right around daybreak there was a little plane
>   come . . . as I'm sitting there on the snow with
>   the plane beside me and Kahiltna Pass up there
>   behind me, I heard a plane come through, [Ed came
>   outside], and we seen it come through and it came
>   out, made a big wide turn over Peter's Basin and
>   come flying back at us. And I waved at it and it
>   tipped its wings back and forth to wave back and
>   flew around a little bit, you know, did that, I
>   don't know, half a dozen times or so. . . .

Mike did not know who was in the plane. There was enough light to see it was red. He heard Hommer say, "Be careful up there Doug." It was cold with very little wind. About an hour and a half to two hours later, another red plane appeared, similar to the first.

After a break for lunch, court resumed at 1:18 with Clouser on the stand. When the red airplane spotted them at daybreak Wednesday, Mike asked Ed what he thought would happen. "[Ed] said that usually they'd send [an Army] Chinook helicopter." When daylight arrived, Mike could see the surrounding area for the first time. Behind and uphill perhaps 200 or 300 feet above them was the summit of Kahiltna Pass, topped by a huge snow cornice. In front and downhill about 150 feet was a cliff dropping to Peter's Basin, 2000 feet below. The slope where the fuselage rested was steep. The snow on the slope was "kind of crusty, but it didn't take much to leave a footprint in it." The temperature was around zero. Between the arrival of the first red airplane and the Army Chinooks, the wind was "5 to 10 mile an hour, maybe."

Mike did not wear a watch. He estimated the Chinooks, approaching from the north, showed up a little over two hours after the first red airplane. One Chinook set down on Peter's Basin, far below, while the other flew up to the crash site. This first Chinook hovered twice. With Mike facing north, looking down towards the second Chinook on the floor of Peter's Basin, the first Chinook hovered in front of Mike "maybe 50 feet over and 100 feet up."

> Q. Could you say whether it was within the
>   dimensions of this courtroom, or was it further
>   away than that?

A. No, it was a little farther than that. . . .

Q. Can you give an estimate of how far in front of you it was?

A. Out direct, 50 feet out this way, but over to the right.

Q. So it wasn't directly in front of you?

A. No. No, it was off to the right.

Q. And how high was it? Was it on your level, higher, or lower?

A. Higher.

Q. How much higher than you?

A. A hundred feet, I'd say.

Q. Do you think you could have hit it with a snowball?

A. Without a doubt.

Q. How long did the Chinook hover there?

A. Close to a minute, I'd say.

Q. What did it do?

A. Just hovered.

Q. What did you do while it hovered?

A. Said, come on down, Buddy. I wanted it to do something other than hover there and I held out my arms and – [Gestures with "come here" motion] . . .

Q. Could you see the people flying the Chinook?

A. You could make out helmets. I could not see faces. . . .

The first Chinook then disappeared over the Pass above and behind them. Mike described the maneuvers of the first Chinook around the summit and on the south side of the Pass, where it could be heard but not seen. The next time Mike saw the Chinook, "it appeared to me that it was attempting to set down on that cornice [at the summit]. It just lowered right down towards it."

Q. How close did it get to the cornice . . . ?

A. From my angle, it appeared to be about five feet
   or so.

Q. What, if anything, did you do?

A. Waved him off.

Q. Why did you do that?

A. I was afraid if he sat down on that cornice, that
   he'd break the cornice off and cause an avalanche
   and take us and the plane and everything over
   that cliff.

Q. Do you know, and you may not, whether the pilot
   could see you waving it off?

A. I don't know. . . .

Q. How long did it hover at the Pass or the cornice?

A. . . . I'd say less than a minute.

The first Chinook disappeared south over the Pass again, then came
north over the Pass to Mike's left, "and then it went through the Pass and
[departed to the south]." With the first Chinook gone, the second Chinook
lifted off from Peter's Basin, "and it seemed like it did a little bit of flying
around but not a lot and then disappeared off to the north the way it came."
The second Chinook did not get any closer "than a quarter of a mile or so."

Q. Did either of these helicopters drop anything?

A. No.

Q. Did they [provide] any assistance to you of
   any kind.

A. None whatsoever.

Q. How long would you say the helicopters were in
   your view, from when you first saw them or heard
   them, and answer that however you want, to when
   they left?

A. Somewhere in the vicinity of half an hour.

Q. While they were there, did Ed Hommer tell you
   these were Chinooks?

A. Yes.

Q. Do you recall at the time what you expected them
   to do?

A. I was expecting them to lower a hoist or
   something and winch us off there. . . . That or at
   least drop something out to us or whatever.

After the Chinooks left, Mike talked with Pat Scanlon. "He could hear them and everything and then when he couldn't hear them, he wanted to know what was going on. Ed and I told him they were checking out other angles. We didn't think they was coming back." But Mike did not tell that to Pat. He wanted to keep his spirits up. Wednesday afternoon and evening, Mike continued to put Pat's mittens back on when he worked them off and tried to keep him comfortable. He gave Pat a small snowball and told him to put it under his tongue and to let it melt. "He was wanting a drink real bad." And, "[I]t seems like I gived him a couple of pieces of candy, but I can't say for sure." When the Chinooks left, the wind "had picked up a good bit."

Q. How was the wind the remainder of [Wednesday] at
   the crash site?

A. Kind of just steadily got worse. . . . [B]y dark
   it was really howling.

Q. How about Wednesday night?

A. It just continued to get worse.

Q. How strong do you think the wind was on
   Wednesday night?

A. Sixty, 80 mile an hour, I would say. You couldn't
   hardly stand up in it. . . .

   The wing was sticking up like a sail, and it
   would go one way and then the other just rocking
   back and forth, and then eventually the wing tip
   went down into the ground . . . and the plane
   slid downhill. It seemed like a hundred feet but

in reality it was only a plane length or so. And
the tail wheel finally dug in and stopped the
slide. And when it stopped, Pat went sliding
through the door into the rear luggage area.

When the plane started sliding in pitch black darkness, Mike "thought
we was going over that cliff."

Q. When the wind started blowing, where [are] you?

A. Sitting crosswise in the plane and trying to keep
Pat from rocking around.

Q. Where [is] Ed Hommer?

A. He was in the tail section back with the cables
and everything. . . .

Q. Where is Pat?

A. Still laying parallel with the center line of
the airplane with his head downhill just like
he was. . . .

Q. Where are you?

A. Sitting crossways, perpendicular to the center
line of the plane. . . .

Q. So Pat was laying underneath your legs and you
were propped over him?

A. That's correct. . . .

Q. As the plane was rocking, was it throwing Pat
Scanlon back and forth in the fuselage?

A. Somewhat, yeah. I wouldn't say throwing back and
forth, but he was rolling around with it. . . .

Q. You've said the plane slid and Pat moved. [What
position did Pat end up in?]

A. He was on his stomach, face down, with his head
and everything through that doorway into the rear
section of the plane up to about his hips or so.

Q. Before the sliding, had Pat been on his back?

A. Yes, he had.

Q. So it had turned him onto his stomach?

A. That's correct.

Q. And slid him down in the airplane?

A. Right.

Q. What did you do then?

A. He begged me to try to get him out. So I tried pulling him out and he –

Q. What was your evaluation of the position he was in?

A. I didn't think I could leave him like that.

Q. Why not?

A. Well, he'd been with his head downhill, I felt like, long enough, and he was more uncomfortable there than he was before, he was more exposed, and I stuck –

Q. Did you talk about it with Ed Hommer?

A. I asked Ed to help me to move him and all and –

Q. Did he agree that moving him was a good idea?

A. I guess. I don't remember him saying that we shouldn't move him.

Q. Did you try to move him?

A. Yes, we did.

Q. [What happened?]

A. Well, first I tried by pulling on his coat tail for to drag him back out, and I told Pat – I says, you're heavy, pal. I says, you're going to have to help us. And we didn't get very far, and kept running out of breath and have to stop and take a break. And –

(Pause.) [Mike was near tears.]

THE COURT: Mr. Clouser, any time you need a recess, just say so.

THE WITNESS: I tried to get hold of his pant legs. I thought maybe that would work, you know, had those bibs on, and told him again, I says, give a push, Pat. And we'd get him about six inches and –

Q. Did Pat give a push?

A. It felt like it. Well, at the same time, he kind of groaned or screamed, whatever you want to call it. Then we took another break and I apologized to him for not being able to help him any more. And he says, don't worry about it, it's just all part of the fun.

(Pause.)

And then he died.

Q. He died during that break while you were resting right after he'd moved?

A. Yes.

Q. Had you done anything with your mittens while you were trying to move Pat?

A. I took them off trying to get a better grip on him, on his clothes, whatever. That nylon material is real slick, and with mittens on, you couldn't get a good grip on it. So I took them off to try to get a better grip. And I never could find them after that. You couldn't even see your hand in front of your face.

[Mike was crying now.] . . .

Chapter 2

Christmas 1981 Press Reports

In the early 1980s, Anchorage had a population of roughly 250,000. Prosperous from the building of the Trans-Alaska Pipeline in the mid-1970s, the city supported two newspapers. The larger, the afternoon Anchorage Times, was locally owned. The morning paper, the Anchorage Daily News, was owned by The McClatchy Company, parent of the Sacramento Bee. The Anchorage Daily News won the Pulitzer Prize for Public Service in 1976 and in 1989. The two newspapers competed vigorously on local stories.

The first mention of an airplane crash with survivors on Mt. McKinley appeared Thursday morning, December 17, 1981 in the Anchorage Daily News. Headlined "**Winds stymie rescue of McKinley plane crash victims**," the Associated Press story reported rescue efforts would resume Thursday to reach a downed Cessna 185 with four persons aboard spotted at the 10,300 foot level of Kahiltna Pass on the slopes of Mt. McKinley, 55 miles northwest of Talkeetna. A Federal Aviation Administration [FAA] spokesperson said the single-engine plane was reported overdue Tuesday afternoon when it failed to return from a sight-seeing trip to Mt. McKinley. An Air Force C-130 homed in on the Cessna's emergency locator beacon after dark on Tuesday afternoon and spotted lights. Lights were also seen by a second C-130 flight Tuesday evening. The Cessna 185 was owned by Hudson's Flying Service and the pilot was identified as Ed Hommer, all of Talkeetna, Alaska. No passengers were identified.

There were unconfirmed reports that at least one survivor was spotted near the downed plane Wednesday. National Park Service [NPS] spokesperson Joan Gidlund said, "They (rescuers) did see one person waving . . . and they thought they saw two people sitting near the aircraft." Two high-altitude Army Chinook helicopters were driven away from the wreckage Wednesday by winds." They couldn't even get close enough to drop anything to them," said Gidlund. Attempts to reach the victims were suspended at darkness Wednesday because of 50-knot winds and poor visibility. The temperature at the crash site was expected to drop to zero Wednesday night. Air Force rescue personnel said plans called for a six-man volunteer civilian climbing party to be inserted below the plane at first light Thursday, weather permitting.

Friday morning, December 18, the Anchorage Daily News carried another AP report under the headline "**Helicopter crew spots plane crash survivors.**" The story reported that on Thursday afternoon an Army Chinook helicopter got through a break in the clouds and spotted the plane and three people, but air turbulence prevented the crew from dropping a hoist. Meanwhile, a six member Talkeetna based rescue team had been inserted on Kahiltna Glacier and was climbing up towards the crashed plane, but was not expected to reach the victims before midday Friday. A special eight-man Army high-altitude climbing team from Ft. Greely near Fairbanks had been flown to Talkeetna and was to be put on the mountain Friday, weather permitting.

The Mt. McKinley crash received national attention. The newspaper in Crawfordsville, Indiana, carried a Friday UPI story headlined "**Blizzards on mountain halt rescue attempt.**" It reported an Army Chinook helicopter dropped six volunteer civilian climbers at 7000' on Thursday and they were climbing to the crash site at 10,300'. An FAA spokesperson said it was necessary to reach the site "within the next 12 to 14 hours" for a rescue to be successful. NPS spokesperson Gidlund was quoted saying: "It is not a pleasant climb. It's a glacier with deep crevasses. They are also dealing with whiteout conditions. It could be as much as two days before they reach them."

Saturday morning, December 19, the Anchorage Daily News headlined "**Climbers in headlamps try daring night rescue on windswept glacier.**" In a story by Ed Truitt, the newspaper reported that at dark Friday the six volunteer Talkeetna climbers reported being within one and a half miles of the plane crash. Led by Art Mannix, the rescue team reported they were sending ahead two or three climbers wearing headlamps to try to reach the victims during the night. The other climbers were Keith Nyitray,

George Ortman, Mark Bloomfield, Brian McCullough and Ron Garrett. Chuck Hudson, son of Hudson Air Service owner Cliff Hudson, said the aircraft carried only enough food to last one person a week. He did not know what survival gear was on the plane. The passengers were identified as the pilot's brother-in-law, Dan Hartmann, 29, and Pat Scanlon, 25, and Mike Clouser, 30.

On Sunday morning, December 20, the Anchorage Daily News headlined "**Two survive ordeal on glacier.**" The story by John Lindback and Ed Truitt reported the volunteer Talkeetna climbers reached the crash site on Mt. McKinley shortly after noon Saturday and found two victims dead and two suffering from severe frostbite and hypothermia. The dead were identified as Dan Hartmann and Pat Scanlon, both of Talkeetna. The survivors were Mike Clouser, of Darlington, Indiana, and the pilot, 26-year-old Ed Hommer. Both were suffering from frost-bitten hands and feet, hypothermia, and abrasions and contusions. With the help of two climbers, Clouser walked through waist-deep snow to a waiting helicopter. Hommer rode in a sled towed by four climbers. After being flown to Anchorage, both were listed in serious condition late Saturday.

The crashed Cessna 185 initially came to rest on the north side of Kahiltna Pass about 200 yards below the summit. In a windstorm Wednesday night, the wrecked plane slid further downhill to within 150 feet of a 2000-foot cliff. "I am getting information now that the first person died the first night [Tuesday] and the second fatality died the second night [Wednesday]," said NPS spokesperson Gidlund.

Also on Sunday, a front page story in the Anchorage Times, written by Patti Epler and Ellis E. Conklin, reported that no survival gear was dropped from rescue aircraft. An Air Force spokesperson said: "There was no way to get close to the site because of the turbulence and cloud cover. We couldn't even see (the plane)."

On Monday, December 21, a front page story in the Anchorage Daily News written by Ed Truitt and headlined "**Rescuers were quick to respond**" reported that the volunteer Talkeetna climbers organized in one hour on Wednesday afternoon. They were flown by an Army Chinook to "the usual staging area for McKinley climbs, not far below Kahiltna Pass," but the helicopter did not land. It returned to Talkeetna Wednesday night. On Thursday morning, the weather was worse and the six civilian climbers were dropped off "at least 10 miles" from the crash site. The climbers, known as the "Mountain Maniacs," encountered whiteout conditions on Thursday and Friday. "Headlamps were useless. We had better luck putting our nose to the compass and guessing. Finally we gave up and . . . dug a huge hole for the tents so we wouldn't blow away," Ron Garrett said. When Saturday dawned clear, three climbers went ahead to the crash site while the others broke camp. Following directions from a National Park Service Ranger who had flown over the wrecked plane, Art Mannix found two survivors at the crash site.

> *"It was a joyous meeting," said Mannix. . . ." They had been eating snow and chocolate bars. They didn't have a stove to melt snow. They were both dehydrated and suffering from bruises and frostbite.*
>
> *"Both of them told me they hallucinated a lot during the four nights they were stranded on the mountain. Mike told me he thought he saw a cabin just a few yards away and he had to stop himself from walking over to it," Mannix said. . . .*

Central Indiana newspapers identified Mike Clouser, 31, as an unmarried mechanic and an orphan who was raised by his aunt and uncle. The aunt, Julia Clouser, said, "He's a strong person." The Indiana press reported that Pat Scanlon was from Clarks Hill, Indiana, not Talkeetna, and quoted a neighbor saying Pat and Mike had driven up the Alaska Highway. Pat was looking for work, but Clouser planned to leave Christmas Day. Patrick Scanlon was unmarried, lived with his parents, and worked as a railroader and farmer.

On Friday, Christmas Day, the front page of the Anchorage Times featured a long interview with Ed Hommer headlined **"Pilot tells story of ill-fated McKinley flight."** (Clouser declined to be interviewed.) In the story by Ralph Nichols, Hommer said the crash was caused by a severe downdraft and that he did not warn his passengers before impact.

> *The three passengers apparently weren't aware of the danger they were in, and Hommer didn't take time to explain the situation "because I knew in the next five seconds all hell was going to break loose." . . .*
>
> *After the impact, they were all unconscious for an hour or more, he continued. . . . [I]t was almost dark when Hommer first*

became aware of his surroundings on the glacier. "It was kind of like something out of a silent film festival with images fading and reappearing, but without sound," he said.

"I remember I was standing outside the plane, but I don't remember getting out of my seat or the plane. . . . [T]he next thing I remember is Mike working with my brother-in-law Dan trying to put him in a sleeping bag."

When Hommer reached his brother-in-law, Clouser left to tend to Pat Scanlon, still inside the wrecked fuselage.

"I was on my hands and knees talking to Dan," Hommer said. "He complained a lot of pain. . . . I knew he was in very critical condition, but I couldn't accept it. I screamed at him that he couldn't die, that he had no right to die."

"I told him that Sandy (Hommer's wife)[and Dan's sister] was having a child in January, and that he would have a new niece or nephew," Hommer said. "He kept saying 'I know' and 'I love you.' I started clearing the snow from his face. He was tossing and turning. I hugged him and told him I loved him."

"He was fighting for life, but he just died," Hommer said.

Hartmann's death came within hours of the crash. . . .

Meanwhile, Mike Clouser worked to make Pat Scanlon, suffering from multiple fractures and internal injuries, as comfortable as possible. The plane rested on a 10 to 15 degree slope, tail downhill, and Scanlon was lying with his head towards the tail, downhill. Neither Hommer nor Clouser wanted to turn Scanlon around in the cramped space because they feared compounding his injuries. "Mike did a good job of stabilizing Pat," Hommer said. That night Hommer stayed inside the plane with Pat, while Clouser walked around outside. 'All through the night he kept calling . . . us by name until we answered. He was worried that we would fall asleep and freeze."

Early Wednesday morning, a Cessna 185 piloted by Doug Geeting of Talkeetna Air Taxi flew over the crash and signaled to the survivors. Later, two Army Chinook helicopters arrived, but "wind conditions were too severe to allow a rescue by helicopter." On Wednesday night, all three men stayed in the fuselage. Hommer was in the tail section and Clouser was in the front, with Scanlon stretched out between them, head downhill towards the tail. With wind gusts of up to 60 mph, the plane rocked loose and began sliding downhill. They knew that below them was a several thousand foot cliff. They thought the plane was going to slide over the cliff. The sliding stopped when the tail wheel and part of the left wing jammed into the snow. The plane now rested on a 30-35 degree slope, dropping Scanlon's head even farther below the rest of his body. Even so,

> "[H]e did not complain. He would moan a little, but he was never hysterical. He was so damned level-headed it was uncanny," Hommer said.
>
> Scanlon asked Hommer and Clouser to move him. For more than an hour, they tried to push Scanlon [uphill] closer to the front of the plane, but with no success. When they apologized, Scanlon said, "'Hey, don't worry about it . . . everything's going to work out. It's all part of the plan,'" Hommer said. "Pat also said, 'It's just part of the fun.'" Scanlon was very tired after this, so they paused to rest. "When we started to try again, he didn't say anything . . . he just died quietly," Hommer said.

While trying to move Scanlon, Hommer's feet became tangled in the cables at the tail of the plane. In freeing his feet, Ed pulled his boots off without knowing it. Exhausted, he fell asleep on top of Scanlon's body. The next morning, standing outside the fuselage, Ed discovered he was not wearing boots.

For the next two days, Hommer and Clouser stayed in the plane "talking and discussing life and death and Dan and Pat--and praying. God, we prayed. We prayed all day long." They were able to melt only one cup of snow for the two of them. They ate candy bars and snow. They were also hallucinating. "Our mental state was pretty shaky. The visions were quite real." Of the rescue by the Talkeetna climbers, Hommer said, "It was just joy like I had never known or experienced in my life before."

On February 8, the Indianapolis Star, in a story by James A. Gillaspy, reported that both of Ed Hommer's feet had been amputated. Clouser was reported to be recovering from amputations of parts of his fingers and feet. Hommer was quoted saying, "I think the thing that kept Mike going was that he's a real strong person." Mike Clouser refused to be interviewed, saying, "I'd just as soon get it all behind me. I lost a good friend up there and I feel like I owe his family that much respect."

Chapter 3

1982

In December, 1981, I had been practicing law in Anchorage for six years, most recently as a sole practitioner. My wife closely followed the press reports. On Saturday, the day of the rescue, she looked out at Mt. McKinley, visible in sunlight far to the north. When Pat Scanlon's name was printed, she recognized him as Tom's brother.

I first met Tom Scanlon in a low-stakes Friday night poker game. He was easy company, a good addition to any game. I knew Tom had a high paying job for Sohio on Alaska's North Slope. He lived in Talkeetna, 100 miles north of Anchorage, where he owned the Fairview Inn, an old hotel and bar he had placed on the National Historic Register. As he prospered, Tom enticed his siblings to move to Alaska. I had represented a Scanlon family member on several occasions, with good results.

It was not surprising to hear from Tom shortly after New Year's Day, 1982. Still grieving over his brother's death, he asked that I talk to a survivor, Mike Clouser. Mike called from the burn unit at Providence Hospital on January 6. He was extremely susceptible to infection so a telephone conversation was the best we could do. I answered general questions and he gave me background information.

Dr. Mills, the frostbite doctor, told Mike he would lose 1/2 of his right foot, 1/3 of his left foot, and the tips or more of most of his fingers. He would be in the hospital until early March. Clouser had been visited by an insurance adjuster, who said the insurance was only $100,000 and the hospital bill "would eat that." Mike was 31, never married, no kids. He had good health insurance through his union. Mike would let me know when he could have visitors. I would not agree to represent him, nor he to hire me, until we met face-to-face.

On January 25, Clouser called to say he could have visitors. To see him in the burn unit, I donned a hospital gown over my suit, replaced my shoes with slippers, and put on a facemask like surgeons wear. Dressed in a green hospital gown and confined to bed, Mike was of medium height, somewhat thin, and had a thick black beard. He looked a bit like Abe Lincoln, but more handsome. We did not shake hands because Mike's fingers were partially mummified. From the last joint to the fingertip, the skin was shriveled and black. The doctors were letting his fingers heal as much as possible before amputating the dead parts. The amputations on his feet had already occurred.

Clouser had a deep voice and a direct, plainspoken way of speaking. He never talked fast. When Mike was less than certain, he said so.

Earlier, Ed Hommer had shared Mike's hospital room. To improve circulation, frostbite victims were encouraged to drink one or two beers a day. After drinking beer, Ed became angry and smashed a beer bottle against the wall. At Mike's request, Hommer was moved to another room.

I explained the potential defendants, the types of damages to which he was entitled, and how attorney's fees could be handled. The basic case was against the air taxi (pilot and owner) and its insurance. The fact of the crash established liability. Alaska law required air taxis to carry at least $100,000 per seat in liability insurance and Hudson carried only the minimum. Mike's case against the air taxi was so good it was questionable whether he needed a lawyer, especially on a contingency fee. I suggested a fee agreement providing for no attorney's fee on the first $100,000 (because he would get that money anyway), 100% of the next $10,000, and then a percentage of amounts over $110,000.

We did not go into detail about events on the mountain, but I was struck by Mike's indignation at the Army Chinooks. I mentioned that the federal government might be liable under the Federal Tort Claims Act (FTCA).

Clouser could next see me on February 9. He signed a contingency fee agreement accepting my fee proposal. Although substantial portions of his fingers had been amputated, Mike could still sign his name--his thumb and index finger were the least frostbitten.

The Scanlon estate did not become a client until later. Pat Scanlon died without a will and it took time to establish that Pat was an Alaska resident, open his estate, and have Tom Scanlon appointed personal representative.

I hired Gary Fye, a private investigator. A big man with a full gray beard and a quiet, friendly manner, Fye resembled Santa Claus more than Robert Mitchum. He would interview witnesses in Talkeetna and research Cliff Hudson's assets. Fye came up with a lead immediately. Dennis Brown, owner of Akland Helicopters in Talkeetna, was ready to fly to the crash site early Wednesday morning with Larry Rivers, a local guide. Supposedly Brown was denied permission to fly into Denali National Park to perform a rescue. Fye also took a recorded statement from Clouser in his hospital room on March 2, but the transcript was not finished until after Clouser departed Alaska.

On Saturday, March 6, after a stay of 11 weeks, Mike Clouser was discharged from Providence Hospital. He delayed flying to Indiana for one day so I could interview him. The two of us settled into my deserted law office and talked for hours.

Two days earlier, on March 4, I had interviewed Dr. Lindholm, the pathologist who performed Pat Scanlon's autopsy. Without mentioning this interview, I asked Mike if Pat was paralyzed. If rescuers had arrived early Wednesday morning, would it have been possible to extract Pat from the fuselage before the plane slid in the windstorm that night? These questions were difficult for Mike.

Mike's amputations left exposed bone on both of his feet and he needed plastic surgery in Indiana. Medical treatment on his fingers was essentially complete. Mike would not be able to return to his previous work, operating a paving machine in road construction, and he was to contact vocational rehabilitation in Indiana for retraining.

My legal research into rescue law was profoundly discouraging. Rescuers were almost never held liable. In addition to proving negligence, a victim had to prove the actions of the rescuers made things worse. The operable phrase was "worsened the victim's plight." A Coast Guard case illustrated the concept. Plaintiff was drifting in a boat without power. No other boats were near. A Coast Guard helicopter winched down a harness, began hoisting her up, and dropped plaintiff to her death. Negligence was established because the victim was improperly attached to the hoist. But was the victim worse off? It was not enough to point to her death because she might have died anyway (lack of nearby rescuers, drowning). The court found the victim's plight was worsened because the water was so shallow (under five feet) that the victim would not have drowned even if a rescue was long delayed.

When we finished, I drove Mike back to his motel. He flew to Indiana the next day. I did not know when I would see him again.

Under the Freedom of Information Act, the FAA provided a copy of its 22 page report on the Hudson crash, but it was of little use. Gary Fye obtained the log from the Rescue Coordination Center (RCC) at Elmendorf Air Force Base, which showed the exact time of many events in the rescue.

Fye travelled to Talkeetna in late March. He did not prepare a written report. Instead, we had a long telephone conversation and I took notes. Fye said he had never encountered so much hostility during an investigation. He was treated as a person up to no good. With so much ill will, he believed it would be a mistake to take witness statements. He took none.

Only Dennis Brown could be described as cooperative. Early Wednesday morning, Brown ordered an Akland helicopter readied to fly to Mt. McKinley. It was fueled and warmed up, with rotors turning. A big game guide named Larry Rivers brought bunny boots, thermal blankets, and other survival gear that was loaded on the helicopter. Brown said it was possible to land the Akland helicopter at the 10,300' summit of Kahiltna Pass, just above the crash site. He believed he and Rivers could have been in and out with the crash survivors by 10:30 a.m., an hour before the Army Chinooks showed up. Brown said he did not fly to Mt. McKinley because he was intimidated by Dick Hunze, an FAA employee at the Talkeetna Flight Service Station[FSS]. Hunze told Brown the crash was in Denali National Park and the rescue would be handled by the military. Brown was concerned that Akland Helicopters would lose its Park Service and military work if he criticized the rescue.

Fye interviewed Doug Geeting, a bush pilot who ran Talkeetna Air Taxi. While talkative, he lectured Fye on lawyers and lawsuits. On Tuesday evening, Geeting spoke to an Air Force C-130 pilot who gave him the Emergency Locator Transmitter (ELT) coordinates. Geeting took off in the dark early Wednesday morning and had no trouble finding the crash site. He radioed the McGrath Flight Service Station and asked them to call Denali Park Headquarters and the Rescue Coordination Center

(RCC) at Elmendorf Air Force Base in Anchorage. At first light, he saw survivors moving about. In daylight, he could see where the Hudson plane hit the south side of the summit of Kahiltna Pass and cart-wheeled over to the north side, ending up tail downhill. He estimated the wind to be a steady 10-15 mph and believed that if the Chinooks had arrived at daybreak, they could have had the victims out by 9:00 a.m. The Army helicopters could have landed without difficulty until 10:00 a.m. The wind increased at 10:30-11:00 and by 11:30 a.m., when the Chinooks arrived, they had missed their chance. Geeting attended a National Park Service rescue critique held in Anchorage in January, one month after the rescue.

Gary Fye also interviewed Ed Hommer, something he had not told me he was going to do. The Code of Professional Responsibility prohibits a lawyer from making direct contact with a person the lawyer expects to sue. Hommer was likely to be sued. Fye was my agent. When he took a recorded statement from Clouser, I was prepared to claim the attorney client privilege because when Clouser gave the statement to Fye, it was as if he was giving it to me. Similarly, when Fye interviewed Hommer, it was as if I interviewed Hommer. In my view, this was unethical. Fye told me what Hommer said and I made notes, filed them away, and did not look at them again.

Ed Hommer was also present when Fye interviewed Jim Okonek [awk-oh-neck], another bush pilot. Okonek had flown for Akland Helicopters, owned by Dennis Brown. He was not available to participate in the rescue because he was in Anchorage Tuesday night and Wednesday morning. Brown had told Okonek his story and Okonek's recollection was that Brown and Rivers were ready to fly at 8 a.m. but heard the Army was coming and decided not to go.

With an initial investigation complete, my focus turned to the air taxi's insurance. Clouser had been offered $100,000 in the hospital and the Scanlon estate would soon be offered the same. While the claims of both clients exceeded the available insurance, the Scanlon family waived my conflict of interest and stated its preference that Hudson's personal assets go only to Mike Clouser. It took several months to learn that these personal assets were not worth pursuing.

In late August, the Scanlon estate was offered $105,675 in full settlement. I recommended acceptance and Tom and his parents soon agreed. My opinion letter explained that an insurance settlement would not prohibit a later rescue claim against the federal agencies involved in the rescue, but made no recommendation on such a claim. The insurance money was paid in October.

Whether Clouser would accept the same insurance offer was unclear. A basic truth about any personal injury claim is the longer you wait, the more you get. Mike could not work pending more surgeries and was living on his savings. He could not hold out much longer. On May 16, Social Security denied his claim for disability benefits. On June 7, he was denied food stamps because he owned a used snowmachine. On July 1, his union notified him his health insurance would lapse because he had not worked enough hours. By mid-September, Mike had borrowed the last $1000 from his life insurance. His expenses were $500 a month and he would be broke by Thanksgiving.

My opinion letter advised that the liability of the air taxi was certain and damages were $750,000 to $1,000,000 on a good day and $300,000 to $400,000 on a bad day. Medicals exceeded $100,000. His union health insurance paid all of the hospital bill and 80% of the doctors' bills, but the unpaid 20% added up to a lot. Grateful for his medical care, Mike wanted to pay his doctors in full. If Mike accepted the offer, he would net about $80,000 after paying all medical bills. This would earn substantial interest, as money market accounts and bank certificates of deposit were paying 8% or more. While I recommended he authorize me to pursue a rescue claim, I asked him to assume he would live the remainder of his life on whatever he received from the air taxi settlement.

On October 7, Clouser rejected $105,675. He wanted to net $100,000 after paying all medical bills. We counteroffered for $25,000 more with an October 29 expiration. As that deadline approached, I sent Mike a draft complaint and asked for authorization to file suit against Ed Hommer and Cliff Hudson. (The insurance company could not be sued directly.) When Clouser granted authority, I filed suit in state court, not federal court. An answer was due by Thanksgiving.

On November 8, Mike entered an Indiana hospital. Two days later, a portion of his back muscle was removed and grafted on to his right foot. He would be in the hospital for weeks.

On November 19, the insurance company agreed to pay the extra $25,000. I called Mike in the hospital. He was deeply pleased. The insurance settlement was paid in early December.

Chapter 4
1983

As 1983 began, Clouser had $100,000 and no unpaid bills. On February 14, he won his Social Security disability appeal. In addition to 14 back payments, he would receive future monthly payments of $600 (to be adjusted for inflation). The Social Security combined with interest earned on $100,000 ($8000 to $10,000 a year) meant his 1983 income would approach his highest net earnings when working full time.

Should two federal tort claims arising from a mid-December rescue on Mt. McKinley be pursued? Even with a "free" lawyer, my clients were responsible for all litigation costs. These could absorb much or all of Clouser's income and eat into his $100,000 principal. If we lost, Mike would live on less money for the rest of his life. The Scanlon estate faced similar risks.

I never filed a lawsuit lightly, but this case was especially daunting. It might be necessary to sue the National Park Service, Army, Air Force, and Federal Aviation Administration. There was much work ahead and I would not be paid if we lost. When I discussed the case with other lawyers, all indicated they would not pursue a rescue claim. I disagreed. Mike's outrage at the Army Chinooks had registered with me at our first meeting in Providence Hospital.

Clouser had given me a green light to pursue a rescue claim the same day he received my opinion letter in the fall of 1982. Eventually the Scanlons did too. I suspected Tom made the decision mostly to support Clouser by splitting litigation costs, an extraordinarily generous thing to do.

A claim against the United States is like a claim against the crown. Kings and queens had "sovereign immunity" and could not be sued. Nor could the crown's administrators or soldiers. When Congress passed the Federal Tort Claims Act (FTCA) in 1935, limited consent to sue the U.S.A. was granted on certain conditions. Trial must be before a federal judge, an employee of the federal government, sitting without a jury. No punitive damages can be awarded.

Under the FTCA, Clouser and the Scanlon estate had two years, or until December 15, 1983, to submit federal tort claims. I had never prepared such a claim, but there were reference books to help. It is necessary to specify the exact amount sought, which becomes the maximum that can be awarded. (A phrase like "in excess of $50,000" limits damages to $50,000.) I arrived at a valuation of $750,000 for Clouser and $250,000 for Scanlon. To be safe, I doubled these amounts and the draft claims requested $1,500,000 for Clouser and $500,000 for Scanlon.

In May, 1983, I travelled to Washington, D.C. on another case and stopped in Indiana. Fifteen months had passed since I last saw Mike. He lived alone in an isolated farmhouse badly in need of repair. In the privacy of his house, I looked at the results of his plastic surgeries, which was difficult.

The main interview took place the next day in a Holiday Inn. We sat near the indoor pool, Mike put his feet up on chairs, and when we got hungry, we ordered food. Twice before Mike had described events on the mountain. He had a "John Dean" memory; he forgot nothing. We went through it again in detail.

Wednesday dawned clear with little wind. Mike was the only person outside the plane. Ed Hommer seldom left the fuselage after Dan Hartmann died, even urinating inside, which angered Mike. (Clouser urinated only once on the mountain. His urine was red.) The first thing he remembered was Doug Geeting's red airplane flying in a big loop. Hommer came out to look at Geeting. Ed went back inside the wreckage. Nothing happened for 2 or 3 hours, "an eternity." The wind blew the opposite of the day before, from south to north or from Kahiltna Pass above and behind them towards the steep cliff and Peter's Basin below. The wind was light enough that Mike could walk around.

Mike described the flying activity of the Chinooks. How close did the lead Chinook get, exactly? I pointed to the dome over the indoor pool. Did it get as close as the dome? Closer. Finally Mike said, "I could have hit it with a snowball."

When I asked about his mental condition, Mike said he was doing okay. He was grateful to be alive. He recognized some depression. He drank less than he used to as he was now hesitant to go to bars. (In his situation, less drinking meant more isolation.) Mike had never dated much, but now it was more difficult. He was concerned about his physical appearance, and he worried any woman he became serious about might be after his money.

Clouser did not attend my interview with Dr. William Smith at Indiana University Medical Center. In his mid-thirties, the doctor was brusque, but helpful. Dr. Smith liked Mike as a patient and had never seen a frostbite case like this. The treatment was partly experimental and used procedures that did not exist ten years earlier. He indicated the Alaska doctor, Dr. William Mills, was on the leading edge of frostbite care. A decade earlier, Mike's feet would have been amputated above the ankle (as were Hommer's).

Dr. Smith described in detail the plastic surgeries on Mike's feet. His hands required no further treatment. The amputations of portions of his fingers caused Mike to lose his power grip on both hands, meaning, for example, he could not remove the top from a jar. For a mechanic, this was a devastating loss of strength and dexterity. Dr. Smith estimated Clouser had another 12 to 18 months of medical treatment ahead, to be followed by job retraining. The doctor was unable to predict the types of work he could do. Even with jobs that seemed within his physical limitations at first, Mike's extremities could break down in unexpected ways.

Overall, Mike's future work outlook was worse than expected. When I talked with Mike on the drive to the airport, my impression was that I had not learned anything he did not already know.

Visiting Clouser motivated me to finish the federal tort claims. On May 31, I drove to Ft. Richardson, an Army base in Anchorage, and hand-filed the federal tort claims with an Army JAG attorney. No further action was necessary for six months.

In late July I telephoned Gary Fye about returning to Talkeetna and wrote my clients that he would finish interviews and take statements from favorable witnesses in the next 30 days. This did not happen.

The FTCA's mandatory six month waiting period expired on December 1, 1983. My clients now had the option to deem the claims denied and to file a lawsuit immediately. Since my schedule for working contingency cases was nights, weekends, and holidays, and Christmas vacation was soon to begin, this was a good time to work on the case. It was not difficult to turn the two claims into one lawsuit. I also checked with an experienced attorney, Mike Moody, who sent over a copy of an FTCA lawsuit the same day I asked for it. I copied some of his language verbatim.

In double-checking my legal research, I discovered I was breaking the law. Congress placed a limit on contingency fees in FTCA cases. My fee agreements, originally directed at the air taxi and insurance, provided that above $110,000, I was to receive 33 1/3% if settled before trial and 40% after trial. The FTCA limited contingency fees to 20% if settled before trial and 25% after trial. I prepared new contingency fee agreements and sent them to my clients for signature.

Friday, December 30, was the last business day of 1983. That afternoon, I went to the new federal courthouse in Anchorage to file the lawsuit. The caption read *Michael W. Clouser, Thomas M. Scanlon, Personal Representative of the Estate of Patrick J. Scanlon, Deceased, Plaintiffs, vs. United States of America, Defendant.* The federal court clerk reviewed my papers, accepted the filing fee of $60, and assigned case number A83-637 Civil. ("A" designated Anchorage and "83" was the year of filing.) *Clouser and Scanlon v. USA* was the last civil case filed in the federal district court for Alaska in 1983.

I expected nothing to happen for sixty days. I was wrong.

Chapter 5

1984

On January 9, 1984, the Mt. McKinley rescue lawsuit was formally served. The U.S.A. had 60 days to respond.

On January 10, the Anchorage Daily News reported the lawsuit in a long article on the front page of the local news section. The Anchorage Times ran a shorter version that afternoon and papers throughout Alaska carried the story prominently. A huge negative reaction followed. Letters to the editor in both Anchorage papers were highly critical. A typical letter came from a resident of Girdwood, where I owned a ski cabin:

Rescue lawsuit ridiculous

I see in the Daily News that Mr. Michael Clouser is suing the U. S. Government for not rescuing him to his satisfaction. They should have been a tad slower and saved themselves the litigation. Mr. Clouser was in a civilian plane and certainly on no military mission. While the military services have always upheld the highest moral standards in their pursuance of rescue missions, I have no knowledge of their being under any legal obligation to do so. Our armed forces have better things to do than airlift cheechakos [newcomers to Alaska].

Over the past decade, . . . the American people in general have become sue-crazy. . . . And now we have reached what I consider to be the ultimate conclusion: a man sues his saviors for not saving him properly.

Mr. Clouser, it surprised me not at all to see that you were not a resident Alaskan. Most Alaskan residents (even relatively short-term

*ones) have learned to appreciate the difficulty of McKinley rescue
attempts (and I stress attempts) especially in the dead of winter. There
are several bodies on that mountain that will never be removed.
They don't have the luxuries of expensive attorneys or the spare time
to dream up get-rich-quick schemes at the expense of the American
taxpayer and the embarrassment of the United States Armed Forces.*

Letters to the editor continued all month. At the end of January, a letter
titled **"Botched rescue suit evil"** appeared:

> *It seems that Mr. Clouser is unwilling to assume the risks and
> take responsibility for a recreational flight that he himself arranged.
> Unfortunately his actions are part of a debilitating trend in our society[,]
> . . . an unwillingness to take responsibility for our own actions and at the
> same time to hold someone, anyone, else responsible. . . .*
>
> *The evil in this lawsuit is Mr. Clouser's assumption that the
> government owes him his safety and well-being for a personal choice
> he made to participate in a risky and potentially dangerous recreational
> activity. What will be the ramifications if his lawsuit is upheld? Will
> anyone, civilian or military, want to be involved in rescue efforts for fear
> of a lawsuit claiming they did not "try hard enough"?*
>
> *While it is sad that two of his friends were killed, I think it is also
> sad that Mr. Clouser cannot see how lucky he was to have been saved
> in the first place and that he cannot appreciate those men and women
> who under no obligation risked their own lives to save his.*

Jim Magowan, flying columnist for the Anchorage Times, wrote
a January 29 column praising the work of the Rescue Coordination Center
titled **"Rescue work filled with uppers, downers"** :

> *[T]he crew at the RCC found a whole new class of downer this
> past week. . . . [The] RCC is being sued by someone who doesn't think
> he was rescued fast enough. The rescue took four days. . . .*
>
> *Generally a four-day rescue when weather and location make it
> difficult is considered pretty good performance. . . . [B]eing sued with
> the implied accusation that they are uncaring and incompetent has not
> slowed down the efforts of the RCC crew. . . . This past week, as they*

were being sued, they proceeded to turn in one of the most remarkable
performances I have ever heard of [describes successful rescue].

John Duggan, an Anchorage lawyer and member of an Anchorage
civilian mountain rescue team (not a Mountain Maniac) who was at the
crash site Saturday, the day of the rescue, wrote the Anchorage Times.
He responded to an earlier letter suggesting that persons climbing Mt.
McKinley should be required to buy rescue insurance. Duggan noted the
Kahiltna Pass rescue involved a downed aircraft, not injured mountain
climbers. He, too, was critical of the lawsuit:

> *. . . had the crash victims been as well equipped for an arctic*
> *survival situation as Denali mountaineers invariably are, then maybe*
> *three, or perhaps even all four of the victims would be alive today.*
>
> *There is not much one can say about the resulting lawsuit. Anyone*
> *with $50 and a typewriter can file a claim, although it takes much*
> *more than that to prevail at trial.*
>
> *As a participant in the rescue effort and a member of the Alaska*
> *Mountain Rescue Group [AMRG]at the time, I can say unequivocally*
> *that Bob Gerhard and his National Park Service team . . . did their*
> *level best to get the survivors out as quickly and safely as possible.*

There was negative publicity in Indiana as well. The largest headline
read **"Michael Clouser sues federal government"** with a lead paragraph
reading: "A Darlington man who survived a plane crash on Mt. McKinley
in December 1981 has sued the U. S. government for $1.5 million, claiming
it mishandled his rescue from the mountain." I was sure Mike did not enjoy
reading the story, but we never discussed it. Nor did I talk with Tom
Scanlon about the Alaska press.

Under the FTCA, the rescue lawsuit would be tried to a federal judge,
not a jury. I strongly preferred jury trials, but wondered if this case would
have been an exception. The vitriol of the letters was troubling. If a person
with this mindset was on the jury, would any amount of evidence change
their opinion?

The custom of the Anchorage newspapers was not to name the
attorneys on either side of a lawsuit, so I was not mentioned in the press
reports or the letters to the editor. However, my name appeared in papers

outside of Anchorage and I received calls from around Alaska. Only one caller was of interest--Doug Buchanan, head of a civilian mountain rescue group in Fairbanks.

On March 8, the mail brought the Answer from defendant United States of America. It was signed by James P. Piper, Senior Aviation Counsel, Torts Branch, Civil Division, U. S. Department of Justice, Washington, D.C. The U.S.A. admitted the basic facts (time and location of crash, injuries suffered) and denied everything else. I had no other contact with Piper.

In April, I accepted a long-standing invitation from Tom Scanlon to bring my family to Talkeetna for a visit. I drove north with my wife and our two young daughters on a sunny day. A very small town, Talkeetna is the jumping off point for Mt. McKinley climbs. Tom gave us a tour of the historic Fairview Inn, the town's main bar, and the B&K, an old grocery store across the street. (He owned both.) Tom introduced me to Doug Geeting, the air taxi pilot who first located the crash site at daybreak on Wednesday morning. I disliked Geeting immediately; he seemed too eager to please. Things were not the same for Tom in Talkeetna and he was thinking of moving to Anchorage.

Although my clients had to pay the travel costs, I decided to interview Doug Buchanan. I hopped a morning jet to Fairbanks and rented a car. Buchanan's modest office was filled floor to ceiling with publications and files. For many hours I alternated between interviewing him and reviewing his material. Buchanan believed NPS personnel were incompetent. "The National Park Service is killing climbers" is how he put it. He believed the requirements of the NPS that climbers "register" and take mandatory mountaineering supplies into Denali National Park created a false impression that the NPS would act when climbers got into trouble on Mt. McKinley. In his view, the Park Service typically did nothing to aid climbers in distress. When it did act, the NPS was slow to respond and often deterred faster rescue efforts. To Buchanan, what happened to the Kahiltna Pass crash victims was typical, the rule rather than the exception.

Doug Buchanan was a superbly qualified mountain climber who specialized in winter climbs in Alaska. Given time and weather and supporting climbers, he believed anything in Alaska could be climbed. He had substantial experience with mountain rescues. He was also trained as a helicopter parajumper and knew how to belay himself from a helicopter to the ground.

Buchanan had not learned about the Hudson crash on the day of the crash, Tuesday. Could his club have responded to a request for assistance that afternoon or evening? Yes. How long would it have taken? An hour or less.

Before the rescue, Buchanan had travelled to Anchorage to inform the Rescue Coordination Center at Elmendorf Air Force Base that his group, the Alaska Alpine Rescue Group, volunteered its services for mountain rescues. To date, the RCC had never utilized his club.

On the return flight to Anchorage, I pondered whether Buchanan was a diversion or a valuable witness. People come from all over the world to climb Mt. McKinley. Some are qualified, some are not. Each season climbing accidents happen. Buchanan's point was that climbers would be better off if they understood they were entirely on their own, that the NPS would not provide assistance. From what I could see, he was right. Still, whether the NPS was "killing climbers" on Mt. McKinley was not my fight. My clients were not mountain climbers. They never expected to be on the slopes of Mt. McKinley or to rely on the National Park Service for a mid-winter rescue. I decided not to return to Buchanan's archives to finish reviewing his documents. Instead, I would keep him in mind as a witness on civilian mountain rescue resources in Fairbanks.

I again contacted Gary Fye to finish the Talkeetna investigation. He refused. I could not tell if he believed further work would be fruitless or he could not stomach the hostility. (Fye visited Talkeetna only once, in March, 1982.) He recommended an investigator I did not know. I talked with the new investigator and hired him, but he, too, did nothing. The investigation of the Mt. McKinley rescue was complete; no one would work on it.

Fye did tell me that Dennis Brown, owner of Akland Helicopters, was moving from Alaska to the lower 48, with no plans to return. If I wanted Brown as a witness, I needed to take his deposition before he moved away. (I could not compel Brown to return to Alaska to testify. If he came voluntarily, my clients would have to pay his travel expenses.) In late May, 1984, I took the deposition of Dennis Brown by videotape.[1] Mr. Piper attended for the U.S.A. and asked lengthy questions.

---

1. A witness in a deposition testifies under oath and answers live questions from lawyers, all of which is transcribed by the court reporter. Depositions can be taken by videotape, which is more expensive. A videotape deposition is also transcribed, but it gives a better feel for the witness. It is a middle step between a live witness (best) and a written transcript read aloud at trial (worst).

Plaintiffs conducted no other discovery in 1984. Nor did the U.S.A.

In the summer of 1984, Mike Clouser drove from Indiana to Alaska. I interviewed him again to help cement his memory. He visited Dr. Mills to show him the plastic surgeries on his feet. He went to Talkeetna to deliver gifts to the Mountain Maniacs. (Mike had brass belt buckles made to commemorate the rescue.) After he returned to Indiana, I heard nothing. In mid-December, I learned Mike had been attending full-time training in computer programming.

1984 ended as it began, with bad press. Each December, the Anchorage Daily News presented what it called "Soapy Smith Awards." Named after a legendary Alaskan scoundrel, the awards were similar to Esquire's "Year's Worst Awards." The Mt. McKinley rescue lawsuit was portrayed as the dumbest lawsuit of the year.

My policy with clients was always to communicate everything that happened in a lawsuit, good, bad, or ugly. No exceptions. I violated the policy twice in this case. The first had already occurred. The second was that I did not mention the Soapy Smith Award to Clouser. If Tom Scanlon saw the depiction of the lawsuit, he never brought it up. It would not have surprised him; Tom knew the emotions in Talkeetna and Alaska first-hand. He had recently moved to Anchorage.

Chapter 6

Discovery and Pretrial Work

In the winter and spring of 1985, Mike completed his training as a computer programmer and began looking for a job.

In May, a full year since the Dennis Brown deposition, I prepared and served a request for production requiring the U.S.A. to produce for inspection and copying numerous documents including witness statements and tape recordings. Eventually, six inches of material was produced from the National Park Service.

Two items stood out. The first was an 84 page "incident report" written by NPS Ranger Bob Gerhard. It included two witness statements from Ed Hommer taken in Providence Hospital immediately after the crash. See *Appendix II*. These closely tracked the Christmas Day, 1981, front page interview in the Anchorage Times. The second was a contemporaneous log of events titled "Original notes and logs. Rescue 12/15 →" and consisted of notes in different handwriting made during the five day rescue.

In mid-1985, Tara Neda replaced Mr. Piper as the attorney for the U.S.A. (She worked in the same office.) When we later met at a deposition, I found her to be a short, dark-haired woman, a little younger than I, who carried herself well. We did not engage in small talk. I never learned where she was from or where she went to school.

In 1986, I took the depositions of one witness each from the four federal agencies involved in the rescue and the lawsuit. Ranger Gerhard was deposed for a day and a half. At the beginning of his second day, I learned that the National Park Service had made a tape recording of what was said at the rescue critique held in Anchorage in January, 1982, one month after the rescue. This tape recording was later produced in the form of three small double-sided tape cassettes.

Dick Hunze, the FAA person on duty at the Talkeetna Flight Service Station on Wednesday morning after the crash, was deposed for less than half a day. Four years had passed and Hunze had no memory of any conversation with anyone that morning.

Bill Strauss, a civilian employee of the Army's Northern Warfare Training Center and the person who trained members of the Army's High Altitude Rescue Team [HART] was deposed at Ft. Greely, Alaska for less than half a day. He took color photographs during the rescue and, on his own initiative, prepared an after action report that was critical of how other federal agencies perceived the HART.

The deposition of Major Sam Baker at Elmendorf Air Force Base in Anchorage lasted less than a day. Baker was a co-pilot on the second C-130 flight that overflew the crash site on Tuesday evening, the day of the crash. Baker had recently been promoted to Chief of the Rescue Coordination Center at Elmendorf and answered questions about the workings of the RCC.

I also travelled to Ft. Wainwright in Fairbanks to review records from the Army's high altitude Chinook squadrons. While there, I boarded a Chinook and talked with Army personnel about fuel capacity, flight times, etc. but no deposition was taken. My clients had to pay the costs of all these depositions and the travel involved.

Ms. Neda took the deposition of Tom Scanlon in Anchorage. We both travelled to Indiana so she could depose Mike Clouser in Indianapolis, near where he lived. We also travelled to Michigan to take the deposition of Dr. Smith, Clouser's treating physician in Indiana, who had since moved to Detroit. Clouser paid the costs of the Smith deposition and my travel costs.

On October 7, 1986, both sides were informed that trial would be held before Federal District Judge Andrew Jay Kleinfeld of Fairbanks. While I was not troubled that Kleinfeld was based in Fairbanks (trial would still be held in Anchorage), I knew little about him. A Harvard Law School graduate, he practiced in Fairbanks, was a recent Reagan appointee, and was probably a conservative Republican. I hoped for a Rabinowitz connection.

For decades, Alaska's finest jurist was Jay A. Rabinowitz, an Alaska Supreme Court Justice who lived in Fairbanks.[2] Rabinowitz made it a habit to hire clerks from Harvard Law School, his alma mater. I soon confirmed that Kleinfeld clerked for Rabinowitz from 1969 to 1971. Our new judge would be very intelligent and one could not live for seventeen years in Fairbanks, 350 miles north of Anchorage, without becoming an Alaskan.

Kleinfeld had been confirmed by the Senate in May, only five months earlier. No lawyer I knew had appeared before him, even for a motion. Several had dealt with him in private practice. I learned he used to have a small insurance defense practice and his main client was State Farm, known in Alaska as a tight-fisted outfit. One lawyer told me, "Kleinfeld is a very conservative guy. To Andy, $100,000 is a lot of money." When I communicated the identity of the trial judge, Mike and Tom could tell it was not good news.

---

2. I held Rabinowitz in high regard from personal experience. As a young lawyer, I represented a plaintiff injured in a car accident. Defense counsel asked my client to sign what I considered an overbroad waiver of the physician patient privilege. Defense counsel filed a motion to compel a waiver of the privilege, which I opposed. The superior court ruled against me. I filed an expedited, discretionary appeal to the Alaska Supreme Court, which accepted the appeal and ruled against me, 4-1. Justice Rabinowitz dissented. His short opinion stated he agreed with everything in the majority opinion, but, when he applied the opinion to the facts of my case, he concluded the waiver of the physician patient privilege was overbroad. In other words, I was right.

Chapter 7
Countdown to Trial

W hen the tape cassettes of the Park Service's January, 1982 rescue critique were provided in mid-1986, I tried to listen to them. The words were often inaudible and I could rarely tell who was speaking. I ordered two transcripts to be prepared, one by R & R Court Reporters and one by Sylvia, a secretary in my office. R & R prepared the better transcript at a cost of $720. While I could now read what was said, most speakers were labeled as "UNIDENTIFIED VOICE." I turned the project over to my secretary/paralegal, Donna Chertkow, who set up a room where she could be alone with the tapes and the R & R transcript. Donna listened to the tapes over and over until she recognized the voices. Then she manually typed the speaker's name on the R & R transcript.

On October 23, 1986, Judge Kleinfeld ordered that trial begin in Anchorage on Monday, April 6, 1987.

In early November, I read the entire transcript of the rescue critique. There was much discussion about why the Chinooks were not moved to Talkeetna on Tuesday night. Terry Bridgman, a Chinook pilot, said, "We sat there [at Ft. Wainwright in Fairbanks] until 12:30 [a.m.] until they finally decided we was not to go." Doug Geeting criticized the late arrival of the Chinooks at the crash site on Wednesday noon. Bridgman described what the Chinooks did at the crash site, but was not specific as to which Chinook did what. Bridgman said they considered unloading the Air Force parajumpers (PJs) on the south side of Kahiltna Pass, but "the PJs were not prepared for an extended stay." Gerhard added, "Neither were the Rangers."

Jim Okonek asked why one Chinook could not be outfitted for a quick snatch and grab rescue and the other Chinook outfitted with a ground rescue party. Lt. Colonel Leavitt, commander of the Northern Warfare Training Center at Ft. Greely, responded that if the Army's High Altitude Rescue Team [HART] had been "in the [Chinook] and they could have dropped us off on the south side, we'd have been good." "We're ready to go forever," he added.

Okonek asked about weather at the crash site. Doug Geeting said: "[I]f they had been there on Wednesday morning and ready to go at first light, . . . they could have landed there. It was smooth."

Bob Gerhard read aloud a letter from Art Mannix, leader of the volunteer Talkeetna climbers, the Mountain Maniacs, questioning why no air drop occurred and stating his opinion that Clouser could have retrieved an air drop. Gerhard said, "I wish we could have dropped something very much. Very badly I wish we could have dropped something." Someone asked why the survivors didn't dig in better. Gerhard answered that Ed Hommer's mental state was "not real good" while on the mountain.

Then the floor was turned over to Dr. William Mills, the frostbite doctor, who had just arrived. Mills first asked for a favor from the military. Beginning April 1 and continuing until July 1, 1982, research stations manned by doctors were to be established at 7000' and 14,000' on Mt. McKinley. "Any of you would like to offer your helicopters to lift two gents in with some gear, we'd be happy to have that." After the laughter died, Dr. Mills said:

> I'll tell you this much so you can all feel a little bit better. Maybe you had problems with your rescue, but you brought two men down alive. No matter what your problems and what you think they are and how you can improve them, the fact is whatever you did or didn't do did not alter what happened to these men, I can tell you that.
>
> First of all, it seems as if one man [Hartmann] was dead upon or soon after impact. One man [Scanlon] was so severely injured he was hypoglemic, he'd lost lots of fluid, he'd lost lots of blood. He [Scanlon] would not have survived probably more than a few hours even after

> rescue, if you had arrived within another 8 or 10
> or 12 to 24 hour period from what we know. . . .

This was disturbing to read. Legal cause was a significant issue for Pat Scanlon. Plaintiffs needed to prove that if the federal personnel had not been negligent and had not prevented the Akland helicopter flight early Wednesday morning, Pat would have survived removal from Mt. McKinley. Clearly, Dr. Mills did not think this was possible. He continued:

> The two men that did survive, though, had
> a very interesting mountain phenomena that's
> one of the major problems [on] Mt. McKinley
> for which there is no recovery. There is no
> reconstitution after an injury like this. They
> both had a freeze and a thaw and a refreeze
> injury. After the refreeze injury, that's it,
> there's no reconstitution. . . .
>
> So this was a tough price to pay, but, again,
> in retrospect, it has nothing to do with your
> operation. . . . You didn't change very much
> for the two survivors and what they lost and
> what they didn't. That was the result of their
> clothing and the freezing and the thawing that
> occurred in the first 24 hours.

Dr. Mills said Clouser suffered a freeze/thaw/refreeze injury in the first 24 hours from which there was no "reconstitution." If true, there was no causation between any negligence by the U.S.A. and Mike's amputations. This statement was so damaging that I checked both transcripts. The R & R transcript had Mills saying 24 hours. Sylvia's transcript had him saying 24 to 36 hours. I listened to the tape recording. Dr. Mills said 24 to 36 hours.

After a break, Julian Mason, head of the civilian Alaska Mountain Rescue Group [AMRG] in Anchorage, took the floor:

> . . . [F]rom my perspective I thought the whole
> response was really excellent. . . . [A]s I look at
> . . . the decisions that were made, the decision,
> for example, to use [Air Force] PJs first, the

> decision to wait until [Wednesday] morning to
> fly rather than trying to fly [Tuesday] at night,
> I think all those decisions were excellent. And
> I think if you were going to make them again
> tomorrow or the next day or the next day, you'd
> have to make the same ones. . . . If it doesn't
> work, it doesn't work . . . I thought that the
> rescue effort itself went very, very well.

None of the Air Force people at the critique, C-130 pilots, PJs, and RCC personnel, would have changed a thing. If another Kahiltna Pass rescue was needed, the RCC would do everything exactly the same.

Initially I was disappointed in the critique transcript. Dr. Mills' comments were especially harmful. After a month or so, I reconsidered. As the tapes contained helpful material, I asked Donna to prepare a tape and a transcript for several speakers, one speaker per tape. The plan was to ask a witness at trial: "Is it not true you said X at the critique?" If the witness denied it, I would play the tape recording of the witness saying X.

On December 10, I got a rare call from Gary Fye, who had received a Christmas card from Mike Clouser. Gary asked who the trial judge was. When I told him Kleinfeld, he said that was bad news. Fye had been instrumental in bringing a legal malpractice claim against Kleinfeld when the judge was in private practice. The judge did not like him. In Gary's opinion, Kleinfeld was a dyed in the wool defense attorney. After the call, I dictated a memo not to call Fye as a witness at trial and to make an attempt at settlement before trial.

I faced two major trials in the first four months of 1987. In mid-February, the "A" trial, a plaintiff's legal malpractice case, was held on schedule. After a two week trial in state superior court, the jury awarded my client substantial damages. The Mt. McKinley rescue trial, to begin five weeks after the "A" trial ended, continued on schedule, providing barely enough time to recover from the "A" trial.

Trial briefs were due on Friday, March 27, 1987. On Monday, March 23, the U.S.A.'s trial brief arrived in the mail. It contained 21 pages, 14 devoted to facts and 7 to law. Ms. Neda summarized the case in one paragraph:

Plaintiffs allege that the United States . . . negligently conducted
the search and rescue attempt of Michael Clouser and Patrick
Scanlon and that such negligence exacerbated the damages incurred
by [them]. . . . Defendant United States alleges that the sole [legal]
cause of the injuries sustained . . . is the negligence of pilot Hommer,
that no act or omission of the [U.S.A.][legally] caused or contributed
to the injuries sustained by Plaintiffs, that the United States owed no
duty to Plaintiffs to conduct the search and rescue, that Defendant
United States' conduct did not worsen their position and that no act
or omission on the part of Defendant United States constituted gross
negligence under Alaska law.

Her factual discussion provided new information. When the Chinooks arrived at the crash site on Wednesday noon, they were bulging with survival gear, which she listed in detail. Ms. Neda offered an explanation for the Chinooks' failure to render aid: "Severe downdrafts and turbulence prevented the Chinook crewmen from positioning their aircraft to permit a rescue attempt or supply drop. The helicopters passed over the accident site several times and one Chinook helicopter attempted to land, but was unable to do so." She argued the U.S.A. spent over $100,000 on the rescue and now it was being sued!

The U.S.A.'s trial brief accurately and impartially summarized Alaska law on negligence. Ms. Neda argued Alaska's Good Samaritan statute, which protected persons rendering emergency aid, made a defendant "immune from liability where his acts constitute ordinary negligence." The only exception to the Good Samaritan statute "is where the defendant had a pre-existing duty to rescue and, therefore, is under an ordinary standard of care." This was a correct statement of Alaska law.

By defendant's analysis, the U.S.A. owed no duty to rescue within Denali National Park and therefore could be found liable only if "gross negligence, recklessness or intentional misconduct is proved." Her brief discussed Alaska law on gross negligence. (It is a lot worse than ordinary negligence.) The U.S.A.'s trial brief concluded: "Alaska law demands Plaintiffs show Defendant United States acted with gross negligence. Yet, they are not even able to show ordinary negligence. Consequently, this action should be dismissed with costs to the [U.S.A.]."

I ignored the discussion of gross negligence. From the beginning, I believed it would be difficult to prove even ordinary negligence. Gross negligence was not pled in plaintiffs' Complaint and would not be mentioned in our trial brief. Instead, plaintiffs argued the NPS had a pre-existing duty to rescue crash victims within Denali National Park, so ordinary negligence applied.

Mike Clouser arrived in Anchorage the day our trial brief was due and came by to say hello, but I did not have time to see him. Plaintiffs' Trial Brief was filed five minutes before the court closed on Friday, March 27. It was 50 pages, the maximum allowed, with 19 pages of facts and 31 pages of law.

The fact section presented three chronologies: (1) events at Kahiltna Pass, (2) federal rescue activities at other locations, and (3) Dennis Brown's rescue efforts. A final paragraph argued:

> A [Chinook] helicopter or, if unavailable, a private helicopter
> (as required by federal rescue procedures) should have been at
> Kahiltna Pass at first light on Wednesday. Defendant should have
> planned for the contingency that the helicopter could not land at
> the exact crash site. Personnel capable of making a ground rescue
> should have been on board. None were. . . . Survival gear to be
> [air] dropped to the victims should have been on board. In short,
> defendant's personnel negligently (and without any real thought)
> put all their eggs in one basket — a quick helicopter [snatch]
> and go rescue. When this proved impossible, defendant had no
> alternative means to assist plaintiffs. . . . Defendant's behavior
> Wednesday morning not only defies common sense, it violates
> applicable federal rescue procedures. Rescue personnel are
> supposed to plan for the worst, not hope for the best.

The next section quoted my transcript of the rescue critique. Another section described seven different search and rescue (SAR) plans, manuals, and interagency agreements applicable to the rescue. The brief then discussed established rescue law and acknowledged that courts have never looked favorably on lawsuits against rescuers. It explained the common law Good Samaritan doctrine, which added the "worsened the victim's plight" requirement, and argued the prohibited Akland helicopter flight by Dennis Brown satisfied this element.

The brief discussed Good Samaritan statutes, also known as "Dr. Kildare statutes" after the television show.[3]

Responding to the public outcry caused by this fictional television episode, a large number of states, including Alaska, passed Good Samaritan statutes. In 1987, Alaska's statute, A. S. 09.65.090, read:

Civil liability for emergency aid.

(a) *A person at a hospital or any other location who renders emergency care or emergency counseling to an injured, ill or emotionally distraught person who reasonably appears to the person rendering the aid to be in immediate need of emergency aid in order to avoid serious harm or death is not liable for civil damages as a result of an act or omission in rendering emergency aid.*

(b) *This section does not preclude liability for civil damages as a result of gross negligence or reckless or intentional misconduct.*

Good Samaritan statutes protect volunteers, not persons whose job it is to give emergency aid. Two Alaska cases held the Good Samaritan statute did not protect state troopers and city firemen. In Lee v. State, a little girl had her arm caught in the jaws of an escaped circus lion. A state trooper killed the lion. While disentangling her arm, the trooper's weapon discharged, hitting the little girl. The Alaska Supreme Court ruled the state trooper was not protected by the Good Samaritan statute because it was his job to render emergency aid. In City of Fairbanks v. Schaible, decided before the Dr. Kildare statute was enacted, a city fire department was held liable for the negligent rescue of a victim in a burning building. The reasoning was the same--it was the fire department's job to rescue fire victims. Plaintiffs' Trial Brief argued NPS Rangers within Denali National Park were equivalent to Alaska State Troopers outside Park boundaries.

With the trial brief filed, I would soon appear before Judge Kleinfeld for the first time at the pretrial conference. A few days later, trial would begin.

---

3. According to my unaided memory from many decades ago, Dr. Kildare, played by Richard Chamberlain, came upon a car accident. The victim was a pregnant woman. Out of the goodness of his heart, Dr. Kildare helped deliver her baby at the accident scene. The baby died. The victim sued Dr. Kildare for negligence. At trial, Dr. Kildare testified he did not spank the newborn baby to make it start breathing; he used a newer, better technique. The jury found Dr. Kildare liable for negligence. Justice was not served.

Chapter 8

Pretrial Conference

The pretrial conference began on time on Wednesday, April 1, 1987 in the federal courthouse in Anchorage. In person, Judge Andrew J. Kleinfeld was a short man with dark, curly hair and obvious intelligence. Mid-40s, he appeared energetic and happy to be a federal district judge.

The judge requested introductions. Ms. Neda introduced herself and James W. Wilson, another Department of Justice lawyer from Washington, D.C. About my age, Wilson was taller than Kleinfeld, slim, and had a pleasant demeanor. He seemed to be below Ms. Neda in the DOJ pecking order. I introduced myself and Mike Clouser. The judge appeared surprised that my client was present.

The judge ordered both sides to identify our witnesses, to state how long each would take, and to describe what each would testify. As plaintiffs had the burden of proof, I went first.

I estimated Mike Clouser would testify for up to two days. Kleinfeld interrupted, saying, "I have never seen a witness who had two days worth of testimony to give." I listed Tom Scanlon, Dennis Brown, Larry Rivers, and Dick Hunze. When I got to Ranger Bob Gerhard, I estimated his testimony at a full day.

THE COURT: A day? What is he going to testify about?

MR. GALBRAITH: He was the rescue coordinator. He prepared an 84 page report which is a detailed description of what happened. . . . He is the key liability witness.

THE COURT: Counsel, I've tried a lot of cases as a lawyer and a number of them as a judge now, and I've just never seen people testify for as long as you say they're going to testify. . . . So far I have what looks like a day to a day and a half here. And that assumes that Clouser takes a long time. Don't run out of witnesses.

MR. GALBRAITH: I've tried some cases, too, and I assure you I will move them along as fast as I believe I can. I try not to mislead a judge by saying it's going to be short and then I go long, because terrible things happen when you do that.

THE COURT: Sure, I understand that. But don't run out of witnesses.

After I named twelve more witnesses, I said plaintiffs' economist was not available until the middle of the second week of trial. The judge replied, "[T]he trial may be all done before the middle of the second week."

Judge Kleinfeld's pronouncements rattled me. At a scheduling conference in October, 1985, I estimated 10 to 15 trial days. A 1985 Scheduling Order allowed 5 to 8 days. Now Kleinfeld seemed to think trial should be much shorter. I could not yield on trial length. Plaintiffs had the burden of proving the case. As their attorney, I was the writer, director, producer, prop manager, casting agent, and one of the lead actors. The judge was the sole critic, but he lacked the ability to walk out while trial was in progress. If I annoyed the trial judge, so be it. Putting on too little testimony would be fatal.

When I finished, it was Ms. Neda's turn. Who would the U.S.A. call as witnesses and what would they testify?

Ms. Neda named Gerhard, Hunze, and Strauss. She listed Doug Geeting, Michael Fisher, and Don Lee "by subpoenas" and said they were air taxi pilots who would testify about the weather at the crash site early Wednesday morning. She named the two Chinook pilots, Terry Bridgman and John Scott Warden, two F.A.A. experts on Hunze's functions and duties and two more witnesses. Near the end, she said, "Ed Hommer will be coming up to testify on behalf of the government."

Judge Kleinfeld announced this "does not seem like an 8 day trial, particularly in a [judge] tried case. It sounds to me more like approximately four days. . . ." The last item on his checklist was settlement.

THE COURT: If counsel settle the case, please . . .
    file a written notice of settlement no later than
    the Thursday preceding trial.

MR. GALBRAITH: That being tomorrow?

THE COURT: . . . Is our trial next week, not the
    following week?

MR. GALBRAITH: It's next Monday.

THE COURT: . . . [I]f you do reach a settlement
    . . ., file a written notice no later than 3
    p.m. Friday. I'm not incidentally attempting to
    put any pressure on either side to settle the
    case. . . . Each side is free to settle the case
    or [to] try the case. I'm equally happy with
    either one. . . .

Experienced judges show a strong preference for settlement, actively pressure the parties, and go out of their way to facilitate settlement, especially at the last minute. I had participated in a judicial settlement conference in federal court before. It was not held by the trial judge, who might be influenced by learning the parties' settlement positions, but by a different federal district judge. (The judges held settlement conferences for each other as a favor.) I suggested a settlement conference in front of another federal district judge. Judge Kleinfeld declined, saying, "it's too late" and "it's not practical."

Ms. Neda said she had witnesses coming from overseas. Intrigued, the judge indicated he would interrupt plaintiffs' witnesses and asked where they were coming from. Chinook pilots Warden and Bridgman were flying in on Sunday from West Germany and Colorado Springs respectively. Both would need to fly out next Thursday night. Ed Hommer was scheduled to testify on Monday of the second week. Hommer "is employed as a commuter professional airline pilot and has been granted permission to take leave on Monday [and] Tuesday of the beginning of next week, Monday being his appearance at trial, Tuesday being just a travel day to go home." I said plaintiffs welcomed the opportunity to call Mr. Bridgman and Mr. Warden before Thursday and I had no problem with Hommer testifying on the following Monday. This was not true. I was not looking forward to a Chinook pilot on the stand and I dreaded Ed Hommer as a witness.

However, as the judge was accommodating their travel schedules, there was nothing to do but put on a brave face.

The pretrial conference ended. I was grateful the judge did not formally limit trial to four days.

The last scheduled task before the start of trial was the filing of exhibits and exhibit lists with the court clerk. On Friday, April 3, Donna and I drove to the federal courthouse with boxes of exhibits. Ms. Neda was present with a paralegal and her exhibits. We deposited the exhibits and exhibit lists with the court clerk and had the opportunity to review the opponent's exhibits on the spot. Plaintiffs listed 189 exhibits. The U.S.A. listed 16, 6 of which appeared on our list.

Judge Kleinfeld's first action after the pretrial conference was to cancel the first day of trial, which would now begin on Tuesday, April 7. Perhaps the change was made to allow the parties to explore settlement. More likely, not.

With no help coming from the federal court, it was time to make a settlement overture to Tara Neda. First, I needed settlement authority from my clients. Clouser's damages were horrendous. As an informal rule of thumb, pain and suffering was valued at 4 times actual medical expenses. With medicals of $135,000, the pain and suffering award could be $540,000. Adding these together, Mike's damages were $675,000 plus lost wages. Mike might never work again. If liability could be proven, Clouser had a $1 million case. If Ms. Neda believed she had an 80% chance of winning at trial, it would be a practical business judgment for the U.S.A. to pay $200,000 to settle. This amount was large enough to make a qualitative difference in Mike's life. Clouser authorized me to accept $200,000 in full settlement.

My belief had always been that Tom Scanlon pursued the case primarily to support Mike by paying roughly half the costs. This generosity was confirmed when I asked for settlement authority. "I'll take anything," Tom said.

I had never dealt with the Department of Justice before, but it seemed likely Ms. Neda had settlement authority. I called her. Any chance of settling this case? She was friendly. She had "cost of trial" authority. She offered what the government thought it would spend to try the case. How much was "cost of trial?" "$20,000," she said. For which plaintiff? For both Clouser and Scanlon, total. No, she would not consider paying some money to settle with Scanlon while still having to go to trial against Clouser. She could spend $20,000 trying the case or she could pay it to my clients. There were no other options. "No thanks," I said. The settlement negotiation was over. I never told her Clouser would take $200,000. Nor did I name a number for Scanlon.

I was not surprised. At all times, Ms. Neda communicated contempt for plaintiffs' case. It was now a matter of crushing plaintiffs at trial.

Her confidence was understandable. The government witnesses regretted the injuries and death suffered by plaintiffs, but believed nothing should have been done differently. (The critique tapes made it clear the next Kahiltna Pass rescue would be conducted exactly the same.) Plaintiffs bore the burden of proving a large number of strangers who put themselves at risk on Mt. McKinley in mid-December owed money to the victims they rescued. The outrage expressed in the letters to the editor (and the Soapy Smith Award) reflected the public perception of the lawsuit. And plaintiffs had to try the case to a conservative, defense-oriented federal district judge.

A trial is not a "win-win" situation. One side wins and one side loses. There cannot be a winner unless there is a loser. A trial lawyer hates losing and may do everything possible not to lose, but when the time comes to give up (settle) or to go to trial, a trial lawyer is willing to lose.

With eleven years of experience, I now called myself a trial lawyer. To date, I had not lost a major civil trial. I expected it would be a devastating experience, emotionally and financially. The Mt. McKinley rescue trial shaped up as the most difficult of my career. I did not expect to win. This is not something I told Mike Clouser or Tom Scanlon, though I suspected both believed the trial to be a long shot. (Mike did not object to my 20-80% analysis in support of a $200,000 settlement.) Why go to trial expecting to lose? Mike deserved a trial. Sometimes justice must be given a chance.

With trial now starting on Tuesday, Monday was open. Clouser had been in town about ten days and I had seen him only sporadically. His testimony was prepared. Mike wanted to see the Talkeetna volunteer climbers, the Mountain Maniacs, who I had never met. So we climbed into my red and beige 1986 Chevrolet Suburban 4x4 and headed north to Talkeetna. It was a glorious, blue sky day that promised to get warm enough to melt the ice on the highway. I bought a new Bruce Hornsby tape and we played it all day.

Talkeetna is about two road hours north of Anchorage. The main highway runs north along the borders of Cook Inlet to a junction near Palmer, where one can head east and north to Tok (and an intersection with the Alaska Highway and points south) or one can turn north and head towards Fairbanks, passing Mt. McKinley and Denali National Park headquarters on the way. We turned north. Past Willow, where Alaskans rejected moving the state capital in the mid-1980s, we turned on a spur road heading 20 miles east and north. Just outside of Talkeetna, there is a viewpoint on the west side of the road with a spectacular view of Mt. McKinley, sixty miles north and west. We stopped at the viewpoint, got out of the car, and absorbed the view.

The mountain was out on a cloudless day. Mt. McKinley has the highest contrasting vertical rise of any mountain in the world. Mt. Everest is almost 10,000 feet higher, but the peaks around Everest are also high, so the contrast is not as great. Mt. McKinley rises to 20,320 feet from a plateau under 2000 feet in elevation. This 18,000 foot vertical rise emphasizes its size. Mike always marvelled at McKinley; he told me he was in awe of it even during the days and nights at Kahiltna Pass.

We drove first to Art Mannix' cabin. Mike slowly walked the trail in through the snow. Art offered tea, which Clouser accepted. I gave Mannix a copy of his January, 1982 letter to the rescue critique, the one Gerhard read aloud. Art said he would read it before trial. We saw Brian McCullough, too. I learned that when the Chinooks set down in a frozen meadow on Thursday morning, McCullough knew where they were. I looked up Larry Rivers, who was involved with his son's athletic career. We talked about the wrestling season, just ended.

We drove to the Talkeetna airport so I could look again at the proximity of the old Akland Helicopters office to the Talkeetna FSS where Hunze worked. The air taxis in Talkeetna had a walk-up tourist trade and we stopped at K-2 Aviation's small log cabin. Mike and I went inside.

K-2 offered for sale some spectacular Mt. McKinley photographs by Bradford Washburn, the pre-eminent photographer of the mountain. Founder of the Boston Museum of Science, Washburn mapped the mountain, pioneering many climbing routes, in the late 40s and 50s. His wife was the first woman to climb Mt. McKinley. One black and white photograph caught my eye. It showed the West Buttress route, the safest and most popular climbing route, which starts just east of Kahiltna Pass. Taken from the south and west, the left foreground of the photograph showed the south side of Kahiltna Pass, where the Chinooks landed Saturday. Several sizes were available. After consulting with Mike, I paid $250 for the largest, a black and white print measuring 24" x 32".

While buying this West Buttress photograph, we met Jim Okonek [awk-oh-neck], the owner. He was friendly and willing to talk. Using the photograph, he showed locations where he had landed an Akland Jet Bell helicopter on Mt. McKinley. Several landing sites were thousands of feet higher than the summit of Kahiltna Pass.

We drove back to Anchorage happy after our day. At my office, I asked Donna to mount the West Buttress photo in a white posterboard frame. Although not on our exhibit list (and late), I expected no difficulty in using it at trial. I doubted Ms. Neda would object; if she did, I believed the judge would allow it anyway. The West Buttress photograph was too beautiful to exclude from evidence.

Chapter 9

Opening Statements

Court convened at 9:02 a.m. on Tuesday, April 7, 1987. Judge Kleinfeld requested opening statements. At the pretrial conference, when I asked the length of opening statements, the judge said he would leave it up to counsel. I practiced a 60 minute opening. Kleinfeld now imposed a 30 minute limit.

Before starting, I asked that witnesses be excluded from the courtroom. Any potential witness, except a party (like Clouser), must be excluded upon request of counsel. (It is human nature that a witness who listens to opening statements or to the testimony of other witnesses may be influenced.) The judge ordered witnesses excluded and told counsel it was our responsibility to identify them "since you know who your witnesses are and I don't." I did not mention that I had never met many of the witnesses.

An opening statement is a preview of the evidence. At trial, facts do not come in logically or chronologically. In their openings, opposing counsel may make different predictions about what the evidence will be, which tells the judge (or jury) what the case is really about. I always urged the fact-finder to hold it against me if the evidence was not what I said it would be and to hold it against my opponent if the evidence was not what the opponent said it would be. During closing argument, the evidence is fitted together like a jigsaw puzzle. Opening statement is the opportunity to tell the fact-finder what the completed puzzle will look like.

In this judge-tried case, I expected the opening statements would be anti-climactic. The 19 pages of facts in Plaintiffs' Trial Brief amounted to a written opening statement. Unlike jurors, who must remain silent throughout trial, federal district judges can ask questions at any time, including during opening statements. Judge Kleinfeld asked questions from the start. Initially, he thought Pat Scanlon was the pilot, not Ed Hommer. After explaining who sat where in the 4 passenger Cessna 185, I briefly described Pat Scanlon's injuries and the death of Dan Hartmann. When I shifted to a C-130 picking up an ELT beacon and a long delay in reaching Ranger Gerhard at his home on Tuesday night, the judge was totally unfamiliar with the Rescue Coordination Center. I explained the RCC and its log of the rescue. Then I continued through Doug Geeting locating the crash site at 8:35 a.m. Wednesday and what the lead Chinook did at the crash site on Wednesday noon.

> THE COURT: Your case will be that they didn't bring along gear that they should have brought and they didn't drop anything that they should have dropped so the people could take care of themselves?
>
> MR. GALBRAITH: That's correct. They could have either dropped gear, they could have dropped people off who could have rendered first aid, or a combination of the two. . . .
>
> THE COURT: Without the [climbing and rescue] gear, [the NPS Rangers and the Air Force PJs] couldn't get out of the helicopter and do anything, is that right?
>
> MR. GALBRAITH: Well, they could get out, but it might have been foolhardy because then they were exposing themselves.
>
> THE COURT: Might not have gotten back?
>
> MR. GALBRAITH: That's correct.
>
> THE COURT: So the gist of the negligence in this case is number one, they didn't bring the gear they should have brought on the trip, and number two, they didn't drop things out the door so the people could take care of themselves, is that right?
>
> MR. GALBRAITH: Yes. And primarily it's planning negligence. [S]omeone wasn't thinking. Nobody was

in charge here. . . . To put it another way, they
put all their eggs in one basket, and the basket
was they'd fly out and land right there and help
the people. And if that didn't work, whoops, they
didn't have a contingency plan. . . .

Resuming the chronology on Wednesday, I covered the lead Chinook refueling in Talkeetna, the Talkeetna climbers volunteering to help, and the Chinook's solo flight on Wednesday afternoon, when it got much higher up Kahiltna Glacier than on Thursday morning. The judge asked how far the Wednesday afternoon location was from the crash and indicated disbelief that civilian rescuers would climb that far to the crash site. "What's your proof going to be?" he asked. It was now clear Judge Kleinfeld had not read the trial briefs and had no idea what the facts were. The judge was telling me to stop wasting his time, to move to my next argument. Fortunately, he had asked for the proof. Starting further away on Thursday morning, the Mountain Maniacs spent two days climbing 10 miles to the crash location. The judge was dumbfounded.

I slowed to a crawl while Kleinfeld regrouped. Backtracking to early Thursday morning, I described the two Chinooks setting down on a frozen meadow to wait for better weather and to receive an airdrop of a military radio from a C-130.

THE COURT: Airdropped to who?

MR. GALBRAITH: To the Chinook and the civilian
   climbers [Mountain Maniacs]. . . .

THE COURT: They still haven't dropped anything to
   the victims of the crash but they dropped the
   radio to the climbers, is that right?

MR. GALBRAITH: Right. At no time does anyone drop
   anything to the crash victims. They spent four
   days [at Kahiltna Pass] with no stove, candy bars
   for food.

Kleinfeld wanted to know if the Mountain Maniacs climbed only in daylight. I answered they also climbed at night with headlamps and a compass.

Continuing the chronology, Gerhard requested the Army's HART, which I described, while the Chinooks were sitting on the frozen meadow on Thursday morning. On Thursday afternoon, Gerhard mobilized the Alaska Mountain Rescue Group from Anchorage. Bad weather Friday prevented any flying. When I reached Saturday morning, the judge interrupted to ask if the Mountain Maniacs reached the crash survivors first, before other rescuers. I answered yes and described where the two Chinooks landed on the south side of Kahiltna Pass.

THE COURT: Your theory is going to be that they could have landed in the same place Wednesday morning, should have, and that the reason they didn't is they didn't have anyone on board with gear to walk up the remaining distance?

MR. GALBRAITH: Right. I don't dispute that the weather started kicking up about noon, but if they'd gotten there when they should have, there would have been no trouble at all.

I described Dennis Brown being told not to fly his Akland helicopter into Denali National Park early Wednesday morning.

THE COURT: Who told him to stay out?

MR. GALBRAITH: Dick Hunze. . . . [t]he Flight Service Station employee, the only one in Talkeetna. It's a small, small office.

THE COURT: That's an FAA position?

MR. GALBRAITH: Yes. Hunze was operating as the communications arm. The Park Service couldn't talk to the Chinooks, et cetera, except through Hunze, so Hunze knew . . . everything that was going on because he was the communications person.

THE COURT: Did he have some authority over Brown?

MR. GALBRAITH: Brown thought he did is the answer. . . .

THE COURT: You've about gone through your half-hour but maybe you could summarize it briefly.

As nothing would be gained by pointing out that the judge was arbitrarily cutting my planned opening statement in half, I hurried through Wednesday night's 80 knot winds shaking the aircraft loose, the fuselage sliding downhill towards the cliff, and Pat Scanlon's death.

THE COURT: Your theory will be that despite his broken neck, he could have been rescued on Wednesday without dying?

MR. GALBRAITH: Yes. Whether he was removed from the site or not, he could have been provided assistance, and I think if rescue personnel had reached there, someone with some energy who wasn't in shock from this crash, easily a snow cave or a tent could have been built and . . . that would have been normal rescue procedure. Unlike [Dan] Hartmann, who had a punctured lung and was going to die within four hours, there was nothing else wrong with Pat Scanlon.

THE COURT: Was his spinal cord severed?

MR. GALBRAITH: That is what he eventually died of, this compression of the spinal cord as a result of the position he ended up in after the airplane slid again Wednesday night.

THE COURT: Your theory will be that his spinal cord was intact until the airplane blew down the hill?

MR. GALBRAITH: Yes. He was not paralyzed. There will be testimony that he was not paralyzed. He had the use of his extremities. There's no question that he had suffered the original injury [broken neck] in the crash.

With my time up, I asked if the judge wanted a summary of damages. He answered "very briefly." I explained Pat and Mike's circumstances but did not name specific dollar amounts for damages. Then I sat down.

Ms. Neda began the U.S.A.'s opening statement by echoing the sentiments of letter to the editor writers. "The Government is being sued because plaintiffs claim the victims of the subject aircraft accident were not rescued fast enough," she argued. The location of the crash had not been pinpointed, she asserted, so the Chinooks could not fly to Talkeetna Tuesday night, adding, "And [tomorrow] I will have for the court the testimony . . . of the two Chinook pilots."

Ms. Neda identified the lead Chinook as tail number 033 and the second Chinook as 525. Judge Kleinfeld asked her to define a tail number and she spelled it out, t-a-i-l, before he understood. She explained the Chinooks' delayed departure from Ft. Wainwright on Wednesday morning, the loading of 3 PJs and 2 NPS Rangers at McKinley Park airstrip, and the flight path from there to the crash site later Wednesday morning.

> MS. NEDA: [Chinook] pilots Bridgman and Warden
> . . . will testify that the severe turbulence,
> the downdrafts and the position of the wreckage
> along that steep gradient underneath a cornice
> or a lip of the [Pass] prevented winching of the
> pararescuers, the PJs. It also prevented the
> dropping of supplies. . . .

> THE COURT: Your case will be, then, that they
> were set up to do winching and to drop
> supplies, but that they couldn't because of
> the turbulence?

> MS. NEDA: Yes. They were also set up to land with
> this crew but were unable to because of the
> turbulence, and then, also, of course, because
> of the critical fuel shortage situation. . . .

> THE COURT: Critical fuel situation. I missed that.

Ms. Neda stated the Chinooks were only able to stay at the crash site for twenty to thirty minutes.

> THE COURT: So your theory will be that the climbers
> weren't dropped, not because they failed to equip
> themselves but because of the turbulence, clouds and
> critical fuel situation prevented it, is that it?

> MS. NEDA: That is true. I am not going to represent
> to the Court . . . that the PJs, however, were
> long-term mountain climbers. However, [NPS
> Rangers] Bob Gerhard and Tom Griffiths were. . . .

She described the flight of the second Chinook, 525, on Wednesday noon. After the lead Chinook, 033, departed south to Talkeetna, "the second Chinook [525] came up from Peter's Basin and tried to hover over and drop something. At the same time, the door was opened on that aircraft to drop supplies, but they were unable to get any closer than approximately 300 meters." Because of bad weather, Chinook 525 could not follow 033 south to Talkeetna. Instead, it flew north towards Ft. Wainwright, landing at Nenana, 60 miles south of Fairbanks, to refuel. The judge corrected her pronunciation of Nenana [banana with an N].

Turning to an Akland helicopter rescue, Ms. Neda argued: "When this court asked plaintiffs whether Mr. Hunze has that authority [to tell Dennis Brown not to fly his helicopter into the Park], the answer is absolutely no and any pilot knows that. He has to know that to be licensed." She outlined testimony from an FAA expert that a weather briefer cannot control traffic; only an air traffic controller can control traffic. "Hunze was just a weatherman?" the judge asked. Ms. Neda answered: "[H]e was an FAA weatherman. . . . He can give advice. He cannot give instructions. . . ." The judge told Ms. Neda she was 10 minutes over her time.

> MS. NEDA: [A]ll involved in this search and rescue
> effort took great risks, yet they must temper
> their risk-taking with the safety concerns of the
> passengers and crew on board and the victims on
> the ground. . . . The plaintiffs sadly forget just
> why they were injured in the first place. . . .
> [T]hey were injured because of the inherent
> danger on Mt. McKinley in the dead of winter,
> and it's this inherent hazardous weather on Mt.
> McKinley that delayed their rescue. We ask this
> Court to find that all of those involved in the
> rescue effort acted with the utmost care and
> skill, and we ask this Court to find in favor of
> the Government.

Ms. Neda sat down. If the evidence established what she said it would, plaintiffs would lose.

The judge declared a ten minute recess, after which plaintiffs would call the first witness.

Chapter 10
Buchanan

Normally Doug Buchanan would not have been the leadoff witness, but the Fairbanks based climber was in Anchorage on other business. By calling him now, I could save my clients the cost of flying him from Fairbanks. As he approached the stand, I informed the judge the witness would testify about Exhibit 84. The judge extracted the exhibit from his copies. Buchanan had the original on the witness stand, while the judge, opposing counsel, and I had a copy. This procedure was followed with all witnesses.

Buchanan hated the National Park Service but I was not calling him to testify the NPS "was killing climbers on Mt. McKinley." Instead the sole focus would be on the mountain rescue group in Fairbanks. I wondered if Judge Kleinfeld, who lived in Fairbanks, was familiar with this group.

39 years old and a Fairbanks resident for 14 years, Buchanan was an experienced mountain climber, especially in Alaska. He received mountain rescue training from his brother, Lynn, a famous central Washington climber and past president of the National Mountain Rescue Association. In 1973-74, Doug had been through the Army's training at the Northern Warfare Training Center at Ft. Greely, Alaska. He was also a helicopter pilot and a fixed wing pilot, receiving his aviation training in the Army. He had participated in mountain rescues involving helicopters. Buchanan taught mountain rescue courses, including field work on glaciers.

He described the Alaska Alpine Rescue Group [AARG] based in Fairbanks. The minimum experience required to be placed on the AARG's roster included three winter climbs in Alaska. He outlined the extensive rescue gear kept by each AARG member and explained the group's one hour response time. All members had to maintain food, fuel, camping equipment, and technical gear for glacier climbing.

Buchanan identified Exhibit 84, a November, 1981 roster of AARG members, which he prepared. He delivered or mailed it himself to the Alaska State Troopers and the Rescue Coordination Center as well as to other mountain rescue groups. When I offered it into evidence, Jim Wilson said there was no objection. Judge Kleinfeld did not remember who he was, so Ms. Neda again introduced Wilson as a DOJ attorney.

Before the Kahiltna Pass rescue, Buchanan had personally visited the RCC at Elmendorf Air Force Base in Anchorage. He was invited in, met with the commander, learned how the RCC worked, and left information about the AARG. Buchanan's group had been called to assist in rescues by the Alaska State Troopers, but never by the RCC. His group was available in December, 1981, to assist in a rescue in Denali National Park. When I asked who was available, Buchanan answered essentially every person on the roster, including several climbers who were about to depart on a month long winter climb in the Alaska Range just south of the Park.

Buchanan first heard about the Kahiltna Pass crash on the radio news. He immediately notified several climbers to be sure they had their gear ready "because it was an airplane crash and you never know about airplane crashes." His group was never contacted to assist in the rescue.

Kleinfeld interrupted to question Buchanan directly. Sitting about six feet apart, the judge and the witness looked directly at each other.

> THE COURT: . . . Is it correct that the Alaska Alpine Rescue Group has given this [roster] to the Rescue Coordination Center at Elmendorf but never has been called by the Rescue Coordination Center at Elmendorf to assist?
>
> THE WITNESS: That is correct.
>
> THE COURT: Has the Alaska Alpine Group been called to assist by the State Troopers?
>
> THE WITNESS: Yes, it has. . . .

Buchanan described his Army training as a helicopter pilot, including flying, rappelling, swing loading, and kicking out loads. By "kicking out loads," did he mean airdrops? Yes.

It had been his experience that the Alaska Alpine Rescue Group was able to respond within one hour of notification. On the day of the crash, the AARG would have responded within one hour on Tuesday evening plus "10 minutes driving time to Ft. Wainwright, [maybe] as long as 15 minutes."

He was knowledgeable about the Alaska Mountain Rescue Group in Anchorage. Which group was closer to Mt. McKinley? The Fairbanks group was closer to Park headquarters and the Anchorage group was closer to Talkeetna. I had no further questions.

Mr. Wilson had no questions. Doug Buchanan was excused and left the courtroom.

The U.S.A.'s decision not to cross-examine was prudent. Wilson undoubtedly knew Buchanan was a sworn enemy of Bob Gerhard and the National Park Service, though this had not been revealed on the witness stand. By not cross-examining, Mr. Wilson avoided all risk of "opening the door" to Buchanan's anti-NPS beliefs. As I called Mike Clouser as the next witness, I wondered how active Wilson would be at trial.

Chapter 11

Clouser II

At 11 a.m., Mike Clouser followed Doug Buchanan on the witness stand. His chronological description of the events at Kahiltna Pass after the crash had reached daybreak Wednesday morning and the arrival of Doug Geeting's red airplane when Judge Kleinfeld called the noon recess.

Trials are like athletic contests. With Mike to be on the witness stand all afternoon, our first priority was to eat a good meal. The federal building had an excellent cafeteria at the opposite end of the block long building, at the limit of Mike's walking ability.

Lunch gave me a chance to take stock. It was disappointing Judge Kleinfeld had not read the trial briefs, but he seemed to track my opening statement. I liked the judge's active questioning of witnesses; it showed what he was thinking. Mike was doing great. From our first conversation in Providence Hospital, I had known he would be an excellent witness. Grounded, truthful, plain-spoken, and blessed with a deep voice, Mike spoke slowly in a central Indiana accent. He was not nervous on the stand and seemed glad to have his testimony underway.

When court resumed at 1:18 with Clouser on the stand, there were spectators in the courtroom. Trials in America are open to the public and it appeared that the spectators were mostly FAA or Park Service employees. I did not like government workers watching the case, but none of them were future witnesses (and subject to exclusion) so there was nothing to be done. Fortunately, no member of the press was present.

After Judge Kleinfeld's five minute recess to let Mike compose himself after describing Pat Scanlon's death, Mike testified Pat's spirits were "real good" from the time of the crash until his death. "He knew he was in trouble and he didn't give up, even to the end there, in trying to help push." Mike did not hear any conversations between Pat and Ed Hommer.

Q. At any time between Wednesday night, Thursday morning, when you lost your mittens, to Saturday afternoon when you were airlifted off, did you find your mittens?

A. No, I did not.

Q. Prior to losing your mittens on Wednesday night, had you felt any pain in your hands?

A. No.

Q. Had you had any discomfort or a feeling of cold in your hands?

A. No. Oh, when I took it off to light that cigarette, they got cold then for just a second and I put them right back on. And they weren't off but 15 seconds or so.

Q. Do you know if when Ed Hommer was attempting to help push Pat out, Ed being in the tail and pushing that way, did anything happen to his boots?

A. Somewhere during that time, and when for sure I don't know, whether it was then or whether it was the next day when he climbed out, but he'd pulled his boots off. . . .

Q. Do you know if Mr. Hommer wore his boots from Thursday morning until Saturday afternoon?

A. No, he didn't.

For the rest of Wednesday night, Mike prayed mostly. The weather was pretty bad most of Thursday. "[S]omewhere around the middle part of the day, it acted like it was going to clear up for a short time, an hour or so. And then it got nasty again." One of the small fixed winged planes came through and one of the Chinooks showed up again.

Q. [Was the Chinook there longer or shorter than on
   Wednesday]?

A. Much shorter.

Q. Was any aid rendered?

A. No.

Q. How close did it get?

A. Not very close.

On Thursday, Mike tried to get the Sterno to burn.

> I had two boxes of those windproof, waterproof
> matches that's got the big, long heads on them.
> It's about half the length of the match. We
> tried to light that Sterno so we could melt some
> snow and have some hot chocolate's what we had
> in mind, but we'd get it to burn a little bit
> and then it'd go out. And eventually we took all
> these old matches and built like a little tepee
> down in that Sterno and put a couple of those
> heads down underneath that. . . . By the time we
> was down to six or eight matches left, we'd had
> maybe half a cup of water and we never did get it
> to burn for any length of time.

Q. [T]o this point, had Ed Hommer done anything
   [to improve] your situation or to increase your
   chances of survival?

A. Up to this Thursday where we're at?. . . No. . . .

Q. Did you dig a snow cave?

A. No.

Q. Did it occur to you to dig a snow cave?

A. No.

Q. Have you ever had any survival training like that?

A. No.

Q. And Thursday you attempted to melt snow for
   water?

A. That's right.

Q. Did Ed help you with the Sterno?

A. Yes, he did. Cupped his hands around it in order
   to try to block the wind.

Mike described the weather Friday as a white-out all day. "There was times you couldn't see 10 feet even during the daylight." They decided to try to make a stove using the dehydrated peaches can, airplane fuel, and a survival can with holes punched in it. They could not get fuel out of the plane's tanks and had to give up on a stove.

Mike testified he did not sleep in a sleeping bag any of the four nights. He tried to use Hartmann's sleeping bag, but Dan's body was frozen into it. Mike asked Ed to help get Dan out of the sleeping bag and Hommer said no.

Q. How were you feeling Friday?

A. Cold and starting to hallucinate off and on,
   slipping in and out of consciousness. . . . I was
   still trying to fight sleep, but I know I was
   dozing off at times, but I'd see a - it looked
   awful real, a restaurant out in the woods and I
   knew we was several miles from even any trees let
   alone any woods.

Q. Were you getting weak?

A. Very weak.

Q. Do you know what kind of shape Ed Hommer was in?

A. He was hallucinating more than I was. I'm sure
   his feet were froze by then.

Q. How were you feeling in terms of your extremities
   Thursday night and Friday?

A. Well, I knew Thursday night something was
   happening to my feet. They hurt real bad and
   they didn't feel right, so I took the right
   boot off and took one of these little foil
   survival blankets and tried wrapping it around
   my foot and put my hands down in there to rub
   it, and it just seemed like it got colder so I
   put it back in the boot.

Q. Did you think your feet were freezing?

A. Yes, I did.

Q. How about your hands Thursday night and Friday?

A. The same. Those hot-liners that I'd had on under the mittens had since gotten wet, so I took those off and tried those cotton work gloves that I had and they had gotten wet too. And my hands felt colder with either one of those on than what they did with them off, so I just left them off and kept them under my armpits.

Q. Did you do anything else to keep your hands warm?

A. Well, before putting them under my armpits, I put them down my crotch, but then eventually my fingers got so stiff that I couldn't mess with the zipper and so then I just went to the armpits.

Q. Could you see your hands changing color?

A. Yeah, they was white, and a couple of spots where I'd bumped against the plane where it took little hunks of skin off, and it was real small pieces.

On Saturday morning, the clouds broke up before daylight and you could see stars "and I thought if we're going to get off here, this is going to be the day." It stayed clear. Shortly after it got light, a small plane flew overhead again.

A. And I don't know, we set there and a couple hours or so went by. And about 11:00, 11:30, I would guess, I heard this voice yelling, hey. And I thought it [was] some more of the mind games that this cold was playing on me. Then I yelled back. And about five minutes later I heard it again, and so I yelled again, and then I turned around and looked up and here comes three of the Mountain Maniacs down – they had come up across the Pass and it was them that I heard yelling.

Q. What did they do?

A. Put warm clothes on, and had a thermos of hot
Tang, and some dehydrated apricots, I believe
it was. Give us warm clothes, food and some
warm to drink. And started shoveling a path.
Some of them was helping us, others were
shoveling a path back up through the Pass at an
angle to it, not straight up but up at about a
45 degree angle.

I think by this time a lot of other people
had come on the scene and had ropes fixed and
all that, and asked if we was ready to go and I
says sure. And they told me to get in this sled
or whatever, and I says, well, why don't we just
walk out? I says, you guys come up all the way
up here to get me. I said, I can walk out.
And I don't know, we had a little discussion
about it, and I asked them, well, what would be
quicker, me walking or you carrying me? And they
thought about it, and it would be quicker if you
can walk.

Roped to climbers fore and aft, Mike climbed to the summit of
Kahiltna Pass.

[At the summit] I asked them if they had any
more of that Tang, and the helicopter wasn't
there yet, and so we sat down and they fired
up a little Coleman stove and melted some more
snow and we had some more Tang. And one of
them, I'm not sure who, I believe it was Art
Mannix, said it's time to go. [He] . . . had
the radio . . . and we could see [the Chinook]
coming, so we started down the [south] side,
then, and they'd cut steps down the [south]
side because it was real icy, and just straight
down, and then they had ropes fixed and all
that. And we walked down and out and onto the
helicopter and they took me off to Providence
here in Anchorage.

THE COURT: The helicopter had landed there?

THE WITNESS: Yes, at the base of the Pass on the
    south side of the Pass. We were on the north side.
    But they cut the steps on the south side also.

Mike went through photographs taken Saturday at Kahiltna Pass. The
first few, taken by Mountain Maniacs, showed the aircraft wreckage, the view
looking from the wreckage up the north side of the Pass to the summit,
and the steps cut into the south side of the Pass. One photo showed Mike
drinking hot Tang at the summit. Another showed a Chinook landed on the
south side of the Pass, waiting for Mike and Ed to be loaded. I also showed
Mike some photos taken by Bill Strauss of the HART. All the photographs
were admitted into evidence.

    Q. Do you remember how you felt when the Mountain
       Maniacs arrived?

    A. Great. I don't know whether elation is the right
       word, but the greatest feeling I have ever felt
       in my life.

    Q. Did you say anything to the Mountain Maniacs
       about the rescue effort?

    A. I couldn't understand why with all the goings
       on around us . . . over those four days why they
       couldn't have at least dropped something out
       to us. . . .

    Q. Did you overhear a conversation between Ed Hommer
       and the Mountain Maniacs to the same effect?

    A. There again, I can't recall any particular
       quotes, but I believe so.

The large black and white West Buttress photograph bought yesterday
in Talkeetna had been mounted and I sought to put it into evidence through
Mike. Everyone wanted the photograph admitted, especially the judge.

    I handed Mike his trip diary, about 3" by 5" by 1." Clouser had it with
him at the crash site but did not write in it. In Providence Hospital on
Monday, December 21, with his hands swollen and bandaged, Mike wrote
entries for Tuesday through Saturday at Kahiltna Pass. He read them aloud
to the judge. They corroborated his testimony in all respects.

Dr. Mills later asked Mike to dictate a frostbite diary. For reasons of privacy, Mike waited three weeks to do so. He testified if there was a conflict between his trip diary and the frostbite diary, the trip diary was more accurate. When I did not ask him to read it aloud, Judge Kleinfeld called a ten minute recess to read it in chambers.

Chapter 12

Clouser Damages

As we moved to damages, Mike described in his slow-spoken, matter-of-fact manner what was done to him upon Chinook 033's arrival at Providence Hospital. He had a core temperature of 97. (Hommer's was 96.) He was lowered into a 100 degree whirlpool bath.

Q. How did that feel?

A. Was painful.

Q. Were you given painkilling shots?

A. Yes, I was. Well, they administered them through the IV's. . . .

Q. Were you hospitalized continuously from December 19, 1981, to March 6, 1982?

A. Yes, I was.

Dr. Mills let Mike's hands and feet heal as much as possible. During the first month, large portions of his fingers and toes mummified. When the exact extent of tissue death was known, modified guillotine amputations of his feet occurred on January 19. Portions of his fingers were amputated later. The amputations were "extremely painful." Photographs of Mike's extremities before and after amputation were admitted. About half of Mike's left foot and more than half of his right foot were amputated, taking all toes on both feet. A portion of the right heel was also removed. As Mike described the amputations, he held his hands up for the judge to see. Kleinfeld asked him to go through it finger by finger, hand by hand.

It is human nature to deny hurt or suffering in the presence of others, but testimony under oath is not the time to do so. His testimony would be the basis for an award of money for what he had endured and would endure in the future, and I asked Mike not to minimize his pain and suffering. Still, he was not disposed to feel sorry for himself. Asked his mental state during ten weeks in Providence Hospital, Mike answered: "For the most part, I feel like it was pretty good. I didn't like what had happened, but I knew the only way I was going to get through it was to just face it and deal with it. I had a lot of bad times, I had down moments."

Moving to treatment by Dr. Smith, Mike described his five operations. In direct questioning, the judge established that Clouser was on crutches continually from March, 1982 until December, 1983.

Mike had significant physical limitations. His balance was bad. The maximum distance he could walk was essentially from the courtroom to the cafeteria and back. He had no sensitivity to hot and cold in his feet or fingertips. His right heel remained prone to infection.

Mike's medical exhibits and reports were admitted by stipulation. He entered his medical bills on his computer (double checked by Donna) and the total was $135,420.48. All bills related only to frostbite injuries. All were paid "far as I know."

We covered his education (high school and junior college) and work experience. Mike described jobs as an auto mechanic, truck mechanic, paving machine mechanic, and paving machine operator. We moved so fast the judge stopped me and asked how I was going to fill in wage rates for these jobs. I answered that I would use income tax returns and union agreements. Plaques and certificates earned by Mike as a master mechanic for G. M., as a snowmobile mechanic, and whatnot were admitted, as were photographs of Mike operating a paving machine.

Clouser was a member of the International Union of Operating Engineers, Local 103, whose membership included both mechanics and operators. Under the applicable collective bargaining agreements, his wage rates rose from $12.15 in 1978 to $19.29 in 1983. Mike also identified the 1984 to 1987 wage rates under the union agreements. He testified he would have continued working as an operator had he not suffered the amputations and his wages would have been covered by the union agreements.

Mike identified his tax returns from 1972 through 1981. His income had fallen in 1980 and 1981, despite higher wage rates. Mike testified there was a recession in the paving industry in Indiana at that time. The judge went through Mike's 1982-86 income tax returns with him. These established income from wages at zero for 1982-84, $1,115 in 1985, and $2,134 in 1986, all from computer jobs during and after vocational rehabilitation.

Mike could no longer work as a mechanic because he could not physically grip the tools. He was unable to do simple mechanic work on his pickup. Nor could he work as a paving machine operator; the machine required good balance and he could not stand for long periods.

The State of Indiana paid an expert with a Ph.D. in vocational rehabilitation to evaluate Clouser. Computer programming was the only plausible fit. Mike attended a nine month, $10,000 program to be retrained as a computer programmer and finished near the top of his class. Although he did well in his internship with Indiana Bell, he had not been able to find employment. Mike was looking for work in the Indianapolis area. His resume and a sample inquiry letter were admitted. He sent out 250 to 300 job packets.

Judge Kleinfeld abruptly adjourned trial until 9 a.m. Wednesday.

Court convened the next morning at 9:28 a.m., almost 30 minutes late. After retraining, Mike was hired by Pilot Systems at $270 for a 40 hour week, but was fired after 8 weeks for being too slow. While only a two-finger typist, the real problem was his programming speed. After 8 weeks, Mike worked at only half the expected speed. In the twelve months since he was fired, he had not found programming work and he was not optimistic. On his own, Mike developed an inventory program on an IBM PC for his brother's business, but he doubted it had commercial prospects.

Because of reduced sensitivity to heat, Mike had burned his feet by leaving them too close to the heater in his rented house. He could not consider working in a cold weather climate. "It'd be awful silly for me to. It'd be a great risk." Medical personnel warned him he was a prime candidate for cold weather arthritis in the joints affected by the freeze--the knuckles, the complete hand, and the ankle joints.

Proving damages for "loss of enjoyment of life" involves a comparison of what life was like before to what life is like now and what it will be like in the future. Mike described his former hobbies as volleyball, softball, water-skiing, and snowmobiling, where he met Pat Scanlon. He could no longer enjoy any of them. Always single, Mike described himself as socially active before the crash. He dated "once a month or so anyway. Sometimes more, sometimes less." Now, it had been "about a year since I've had a date."

```
Q. Why is that?

A. I don't feel comfortable going out to those kind
   of places.

Q. Did you used to dance?

A. Yes.

Q. Do you dance now?

A. No. . . . Not without causing damage to my feet.

Q. Did you used to go to bars near Darlington,
   Indiana?

A. Yes, I did.

Q. Do you still do that?

A. Just the American Legion. . . .

Q. How is your mental outlook now?

A. I still feel it's pretty good. I get awful
   discouraged but that's to be expected I think.

Q. Do you think you are going to marry?

A. I don't see it happening in the immediate future.
   I haven't excluded the possibility.

Q. Are you looking forward to old age?

A. Not at all.

Q. Why not?

A. Mostly because of the arthritis. I've got fears
   of being in a wheelchair when I get old because
   of the arthritis.
```

Clouser had not seen a mental health counselor. He sustained horrific injuries and kept his head up as best he could.

When Ms. Neda cross-examined, all her questions were on damages. She brought out that in 1977, when his wages totaled $24,000, Mike had employee business expenses of $5708. The expense was this high because "I stayed in a motel [in Illinois] from April to December, so it's quite a hunk I'm sure." Her purpose was to show that Mike's adjusted gross income was substantially less than his gross income in the years before the crash.

She established that his $270 weekly wage as a computer programmer was comparable on a yearly basis to what he earned operating the paving machine. She questioned why he could no longer operate the machine.

Q. And finally, when operating the concrete paving
   machine . . ., you didn't stand to operate the
   machine did you? You sat on a stool, didn't you?

A. You sit on a stool, and walk around the machine,
   be climbing off, and up and down it. Working
   on it while it was in motion. It wasn't just
   sitting there.

When he was excused, Clouser had been on the witness stand from mid-morning Tuesday until mid-morning Wednesday, or one full trial day.

Chapter 13

Bridgman

As Clouser returned to our table, the judge directed me to call another witness. I reminded him Ms. Neda wanted the Chinook pilots to testify next. She called one pilot while the other waited in the hall because of the exclusion rule.

A sense of foreboding swept over me as Terry Bridgman entered the courtroom. I did not know what he would testify nor even which Chinook he flew. The decision not to take depositions of the pilots stemmed from cost (neither was in Alaska) and strategy. Early on, I decided not to argue the pilots flew negligently. Instead, I hoped they would not be called as witnesses. No such luck.

Dressed in civilian clothes, Mr. Bridgman had been a Chief Warrant Officer 4 in the U. S. Army, Aviation Branch, until retirement on March 31, 8 days ago. He had a master's degree in procurement and materiel management. He flew two tours in Viet Nam, had about 4000 hours in a helicopter, and held numerous pilot ratings for fixed wing and rotary aircraft. He arrived in Alaska in 1977 and began flying high altitude rescues as pilot in command of a Chinook soon after. He was also operations officer, taking care of crew, aircraft, and flight scheduling for daily mission support.

A twin rotor Chinook helicopter carries troops and equipment internally and cargo externally, from a hook. It has a winch with 120 feet of cable operated from a center hatch. Chinooks in Alaska were not outfitted for rappelling.

A Chinook flies with a pilot, co-pilot, and two flight engineers in the rear. All crew members were required to carry at all times an Army rucksack of survival gear, the contents of which he described. With Army funding, the crews bought one "mountain survival kit" per Chinook with extra sleeping bags and gas stoves.

At 6 p.m. the day of the crash, Tuesday, Mr. Bridgman received a call from the RCC about a high altitude rescue mission near Mt. McKinley. As air mission commander, he called the flight crew, who had departed for the day, and the maintenance section to request two high altitude Chinooks. He chose Scotty Warden as the other pilot (3500 rotary hours and two years of McKinley flying). Bill O'Halloran (4000 hours) and Jim Holt (3000 hours) were chosen as co-pilots. The RCC gave him "an approximate lat/long and we plotted it on the map there. Within about a one inch radius of the lat/long they gave us, we could have been required [to rescue] . . . anywhere about 7000 feet to 20,000 feet." Would a Chinook have flown with the Army's High Altitude Rescue Team [HART] aboard if the crash site had been at 17,000 or 18,000 feet? "No, ma'am, we would not."

By 7 p.m. the flight crews had arrived and the two hour preflight on the outdoor ramp was underway. Crew rest waivers were needed and these were obtained. Bridgman checked the weather with Eielson Air Force Base, also in Fairbanks. "They were forecasting severe turbulence [and] icing conditions. . . . [T]he Chinook, by regulation, is authorized to fly into light icing conditions, [but] we were looking at approximately a two hour flight [which] allows ice to accumulate to a point where it severely degrades performance." "If we could have gotten legal and reasonable weather to fly in, we would have flown."

The crews waited on the flight ramp until midnight for a final C-130 report about the precise crash location "and also to get a weather report from him." Bridgman was concerned that if the Chinooks flew to Talkeetna after midnight, the crews would get only two or three hours sleep. All four pilots and co-pilots and the Battalion Commander recommended not to fly. "[T]he decision was made not to fly at night because of the severe turbulence and because of the icing conditions."

Wednesday morning, he reported at 6 a.m. and the crews were present at 7. The planned 9 a.m. departure was delayed because Bridgman's Chinook, 525, had a broken "lord mount." The two Chinooks left Ft. Wainwright about 9:30 and flew directly to McKinley Park airstrip, a one hour flight. On arrival, they kept rotors turning and, in about 10 minutes, three Air Force PJs and two NPS Rangers, Gerhard and Griffiths, boarded Mr. Warden's

Chinook, 033, because the hoist on 525 was not working. Bridgman did not learn the exact crash location until after the Chinooks departed the airstrip. The flight to the crash site took about 45 minutes. "The closer we got to McKinley, the more turbulent it became. By the time we got there, it was very turbulent."

The rescue plan had three options. (1) "We always prefer to land at the crash site if at all possible." (2) "The next thing we do is land as close to the site ['within 200 or 300 meters']." (3) "If we're unable to land anywhere near the site, our next method of picking people up is the hoist operation." "[T]errain permitting, we would lower PJs on the rescue hoist, and they would do whatever they had to do to climb to get to the accident site, recover the victims and then they would bring them back to the point where we could hoist them back into the aircraft." The Army preferred the PJs remain attached to the hoist at all times. When Ms. Neda asked about other options, Bridgman answered, "We had never planned or made provisions for landing somewhere and dropping a crew off. . . . We weren't basically in the search business. We were basically in the rescue business." Asked point blank if he would airdrop equipment and supplies, he testified, "It was always a consideration."

The crash site on the north side of Kahiltna Pass was so narrow that only one Chinook could maneuver at a time. Bridgman landed 525 on Peter's Basin at the base of the cliff and idled the engines to conserve fuel. He watched some of Chinook 033's maneuvers and talked with Mr. Warden during events. He saw 033 make several attempts at hovering, both at the crash site and at the summit of Kahiltna Pass. Warden " . . . made several attempts . . . to come to a hover, and he was unsuccessful."

Mr. Warden soon indicated 033 was low on fuel and the weather was closing in and he was going to fly to Talkeetna to refuel. As 525 had additional fuel remaining, Bridgman made two rescue attempts. On the last, he came within 900 to 1000 feet over the crash site. "[W]e ended up at maximum power and we were in a 3000 foot per minute rate of descent and unable to control the aircraft and we finally had to just pull the aircraft over and let the wind push us back out of there."

Q. Was it possible at that time to drop any
   equipment or supplies to the wreckage site? . . .

A. My aircraft, 525, . . . had intended to do
that and we had unsecured from its tie-down
positions our mountain survival kit [for the
Chinook]. . . . I had a crew member position
himself in our cabin door, which is right
behind the right pilot station, and open the
door. On that last attempt . . . the turbulence
was shaking us so bad I . . . could no longer
read the instruments inside the cockpit. . . .
The [wreckage] was on a slope that was
probably, and I'm just guessing, 30 to 45
degrees. Very, very steep, and we were unable
to throw the [survival kit] out the [door]. . . .

Judge Kleinfeld clarified that 30 to 45 degrees referred to the slope of the ground. The Chinook was level and the crew could have pushed out the mountain survival kit, "but we were approximately 1000 feet above the slope and . . . we were still a considerable ways away."

Bad weather prevented 525 from following 033 south to Talkeetna, so Mr. Bridgman flew north towards Ft. Wainwright in Fairbanks and landed in Nenana with only 10 minutes of fuel left. The judge asked, "So that wasn't 10 minutes plus 30 minutes [reserve] you had in Nenana, that was 10 minutes?" A. "No, sir, that was 10 minutes." Bridgman explained, "We had planned to have 30 minutes of fuel remaining when we landed at Talkeetna, so the only alternative I had was to go to Nenana. Had we not been able to make it to Nenana, we would have had to [land and] wait until somebody could bring us fuel. . . ." After partially refueling in Nenana, Bridgman flew 60 miles further north to Ft. Wainwright. His co-pilot, O'Halloran, had developed an ear blockage, so Bridgman replaced him with Donald Olson. After refueling at Ft. Wainwright, 525 flew directly to Talkeetna, arriving in darkness at 4:30 p.m.

On Thursday morning, all ground rescue personnel were again loaded on 033 and 525 flew chase, empty. Unable to fly up Kahiltna Glacier because of bad weather, the Chinooks set down on a frozen meadow and turned off their engines. After recovering a radio airdrop from a C-130, the weather improved somewhat and Mr. Warden inserted the Mountain Maniacs at 6700 feet on Kahiltna Glacier. Both Chinooks returned to Talkeetna to refuel.

Thursday afternoon the two Chinooks flew back to Kahiltna Pass. Bridgman was able to overfly the crash site but could not descend to a safe level or execute a hover. "We didn't run into the same kind of downdrafts but, again, it was so turbulent that I was not able to read the instruments inside the cockpit . . . as we got around 1000 feet [above] the rescue site."

Friday's plan was to load 525 with the Army's HART, which had arrived Thursday. Chinook 033 was to keep the PJs and add 6 civilian AMRG climbers from Anchorage, and the NPS Rangers were not to fly. Nothing was accomplished Friday because of bad weather. When Ms. Neda reached Saturday, the judge ordered a long lunch break.

When court resumed, Bridgman testified the weather on Saturday was perfect all day, clear and windless. 525 took off on schedule with 13 HART members aboard. Mr. Warden in 033 had 6 AMRG climbers, 3 Air Force PJs, and Gerhard. 525 soon developed an engine malfunction and Mr. Bridgman flew back to Talkeetna. Mr. Warden continued, solo, to Kahiltna Pass, where he landed on the south side of the summit and unloaded the AMRG climbers. When 525 was repaired, Bridgman flew to Kahiltna Pass, landed above where 033 landed, and offloaded the HART. Both Chinooks flew back to Talkeetna, refueled, waited, and returned to Kahiltna Pass about 2 p.m. Mr. Warden flew the two survivors to Providence Hospital in Anchorage and Mr. Bridgman flew the civilian climbers, 6 Mountain Maniacs and 6 AMRG, to Talkeetna. The HART remained on the mountain Saturday night to extract Pat Scanlon's body. The team and the body were evacuated Sunday morning.

As direct examination ended, Ms. Neda asked Mr. Bridgman, "Do you feel prior to [Saturday] that there was a time when you felt that the benefit warranted the risk of setting down your aircraft and letting off either military or civilian personnel?"

```
A. No, ma'am, I do not. We made many, many
   attempts from many different positions, from
   many different altitudes to many different
   sites on the mountain. Had we felt . . .
   reasonably assured of making a successful
   landing at any time during that operation, we
   would have done so. . . .
```

Q. It's for you as pilot in command to make those
decisions?

A. Yes, ma'am. That is my responsibility. That is
my duty. And my first responsibility has to be
to the safety of my crew and the safety of my
aircraft. I would be remiss to the people on
the ground that we're trying to rescue, and
to my crew, and to the government, if I . . .
went beyond the aircraft's capabilities and my
capabilities and damaged the aircraft or crashed
the aircraft up there. . . .

Cross-examination began with Bridgman referring to a 1:250,000 scale
Washburn map and tracing his flight route. Starting from McKinley
Park airstrip, the Chinooks flew west through the Park, around the north
side of Mt. McKinley, and south up Peter's Basin to the crash site on the
north side of Kahiltna Pass. Was Bridgman familiar with a 1:50,000 scale
Washburn map of Mt. McKinley with 100' elevation contours? Yes. (Both
maps were in evidence.) Using the West Buttress photo, he showed the
judge where Chinook 525 landed Saturday on the south side of Kahiltna
Pass. (This may have been the first time Judge Kleinfeld understood the
West Buttress photo.) He agreed the ELT coordinates he received from the
RCC on Tuesday evening were "quite accurate."

Q. It was your testimony that within an inch of
those coordinates, you could have had a mission
between 7,000 and 20,000 feet?

A. On our planning map that I had on my wall, which
is not the same map that you have here [1:50,000
scale Washburn map], that is a true statement. . . .

Q. Did you have a [smaller scale] map available
to you?

A. I probably had one of the Washburn maps.

Q. Did you put the coordinates on the Washburn map?

A. I don't recall doing that.

On the Washburn map with 100' contours, within an inch of the coordinates, the elevation of the crash site would have varied no more than 500' from a starting elevation of 10,300'.

Bridgman had flown 40 to 50 missions in Denali National Park. He stopped counting rescues after eight or nine. Initially, he denied flying any military personnel in the Park. When asked about the HART, he admitted he may have flown the team in for their exercises on Mt. McKinley in 1980, 1981, and 1982. Yes, the Chinooks "could carry a ground rescue team from [the HART]." Yes, he had trained to do so.

As I cross-examined Mr. Bridgman, I made use of what I learned from talking to Army personnel at Ft. Wainwright in June, 1986, when I was allowed to board a Chinook. If Bridgman disagreed with what I had been told, I had no way to contradict or impeach him but at least I knew what questions to ask.

He agreed a Chinook has a hatch one yard by one yard in the center of the fuselage floor through which the hoist operates. "You can actually open up the hatch and there you've got a square yard literally." Judge Kleinfeld smiled during this testimony.

Bridgman had never seen the controller's log from the RCC mission folder, but he agreed with all the times and events in it. He agreed the RCC log reflected that a civilian [Doug Geeting] spotted the crash site at 8:35 a.m. Wednesday. He did not learn of this sighting for 2 ½ hours.

He remembered attending the rescue critique on January 18, 1982. Ms. Neda had played "a very small part" of the tape recording of the critique for him three days ago. Yes, his memory of these events was better at the critique than now, more than five years later.

Backtracking to Tuesday night, Mr. Bridgman agreed the Chinooks were ready to fly at 9 p.m. and the decision not to go was made at about midnight. Colonel Parrish, Commander of the 222d Aviation Battalion [parent of the 242d], made the final decision. Bridgman's memory of the weather that night was "very clear, sir," but he had no records to refresh his memory of the weather. He repeated the Chinooks would have flown if they could have gotten reasonable or legal weather. He made a recommendation to his superiors "that we not fly." "[W]e were legally prohibited from flying by the regulation, which my Commander nor did the Commanding General of the Brigade have the authority to waiver. . . . We're not allowed to fly into severe turbulence." He could not recall if he mentioned the severe turbulence regulation at the rescue critique.

Bridgman agreed Talkeetna was the preferred staging area into the Park because the mountain can be seen from Talkeetna, fuel is available, and it is a much shorter flight. He would have flown the Chinooks to Talkeetna on Tuesday night if he could have.

Bridgman agreed the rucksack of survival gear required to be carried by each Chinook crew member was for their own protection and was not available to be airdropped to a crash victim. None of the four crew members could leave the Chinook at any time during this mission.

Whether to land Chinook 033 on Wednesday noon was Mr. Warden's decision, not Bridgman's. "I never meant to infer to the court that I had control of both helicopters. Only over mine." He agreed that when 525 was sitting on Peter's Basin, 2000 feet below the crash site, the survivors on the ground could see Chinook 033's maneuvers better than he could. He remembered seeing Chinook 033 attempt to hover over the crash site and later try to land at the summit of Kahiltna Pass.

> Q. Is it your testimony that the Chinook squadron
> . . . was not trained to carry a ground rescue
> group to a vicinity near a crash site . . . ?
>
> A. We were trained to land anywhere we could land
> the aircraft, sir. . . . The landing procedures
> are the same. Our training with the PJs in the
> past, which is the party we had on board there,
> was to extract through hoist operation at or very
> near the crash site.
>
> Q. But you testified there was no provision for
> landing . . . near there and dropping people off.
> Particularly no provision for dropping equipment
> and supplies off.
>
> A. We did not have any provision in the United
> States Army, nor are we equipped, nor do we have
> the equipment to drop rescue supplies. That's not
> something that we have available to us.

As the mountain survival kit for each Chinook was "extra" protection, it did not have to be carried at all times. Bridgman wanted to airdrop 525's mountain survival kit on Wednesday noon but never got close enough. He did not know why Chinook 033 did not attempt to drop its mountain survival kit.

According to Bridgman, the fuel capacity of a Chinook was two hours and forty-five minutes including a thirty minute reserve. "You would plan on being at your destination at two hours and 15 minutes." "The maximum flight time, if you weren't going to violate your reserve requirement, was two hours and 15 minutes." His testimony contradicted what I learned from the 242d Chinook personnel at Ft. Wainwright. They told me the total flight time was 3 hours and 30 minutes with a 20 minute reserve or 3 hours and 10 minutes total. Was Bridgman deliberately understating a Chinook's flight time? Rather than contradict him, I brought out the obvious point.

"Q. [I]t was going to take you an hour to fly from Wainwright to McKinley Headquarters and 45 minutes to fly from McKinley Park strip to Kahiltna [Pass] and 25 minutes to fly from Kahiltna [Pass] to Talkeetna?" "A. [That flight time is] two ten. That looks right." He agreed this would allow the Chinooks only five minutes at the crash site before they began to violate their fuel reserve. Judge Kleinfeld abruptly called the afternoon recess.

During this break, I decided to focus on a flight that had escaped notice. The flight route from Ft. Wainwright directly to Talkeetna is southerly and well to the east of Mt. McKinley. Kahiltna Pass is on the west side of the mountain, where the weather often is different. Late Wednesday afternoon, after refueling in Fairbanks, Mr. Bridgman flew Chinook 525 in darkness from Ft. Wainwright directly to Talkeetna at a time when there was known bad weather (becoming terrible) at Kahiltna Pass.

When court resumed, Bridgman wavered on when 525 arrived in Talkeetna from Wainwright (4:30 or 4:00 or 6:00) but agreed "[i]t was dark, well after the sun had gone down." [In Fairbanks, the sun set at 1:41 p.m. on Wednesday.]

Q. Do you remember how the weather was . . .
   Wednesday afternoon when you flew from Wainwright
   to Talkeetna?

A. It was VFR, which means I was able to fly visual
   flight rules through Windy Pass. . . .

Q. It was VFR on Tuesday night also, wasn't it? . . .

A. . . . There was not conditions that would have allowed us to fly VFR from Ft. Wainwright to Talkeetna [on Tuesday night]. Therefore, we had to go under instrument flight rules at 10,000 feet and they were forecasting severe turbulence at 10,000 feet.

THE COURT: I didn't understand that. . . . 4:30 at night, middle of December, it's pitch dark around Fairbanks, Mt. McKinley, isn't it?

THE WITNESS: Yes sir, it is dark. It is dark at 4:30.

THE COURT: What was the difference between Tuesday and Wednesday in your ability to fly from Fairbanks to Talkeetna?

THE WITNESS: There are a couple of differences, sir. One is that in order to get to Talkeetna in VFR, you go through Windy Pass. Which means you only have to climb to an altitude of 3000 feet.

THE COURT: I understood that.

THE WITNESS: Additionally, the crash site [was] on the west side of Mt. McKinley, [and] as far as I knew, it was somewhere between 7000 and 20,000 feet.

THE COURT: That's where I am confused. What does the crash site have to do with your ability to fly from Fairbanks to Talkeetna Tuesday night or Wednesday night?

THE WITNESS: Well, he had asked – oh, I'm sorry. . . . There was a significant difference in the weather along that route between Ft. Wainwright and Talkeetna on Wednesday than there was Tuesday night. Tuesday night, there was weather . . . reported by [the] C-130 as severe turbulence, which prohibited us from flying in those conditions, sir.

The judge seemed satisfied, but I was not. On Tuesday night, the C-130 (with future witness Major Baker aboard) was circling the crash site at Kahiltna Pass and the turbulence it reported was at Kahiltna Pass, far from the flight route from Fairbanks to Talkeetna.

> Q. I understand your answer to mean that when you
>   were going to fly from Wainwright to Talkeetna
>   on Tuesday night, you were going to overfly the
>   crash site.
>
> A. I don't think – no. My flight plan for – I'm
>   confused now.
>
> Q. I asked you Tuesday night . . . was it to go to
>   the crash site or was it to go to Talkeetna?
>   And you said "No. We ruled out the crash site
>   quickly because the weather was bad. The C-130
>   told us that."
>
> A. That's correct.
>
> Q. . . . [Y]ou were going to fly from Wainwright to
>   Talkeetna Tuesday night . . . [f]ollowing the
>   same route you followed on Wednesday afternoon?
>
> A. Yes, but at a different flight altitude.
>
> Q. Why?
>
> A. Because I was able to fly there VFR on the
>   second night. I was not able to fly that route
>   VFR the first night.
>
> Q. Why not?
>
> A. I had to fly instrument flight rules [based
>   on the weather report from the C-130 over
>   Kahiltna Pass].

Bridgman abruptly retreated to his earlier testimony that all four pilots and copilots recommended against flying to Talkeetna on Tuesday night. "This was not my sole decision. . . . There's also the other pilots involved in here." With this bizarre answer I was content to move on.

Judge Kleinfeld was not. He asked three pages of questions to clarify why flying conditions supposedly were IFR on Tuesday and VFR on

Wednesday. The judge asked about lights on the highway that runs through Windy Pass, moonlight available either day, and cloud cover.

When Kleinfeld finished, it was time to play the tape of Bridgman at the rescue critique. Ms. Neda's numerous objections were overruled. Judge Kleinfeld wanted to hear what Bridgman said one month after the rescue. Initially, the judge had trouble hearing the tape recording. We moved my black boombox to the judge's desk and Kleinfeld adjusted the base and treble, which made the voices much more audible.

```
(Tape recording playback.)

Bob Gerhard [to Bridgman]: I know there's been talk
    about the response both that Tuesday night and
    [on] Wednesday morning. And if it would have been
    possible to get in there Tuesday night, into
    Talkeetna, and get in earlier Wednesday morning.
    What was the problem involved in that?

Mr. Bridgman: Our crews got assembled by about 9:00
    o'clock that night; went out and prepared the
    aircraft for launch and they were completed with
    that by about 10:30. But there was some confusion
    as to, number one, were the coordinates accurate?
    And, number two, had they actually confirmed
    the sighting of the aircraft. I think for those
    two reasons the command structure above me . . .
    elected for us not to go that night. We sat there
    until 12:30 until they finally decided we was not
    to go.
```

At the rescue critique, Mr. Bridgman never mentioned bad weather as a reason not to fly to Talkeetna Tuesday night.

As cross-examination continued, I played more of Bridgman's rescue critique statements to contradict his trial testimony. At trial, he thought the Air Force PJs had an extended ground rescue capability. At the critique, he admitted they did not.

```
Q. Do you recall stating that if . . . you'd been able
    to stage out of Talkeetna on Wednesday morning, it
    may have made a difference in the rescue?
```

A. Yes, sir. If the weather . . . was, in fact,
   good [Wednesday] morning, it could have made a
   difference if all those conditions existed. . . .

Q. Do you recall stating that in retrospect, you
   think perhaps the decision to go to Talkeetna
   [Tuesday] night should have come out differently?

A. I heard that on the tape. . . .

Bridgman could not recall whether he stated at the critique that he would always notify the Army's HART on future missions. As the tape recording of him saying this was playing in court, Bridgman began arguing with the boombox. I stopped the tape, asked him not to speak while it was playing, and replayed the entire excerpt. Finally, he agreed that if the Park Service had put 100 pounds of survival gear on one of the Chinooks, "[i]t would not have affected my performance and my aircraft."

When I finished at 3:50, Tara Neda had no questions. The judge excused Mr. Bridgman as a witness. Court was adjourned until 9 a.m. Thursday.

Chapter 14

Warden

John Scott Warden, pilot of Chinook 033, was the first witness on Thursday morning, day 3. A Chief Warrant Officer, Scotty Warden was an instructor pilot in Army Chinooks stationed at Schwabisch Hall, Germany. He joined the Army in 1969 and flew Chinooks in Viet Nam. He arrived in Alaska in December, 1977, and volunteered as a high altitude pilot in 1979. He held a commercial helicopter pilot rating but no fixed wing ratings.

On the day of the crash, Tuesday, Mr. Warden received a call after dinner from Bridgman to report for a rescue mission. He did so. When Ms. Neda asked what Warden learned about the weather Tuesday night, he answered, "Mr. Bridgman called the weather station" and then repeated Bridgman's testimony yesterday about "high winds at altitudes" and "severe turbulence forecast for the [flight route]."

```
Q. Do you recall whether there was a discussion
   as to whether you should proceed to Talkeetna
   [Tuesday evening]?

A. Yes, ma'am. We discussed that [at] length, the
   options that were open to us. Could we make
   it VFR? Could we make it IFR? Could we find
   a route that would avoid possible turbulence?
   . . . The answers to all those questions ended
   up being no, we couldn't avoid the turbulence,
   no, we couldn't fly VFR.
```

Like Bridgman, Warden testified that after plotting the RCC's coordinates Tuesday night, the crash site "could have been anywhere from the bottom of Peter's [Basin], which is, what, about 7000 feet, all the way up to near the top of McKinley [20,320 feet]." Chinook 033 carried the same survival gear as Chinook 525. Each Army crew member had the required individual rucksack and each Chinook had one mountain survival kit with extra sleeping bags and stoves. This kit measured two and a half feet long, a foot and a half wide, and two feet tall.

On arrival at McKinley Park airstrip Wednesday morning, the three Air Force PJs and two NPS Rangers were waiting for the Chinooks. "Approximately 10 to 15 minutes is what it took us to load those people on, get them strapped down, get them ready to go." Like Bridgman, Mr. Warden did not learn the precise location of the crash site until after the Chinooks left McKinley airstrip. The flight to the crash site "probably took us between 30 and 45 minutes."

Option 1 of the rescue plan was to land near the wreckage, "let the PJs get out, walk the short distance to the site, effect whatever they needed in victim rescue, first aid or whatever, and bring them back to the helicopter. That was the preferred method." Option 2 was to use the rescue hoist to "get close to the site and allow the PJs to go out on the hoist and, again, effect whatever they needed, and then pull the victims back up the hoist into the aircraft while we were hovering there." Option 3 was to land "at some distance from the site" and allow the PJs to walk to the site and effect the rescue. Asked if there were "any other things you could do for a rescue," Warden answered, "[O]bviously, if we had the opportunity, . . . we had gear on board, we could have perhaps thrown it out to them, dropped it to them."

When Warden arrived at the crash site, he realized Chinook 033 could not land nearby because the north side of Kahiltna Pass was too steep.

```
     I knew that I wasn't going to be able to make
an approach direct into the site because of the
winds coming over. You could see the wind coming
over. It comes up Kahiltna Pass [south to north]
and then it would drop down on the back side, on
the north side, down towards Peter's [Basin]. My
options, then, were to attempt to climb up under
the wind or in close to the face of the cliff
```

there above Peter's [Basin]. I attempted to do
that. The turbulence was vile. . . . It was severe.
I lost control of the helicopter a number of times.

. . . [T]he way the Pass sits there with the
Kahiltna Dome over on one side [west] and the
west buttress [of McKinley] over on the other
side [east], the Venturi effect of the wind as it
was whipping through there, it was accelerating
and zipping down the mountain. So I figured maybe
I can get in from the sides. I tried from the
east side, I tried from the west side, and both
times, as I got close to the top of the Pass and
in where the crash site actually was, I would run
into this turbulence again, severe turbulence and
it would throw me around. . . . So I couldn't get
close to the accident site in that method. It was
quite impossible to do.

"It was impossible" to hoist down the PJs over the wreckage. Later, he
did achieve a hover.

At one point, I came to a hover after several
attempts. I managed to bring the aircraft to
a hover right over the top of the Pass, right
at the very top of the Pass. At that point, I
evaluated the area and there was no way that I
could land up there. There's just not a flat
enough, large enough spot to land. So at that
point, I said, well, my goodness, you know, if
I [can] hover here, maybe I can back it off a
little bit, because the crash site was to my
right rear. . . .

I put in the aft input. I attempted to back
off the [top] of the Pass hoping that by backing
off and staying in close I could move the
aircraft over the site. As soon as the back rotor
came over the lip of the Pass, it started to fall
because of the downdraft. At that point I said,
Hmm, Um, this isn't going to work. So I kicked
left pedal, pushed the cyclic over on the side,

`turned the aircraft around and flew back out of`
`the site [north, towards Peter's Basin].`

During this hovering, he remembered Gerhard "and Sgt. Tanner [a PJ] talking about whether or not they had enough gear to actually work the site. To land it there and to spend some time up there." They were all on headsets. "Sgt. Tanner, Mr. Gerhard and myself, . . . we were all talking." He told them "[i]t was a moot point at that time because . . . I didn't have enough gas. I would have to return to Talkeetna right now or I wasn't going to make it and I departed . . . the area." The flight to Talkeetna took 20 to 25 minutes. On arrival, 033 had only 15 to 20 minutes of fuel.

In Talkeetna, Warden refueled 033 and loaded 5 Talkeetna climbers (Mountain Maniacs), 3 PJs, and two NPS Rangers. Chinook 033 took off at 1 to 1:30 p.m. Wednesday. Because Chinook 525 was refueling at Ft. Wainwright, Mr. Warden flew solo towards Kahiltna Pass even though "it was not customary." "Had we been working at a higher altitude than 10,000 feet, I probably would not have departed Talkeetna en route to the mountain without a backup aircraft." "But my judgment at the time, the severity of the situation, the altitude that was involved, I took it upon myself to attempt the rescue even though we didn't have two aircraft."

On this Wednesday afternoon flight, "the light [was] very flat up there, . . . [and] the light rays . . . weren't showing me shadows and contours, things that I need to fly the aircraft on." "[W]e use a term in the Army, like flying inside a ping-pong ball. It's hard to determine where the horizon is and what's up and what's not up." He flew as high up Kahiltna Glacier as he could and made several attempts to land. "There is no visual cues, there is no rocks, there is no bumps, there is no white, there is no shadows, there is no nothing. It's just a flat nothing, like flying on top of a haze layer." At one point, his crew attached a smoke grenade to a nylon strap and threw it out, hoping the strap would buoy it in the snow. "We couldn't find it." Retreating back down Kahiltna Glacier, the weather was good enough for a landing at 4000 feet, but Gerhard said it was too far from the crash site and "it wasn't a realistic option." Chinook 033 returned to Talkeetna for Wednesday night. Asked if he was required to carry horizon or ground markers like dye or spruce boughs, he answered, "No, ma'am, we certainly weren't. Were it not for the fact that we were involved in a rescue mission, I wouldn't have been anywhere near that Glacier that day. That was dangerous flying."

On Thursday morning, Chinook 033 took off at 9 a.m. with 6 Mountain Maniacs, 3 PJs and Ranger Gerhard. 525 flew empty. When the Chinooks set down on a frozen meadow, Mr. Warden radioed to the C-130 overhead Gerhard's request to mobilize the Army's HART. After the weather improved somewhat, Warden successfully inserted the 6 Talkeetna climbers at 6700' on Kahiltna Glacier. The landing was "hairy." After refueling back in Talkeetna, the Chinooks departed for Kahiltna Pass in the afternoon, but he had no memory of that flight. "[T]hat afternoon, to me, is blank. . . . I didn't have anybody on board except the PJs that afternoon."

On Friday, the two Chinooks launched morning and afternoon missions but were unable to fly any distance because of bad weather.

On Saturday, Mr. Warden took off at 9 a.m. loaded with 3 PJs, 6 AMRG climbers, and Gerhard. Bridgman had the 13 member HART aboard but 525 soon turned back with mechanical problems. Warden again flew to Kahiltna Pass alone. "My job was to take the Alaska Mountain Rescue Group up the mountain, land them as high up as I could to support the Talkeetna climbers who [had been climbing for two days]. . . . And that's exactly what I did." Warden got as high as he could and used the Talkeetna climbers' trail in the snow as a visual reference for landing. "And we landed between the two groups [of Mountain Maniacs] . . . and discharged our passengers."

Mr. Warden started back to Talkeetna to transport the HART, but 525 was repaired before 033 reached Talkeetna. Mr. Bridgman inserted the HART on the south side of Kahiltna Pass above where 033 had landed. Both Chinooks then flew to Talkeetna, refueled, and awaited a summons to return.

> [A]bout 1:30, we got word that the crew on the hill was ready for us. So we took off and we flew up to the top of Kahiltna Glacier. . . . The 9,500 foot level was about as high as we could get on the mountain at that time. . . . We landed up there and waited . . . maybe a half an hour . . . while they brought the two survivors over the lip of the Pass and down and loaded them on our aircraft.
>
> . . . we proceeded from the mountain direct to Providence Hospital [in Anchorage] where we dropped them off. The entire [hospital staff] was

```
standing by down there with their ambulances and
everything. We dropped off the two survivors,
went to Elmendorf [Air Force Base], refueled the
aircraft, [dropped off the PJs], and then got
back to Talkeetna. . . .
```

In her final question, Ms. Neda asked, "On [Wednesday] morning, in your judgment as pilot in command of Chinook 033, could you have landed at the 9,500-foot level on Kahiltna Glacier [where you landed Saturday]?" A. "No."

Because Warden did not attend the rescue critique, I anticipated his cross-examination would be more difficult than Bridgman's. Yet as I listened to his testimony and watched him on the witness stand, he struck me as different from Bridgman. He was a Chinook pilot for the U. S. Army, no more, no less.

Cross-examination began with standard questions about what he did to prepare to testify. In other words, how much coaching had he received? He had no personal records to refresh his recollection of what happened during those four days. Nor had he been deposed. No, he did not attend the rescue critique in January, 1982. (At this point, Judge Kleinfeld knew plaintiffs had nothing on Mr. Warden.) He met with Ms. Neda at length from Sunday onward and talked with Mr. Bridgman before and after his testimony yesterday. Bridgman was always present when Warden met with Ms. Neda. Now excused as a witness for trial, Terry Bridgman was in the spectator section watching Warden testify.

```
Q. What documents have you reviewed to refresh
   your memory?

A. I was given [Gerhard's] after action report. . . .

Q. In particular, you reviewed the narrative of
   events that Mr. Gerhard wrote [in Exhibit 1]?

A. That's correct.

Q. So that if some of your testimony sounds as
   if it's almost word for word the same as the
   language in Exhibit 1, could that be because
   you'd reviewed this report before you testified?
```

A. I suppose that's possible.

This answer was more honest than expected. I asked the question because of a gap in Warden's memory. He recalled all his rescue flights from Talkeetna except for Thursday afternoon, the only flight Gerhard was not aboard and that Gerhard did not write up. Warden agreed that before reviewing Gerhard's report and talking to Bridgman, his memory of these events "was not very good at all."

If the weather was so convincingly bad on Tuesday that a flight to Talkeetna was not possible (or legal), why did the Chinooks and their crews sit on the flight line, ready to go, until past midnight? When asked when the preflight was finished that night, Warden gave a long, confused answer. I suggested, "[i]f you don't know, just say I don't know. Okay?" A. "Okay."

Warden agreed the battalion commander's final decision not to fly was made at a late hour. He agreed that if the Chinooks had left Ft. Wainwright when the preflight was complete at 9 p.m., they would have arrived in Talkeetna by 11 p.m. and he would have gotten as much or more sleep as he did in Fairbanks Tuesday night.

Q. Then you went back to Wainwright at 6:30 [Wednesday] morning . . . being at least an hour and a half from the crash site?

A. That's correct. But there was no way that we could fly down there [Tuesday] night so it's really a moot point when we would have left.

Q. I didn't ask you that. And I'll ask you to just answer the questions that I ask.

MS. NEDA: May I ask that if counsel has a request of the witness with regards to the mode of his responses that he direct them through you, Your Honor?

THE COURT: [To Ms. Neda] Counsel, it's perfectly appropriate for the attorney to advise the witness of what questions he's asking.

[Facing witness] I will advise the witness. Counsel is permitted on cross-examination to ask the questions he wants to. It's appropriate

for you to respond to the question he asks
and not a question that you think he might
have asked or should have asked but didn't
ask. If counsel for the government feels that
the answer is misleading because of something
else that wasn't asked, then counsel for the
government will have the opportunity to bring
it out on her redirect examination.

THE WITNESS: Yes, Your Honor.

Moving to Wednesday morning, Warden did not recall the weather being a problem on the flight route from Ft. Wainwright to McKinley Park airstrip. Eventually he agreed a Chinook could have left as early as 8 a.m. instead of the planned 9 a.m. departure or the actual 9:30 a.m. departure.

Mr. Warden initially testified he had never flown over Kahiltna Pass before. Using a combination of the two Washburn maps and the West Buttress photo, his answers changed from "I have never flown near it" to "I can't say yes or no" to recognition that he had flown there many times. The Chinooks trained on the West Buttress route and landed often at 14,500 feet. Kahiltna Pass, just below the West Buttress route, is at 10,300 feet. Warden agreed that if he had known the crash site was at the north side of Kahiltna Pass, he would have known where it was from his previous flying in the Park. He also agreed that if he had known there were survivors as of 8:30 or 8:45 a.m. Wednesday, it would have been possible to fly from Wainwright to the crash site, following the route he later took, without [a] backup helicopter. "I could have done that, yes, sir." He agreed the Chinooks departed McKinley strip at 10:50 and arrived at the crash site at 11:35 a.m.

Q. You said while you were at McKinley Park strip you
   loaded the three PJs and the two NPS rangers, --

A. That's correct.

Q. And you tied their gear down?

A. Yes, that's correct. . . . That's a standard
   operating procedure in a Chinook.

I slowed the pace of my questions. Warden slowed his answers, too.

Q. Now let me jump ahead. After you got to the
   Kahiltna Pass crash site on Wednesday morning,
   did you at any time attempt to drop anything to
   the crash survivors?

A. I never threw anything out of the helicopter
   toward the crash survivors, that's correct.

Q. Sorry. I didn't ask you if you ever threw
   anything out, I asked you if you ever attempted
   to throw anything out.

A. I never attempted to throw anything out. . . .

Q. At the time you were there, did you <u>think</u> about
   dropping anything to the crash victims?

A. I don't recall thinking about that, in all honesty.

Q. In all honesty, it never even crossed your mind
   that morning to drop something to them?

A. I - no, it never came into my mind.

(Pause.)

   I don't know why. I just - [stops speaking]

Mr. Warden was staring at the floor. The courtroom was completely
still. Judge Kleinfeld moved his eyes from the witness to me. After a pause,
I continued, "So you never even untied the gear of the PJs or the park
rangers that had been tied down at McKinley Park strip, correct?" A. "I
never had that untied, that's correct, sir."

Placing the two Washburn maps in front of him and positioning
the West Buttress photo nearby, I asked Mr. Warden to take his time and,
using the maps, to tell the judge where and how he flew on Wednesday. Ms.
Neda had asked the same questions without any visual aids. As he answered,
Judge Kleinfeld interrupted often. When I asked Warden to show the judge
where he attempted to hover, Judge Kleinfeld corrected the wording of the
question to "where you succeeded in hovering."

THE WITNESS: Where I succeeded in hovering. It was
   probably this, right in this small dip right here
   [indicating on West Buttress photo].

THE COURT: Right over on the north side [of the
    Pass]? Or the south side?

THE WITNESS: It was right over the top. Right on –

THE COURT: Right on top?

THE WITNESS: -- the top of it. It wasn't on the south
    side or the north side. It was right, right
    square on top of the thing. . . . I was hovering
    right here. And I wasn't this side or this side
    of it. . . .

Q. What happens next?

A. At that point . . . I attempted to back off the
    Pass so that I could slide sideways perhaps and
    get over [the crash site] sideways. I knew the
    site was behind me and to my right rear because I
    was hovering facing this way.

Q. So you're facing south [towards Talkeetna]?

A. South. . . .

When Mr. Warden hovered at the summit of Kahiltna Pass and Clouser
tried to wave him off the snow cornice, Chinook 033 was facing the wrong
direction for Mike to be seen.

Q. At any time, did you reach a stationary position
    near the crash site on the north side of the Pass
    . . . ?

A. No. No, sir. The only time I got stationary at any
    point was when I came to the hover at Kahiltna
    Pass that one time.

Q. How close do you believe you got to the crash
    site coming up from Peter's Basin towards the
    crash site as you described?

A. Oh, probably 1,000 meters, 800 meters. Almost
    a kilometer. . . .

Q. If one of the survivors testifies that you got so
    close to the crash site that he could have hit
    you with a snowball, would he be mistaken?

A. Yes, sir, he would be mistaken.

Later in cross-examination, when explaining his actions, Warden testified, "I don't remember being told of any all-encompassing plan."

Q. Was anybody even telling you what the plan was up till this point? Or were you setting it yourself as you went?

A. I don't understand. . . .

Q. Wednesday morning, you hadn't ordered up the people who got on your Chinook at McKinley strip, you just picked up people you were told to pick up, correct?

A. That's correct. . . .

Q. . . . The point I am establishing is you, the [Chinook pilot], didn't decide whom you were going to carry, whether it was the HART, whether it was park rangers or [anybody] else. You just picked up who you were told to pick up by the Rescue Coordination Center.

A. That's correct, sir.

At 11:50 a.m., Judge Kleinfeld called an early lunch recess because Thursdays were "the judge's luncheon and it takes a bit longer." He suggested a recess until 1:45. I informed him I had Dr. Mills scheduled for 1:30 and asked for permission to interrupt Warden to take Dr. Mills' testimony. Ms. Neda stated Warden needed to fly to Europe that night. I assured the judge the testimony of both Dr. Mills and Mr. Warden could be completed this afternoon. Judge Kleinfeld granted permission for the doctor to interrupt Warden and said he would try to resume court at 1:30 p.m. We adjourned for lunch.

Chapter 15

Dr. Mills

C ourt resumed at 1:35 with Dr. William J. Mills, a 1949 graduate of Stanford Medical School, on the witness stand. After a 5 ½ year orthopedic/general surgery residency at the University of Michigan, he moved to Alaska in 1955, before statehood. Mills was board certified in orthopedics and specialized in orthopedic surgery, with interests in various forms of cold injury and in children's orthopedics.

After trial adjourned yesterday afternoon, I drove to Dr. Mills' office to conduct an interview I had been avoiding for more than five years. In January, 1982, Dr. Mills told the rescue critique that by the time the Chinooks arrived at Wednesday noon, the fate of the victims was sealed and nothing the rescuers did or did not do had any effect on their injuries. Mike had warned me the doctor opposed the lawsuit. In the summer of 1984, when Clouser showed him the plastic surgeries on his feet, Dr. Mills asked why he was bringing the rescue lawsuit. Mike did not answer.

The interview began with the doctor greeting me coldly. When I outlined what I wanted his testimony to cover, he stated he was not in favor of the lawsuit. I said I was not there to talk about the merits and got another frosty response. Nervous and tired from a day of sparring with Bridgman, my instincts took over. With a flushed face and emotion in my voice, I told Dr. Mills I had to call him as a witness because he was the primary treating physician. All I wanted was a description of how he treated Clouser's injuries. I was so angry I was about to walk out. The doctor then cooperated in a neutral fashion.

It was a short interview. His testimony would be a chronological explanation of Mike's treatment with detours into what causes frostbite, how it manifests itself, and the best course of treatment. I prepared him for cross-examination, too. I did not like what he said at the rescue critique, but it was my responsibility to remind him of it. As my boombox was left in the courtroom at night, I could not play him the tape of his comments. Instead, I told him the gist of what he said, brought up some countervailing points, and asked him to think about it overnight.

My approach to unfavorable evidence from my witness at trial was to bring it out myself on direct, rather than let the opponent have a field day on cross. I had not seen enough of Ms. Neda or Mr. Wilson to know if either would conduct an effective cross-examination, so I decided to deviate from this approach. Perhaps they had not listened to Dr. Mills' comments at the critique. Perhaps they did not have a tape recording ready to play in court. Perhaps I was dreaming.

On the witness stand, the doctor outlined Clouser's frostbite treatment. From the outset, Dr. Mills was greatly concerned about freeze/thaw/refreeze injuries.

A. ... it [appeared] that he had, from his history, from the history given us by others, a freeze/thaw/refreeze injury. And if that was true, ... he will lose the part usually about the level of the second freeze or thereabouts. And that's been true for almost all of our cases from McKinley. ...

Q. [Why is it that] with freeze/thaw/refreeze injuries the extremity will be lost from the [location] of the second freeze?

A. [Explains what happens in initial freeze.] Now when you have a freezing injury one time, that occurs. ... And now before you can handle that, now there is refreezing of already injured cells, and then ... there is total destruction ... so that the second injury is the coup de grace. It just absolutely wipes out the normal living tissue.

For now, I was trying to stay away from two critical questions--how did Dr. Mills know there had been a freeze/thaw/refreeze injury and when did it occur. Judge Kleinfeld had different ideas.

> THE COURT: [W]hat . . . led you to believe there was
> a freeze followed by a thaw and a refreeze?
>
> THE WITNESS: Well, on [Hommer], we had a definite
> history from him. On this patient [Clouser], we
> had a history of not only the timing but that
> he had cooling of his hands and thought he had
> some cold injury to his hands, then he thawed his
> hands or tried to rewarm his hands in his groin
> and his [armpit], . . . and then he got them cold
> again, and probably froze them again. And the two
> survivors just finally, because of all the other
> things they had to do to stay alive, just gave up
> and probably remained in the frozen state until
> they were rescued. . . . So my colleague and I
> putting it all together . . . figured that there
> may have been two or three or four occasions when
> they had freezing and refreezing.

The judge did not ask and Dr. Mills did not say when the first freeze/thaw/refreeze occurred.

As direct continued, the doctor listed several possible causes for Clouser's injuries including a freeze/thaw/refreeze injury and using an extremity while still frozen such as walking on frozen feet (causing injuries at the intersection of frozen and unfrozen arteries and tissues). Asked the most likely of these possibilities, he answered: ". . . the freeze/thaw/refreeze injury certainly is a major possibility, plus the fact that he did a lot of walking and hiking and slogging on frozen feet."

On Sunday, the day after the rescue, Dr. Mills performed a fasciotomy on Mike's feet to relieve very high blood pressure where healthy arteries intersected with damaged or dead blood vessels. To maximize tissue retention, he waited one month to perform amputations on Mike's hands and feet. "You have to wait until [the dead skin/live skin interface] demarcates and begins to pinch in, because if you cut too soon the tissue will retract and every half centimeter is important on a finger." Using before and after photographs, the doctor explained the amputations on Mike's fingers. Dr. Mills brought an artificial foot to court; he used this, plus photographs, to show the amputations on Mike's feet.

Remaining surgical procedures were covered rapidly. On January 29, he did a closure of the wounds of the hands and a skin graft to some areas of the feet. On February 17, he did further skin grafting to the right and left heels. On February 26, there were more skin grafts to both heels and corrective surgery to the right index finger. The rest of the treatment was physiotherapy, occupational therapy, range of motion therapy, and application of casts so Mike could travel home.

Q. [How] would you describe Mike Clouser as a patient?

A. Oh, he was an excellent patient. We have a great deal of trouble with some of our patients in the thermal unit . . . particularly if there is going to be a loss of extremity and the gangrenous changes appear, and it's very frightening and they're very disappointed. And then we have many of them who have such stress that they need psychiatric care. But he was very helpful, very cooperative, and he just responded well to all the treatment and we had no trouble with him.

Q. Mr. Clouser did not require any psychiatric care?

A. No.

When did the first refreeze injury occur?

A. . . . it's pretty difficult to say exactly when, but I can name Thursday as a time where he obviously commented that he was having trouble with his hands and some of his feet.

. . . I would be surprised if he didn't have some cold injury from the beginning. But I think . . . the problem with his hands must date to about the time he lost his mittens because he seemed to have not too much difficulty [before] then, and this was about the time that I think the plane slid [Wednesday night] and they were doing a great deal of work [with Pat]. [S]o far as I can tell, [he] had removed his mittens about the second night, which would be Wednesday, and then was wearing the little liners. And I think they probably were very, very little protection.

> . . . I really am hard put to determine as
> to all the things I gave you exactly [when] the
> worst damage to the feet occurred. . . .

Q. You were also Ed Hommer's treating physician,
   were you not?

A. Yes.

Q. . . . [I]sn't it correct that Mr. Hommer did not
   require any amputations [on] his hands?

MR. WILSON: I object to this as irrelevant and
   immaterial to any of the issues in this lawsuit.

THE COURT: What is the point?

MR. GALBRAITH: The point is that Mr. Hommer
   did not lose his gloves during the four days
   and didn't —

THE COURT: Overruled.

THE WITNESS: Yes. He had very minimal injury to
   his fingers.

Q. And is it your understanding that Mr. Hommer did
   not lose his gloves during the four days?

A. My understanding is that he had some early
   mitten trouble but he was able to recover and
   replace those.

Q. Mr. Hommer, on the other hand, did lose all of
   his feet, correct?

A. Yes, he did.

Q. Is it also your understanding that on the same
   Wednesday night, Thursday morning plane slide,
   that Mr. Hommer lost his boots . . . ?

A. Yes, that's my understanding.

Jim Wilson began cross-examination by focusing on possible injury to Mike's feet when Clouser walked over Kahiltna Pass on Saturday afternoon. Dr. Mills repeated what happens at the intersection of a frozen with a non-frozen part of a foot and agreed "that's one of the possible scenarios in this case."

Then Wilson went where I most feared. Yes, the doctor remembered attending the rescue critique and expressing his opinions about the cause of Clouser's injuries.

Q. Do you recall what you said during that critique relative to his injuries?

A. I was reminded of it by Mr. Clouser's attorney yesterday and you might recall it again for me.

Q. Sure. What did Mr. Clouser's attorney tell you about it yesterday?

A. He reminded me that I had made a comment to the effect that I didn't think that any of the rescuers should be held at fault for whatever –

[Hearsay objection overruled.]

Q. Did Mr. Galbraith tell you anything else about your comments during that particular critique?

A. No, just that he reminded me that I made that comment, or a similar comment, and I presumed that I would be told what it was today. . . . .

Q. I want to be totally fair to you, and what I've got is just a very short portion of this tape, and if you would like me to play it for you, I'd be happy to because I want you to know what was said.

A. Fine.

[Hearsay objection overruled.]

(Tape played).

Dr. Mills: I'll tell you this much so you can all feel a little bit better. Maybe you had problems with your rescue, but you brought two men down alive. No matter what your problems and what you think they are and how you can improve them, the fact is whatever you did or didn't do did not alter what happened to these men, I can tell you that.

(end) . . .

Q. And did that statement accurately reflect what your opinions and conclusions were at that time?

A. Yes.

Mr. Wilson was finished. His cross-examination pinpointed the most damaging opinion from Dr. Mills — nothing the U.S.A. did in carrying out the rescue had any effect whatsoever on the injuries suffered. In legal terms, any actions by the U.S.A. were not the legal (proximate) cause of plaintiffs' injuries. Even if plaintiffs proved defendant was negligent and worsened the victim's plight, defendant's conduct was not a legal cause because the freeze/thaw/refreeze injuries had occurred before Wednesday noon. My redirect needed to move Dr. Mills from this opinion.

Q. On that last point, doctor, does that statement reflect your current opinion?

A. Well, I don't think that - if I may explain this, and I have - I said that. And what I meant by saying that was that when the freezing occurred, whatever happened with the freeze and the thaw and the refreeze, nothing in the rescue would alter that. The question, of course, can always be raised as [to] when did the freezing occur. . . .

   And I also said that, too, because . . . I am very much involved in rescue, I have been a passenger as a medical officer in a helicopter in blizzards and . . . I thought that . . . it was enough to risk everybody's life over and over again in effecting these rescues, and I was a little put out that our program of rescue . . . was under fire from anybody. . . .

Q. Let me focus on the point that counsel was making. At the critique you may have said that what these men endured the first 24 hours had an effect on their frostbite injuries.

A. Yeah, I think it did.

Q. But it is now your opinion, is it not, that Mr. Clouser did not suffer an initial freeze of his fingers until after he lost his mittens Wednesday

night, Thursday morning, some 36 hours after
the crash?

MR. WILSON: This is objected to as leading
and suggestive.

THE COURT: At this point, I think leading questions
are permissible because of the developments
during cross.

The judge's ruling reflected that Wilson's cross-examination turned Dr. Mills into a hostile witness. Put another way, the cross-examination showed that Dr. Mills had always been a hostile witness.

Q. [Please] repeat what your opinion is now about
when Mr. Clouser suffered his initial freeze
injury to his hands.

A. Well, I think that all of the individuals
involved . . . had cooling from the very
origin. . . . [T]hey had very little food, they
had very little water, and they were obviously
dehydrated, they were hustling around, and
it's very difficult to pick up exactly what
happened. . . . [T]he patient on the second
night was having difficulty and had cold hands
and then he thought perhaps he might have some
freezing. . . . [No] mention was made of his feet,
at least of Mr. Clouser, until about Thursday,
and it was my assumption . . . he had either
severe cooling or early freezing at that time and
wasn't even aware of it. . . .

Q. You testified . . . Mr. Clouser walking on his
frozen feet on the day of the rescue, Saturday,
. . . [possibly] could have been an aggravation
of his frostbite injuries?

A. Yes.

Q. It's a simple point, but is it correct that had
his feet not been frozen at the time he made that
walk, there would have been no injury?

A. Yeah, I think that's true.

Wilson had no questions. Unlike counsel, the judge was not afraid of Dr. Mills. As the ultimate trier of fact, Kleinfeld wanted answers to some basic questions.

BY THE COURT:

Q. Doctor, based on what you know of the history of
   the accident, would it have made any difference if
   a sleeping bag, stove, tent, other survival gear
   had been dropped to Mr. Clouser and the remaining
   survivors on Wednesday around midday? . . .

A. It might have made all the difference in [the]
   world if they could use it, yes.

Q. What are the probabilities and why would it have
   made a difference?

A. If they had a tent so there was shelter from the
   wind, they could have avoided the severe extra cold
   from wind chill. It could have made a difference
   of many degrees Fahrenheit. If they had had warm
   food and had a stove so they could melt water and
   stay hydrated, their tissues would have been able
   to resist cold injury in a much better fashion. And
   they would have been able to dry clothing. It's the
   matter of proper survival or not. . . .

Q. Assuming that they had some cold insult during
   the first 24 hours, would Mr. Clouser have lost
   the portions of his hands and feet that he did
   lose . . . if supplies had been dropped at around
   midday that second day, Wednesday?

A. . . . I think none of them would have had the
   severity of injury and then the loss would have
   been very minimal if they had been able to have
   shelter, food, water, heat, dry clothing.

The doctor was excused. The court called a 10 minute recess.

Dr. Mills did not send a bill for his trial testimony or for the interview the night before. The doctor wanted only a color slide showing the wrecked aircraft fuselage where Hommer and Clouser survived for four days and nights in mid-December at 10,000 feet on Mt. McKinley.

Chapter 16

Warden to Gerhard

Resuming the witness stand after Dr. Mills' one hour testimony, Scotty Warden agreed weather conditions on Saturday were perfect for a rescue. Yet even with perfect weather, he did not attempt a hoist rescue. When the two survivors were loaded on his Chinook that afternoon, he estimated the distance from his landing site to the summit of Kahiltna Pass to be 800 to 1000 meters.

I had Warden read aloud several entries in the RCC log reflecting "real time" communications with him on Wednesday noon. One read: "[Warden] reported an attempt to hover over crash site and was unable to. Attempted to land 1000 feet above site. Started to lose power. . . . Turned from there to attempt landing on south side of Pass. Weather then closed in on them." Mr. Warden disagreed with this entry because "an attempt to hover over crash site" supported Clouser's testimony. He also disagreed that he attempted to land on the south side of Kahiltna Pass. Finally, he did not remember a request he passed on to the RCC from Sgt. Tanner, a PJ, for "some smokes and sea dye marker to help helicopter pilots hover."

Ms. Neda's redirect was brief. Mr. Warden did not believe conditions on Wednesday afternoon's flight were safe enough for the Mountain Maniacs to rappel, winch down, or jump from Chinook 033 onto Kahiltna Glacier. He believed it would have been foolhardy. Of rappelling, Warden said "It's an operation that I had never done before." On Wednesday noon, he could not land on the south side of Kahiltna Pass because the wind was too strong, there were no visual clues, and he would have had to land down slope flying against the wind. Horizon markers would not have helped in those conditions, he testified.

When counsel finished, Judge Kleinfeld was still interested in the flight route from Ft. Wainwright to Talkeetna on Tuesday night. Judge and witness held a lengthy discussion of the geography from Fairbanks south to Healy, then south to McKinley Park Headquarters, and then further south to Talkeetna. I understood their discussion only because Healy was the southern boundary of an extra gang I worked on while a track laborer for the Alaska Railroad between college and law school. When the judge finished, Mr. Warden was excused as a witness. He flew back to Europe that night.

With no break, I called NPS Ranger Robert Gerhard. It was late and I was tired, but I could feel myself relax as the clerk swore him in. By calling Gerhard as a hostile witness, I could cross-examine before Ms. Neda's direct. I even had a script to follow; the transcript from his day and a half deposition was in my three ring trial notebook. If his trial testimony differed from his deposition testimony, I would impeach him.[4]

Almost exactly my age, Bob Gerhard was a little shorter than I but still over six feet. He seemed fit. Gerhard was dressed in a National Park Service uniform, which underscored the first point--within the boundaries of Denali National Park, a Ranger has the same authority an Alaska State Trooper has elsewhere in Alaska.

```
Q. The National Park Service retains authority and
   responsibility for search and rescue missions within
   the boundaries of Denali National Park, correct?

A. Yes, I believe that's correct. We do search and
   rescue in the Park.

Q. Not only do you do them, but you have the
   responsibility and the authority to do them.

A. I believe we have the responsibility. I'm not
   sure where our authority comes for that. . . .
```

---

4. Impeaching a witness with prior deposition testimony is simple. The trigger is a significantly different answer at trial. After the answer, the original of the deposition transcript is given to the witness. A motion to publish the deposition is routinely granted. The witness is directed to page so and so, line such and such. Opposing counsel and often the judge turn to the same place. Either the witness or counsel can read the question and answer aloud. It is optional to ask, "In your deposition, you answered X and now you are answering Y. Please explain." This translates to "Were you lying then or are you lying now?"

Q. Would you turn to the third page of Exhibit 7, the Mt. McKinley National Park SAR [Search and Rescue] Plan [Denali SAR Plan], and read [aloud] the first paragraph under the heading "Purpose"?

A. [Reading] "Mt. McKinley National Park has legislated exclusive jurisdiction over its land and all activities thereon. As a result, the responsibility and authority to carry out search and rescue activities within the boundaries of the Park lies with the National Park Service."

Gerhard acknowledged that for eight and one half years, he was the NPS Ranger in charge of search and rescue operations within Denali National Park. He was rescue coordinator for this rescue. Questions asking for "the first action you took to direct the rescue" or "when did you first realize you were in charge of this rescue" elicited only testimony that he got a call from the RCC at 11:21 p.m. on Tuesday and that he immediately called his boss, Tom Griffiths. Gerhard gave no indication he ever realized he was "in charge" or that it was his job to plan the rescue. Instead, he acquiesced in the actions already taken by the RCC (alerting Air Force PJs and Army Chinooks).

He agreed that climbers come from all over the world to climb Mt. McKinley. The number of rescues of climbers per year varied from half a dozen to as many as twenty-one. As rescue coordinator, he had three aviation resources available. Commercial air taxis in Talkeetna offered helicopters (Akland) or fixed wing (Talkeetna Air, Hudson, K-2 Aviation). Military helicopters (Chinooks) were also available. At various times, he had used all these resources for Park rescues.

He admitted that Jim Okonek, who he considered a skilled helicopter pilot, had flown many rescues within the Park for the National Park Service using a Bell Jet Ranger owned by Dennis Brown's Akland Helicopters. Yes, he knew that Okonek had received the International Helicopter Association's Pilot of the Year award for 1980 for numerous rescues within the Park.

Q. To your knowledge, [the Akland] Bell Jet Ranger could have landed at the 10,300 foot [summit] of Kahiltna Pass without difficulty,

```
assuming weather and wind conditions were
acceptable, right?
```

A. . . . [Y]es. . . .

Q. There was a Bell Jet Ranger in Talkeetna on
Wednesday morning, wasn't there?

A. I'm not sure that I knew that for sure.

Q. What did you do to find out?

A. I believe I talked with Doug Geeting [on
Wednesday morning]. I really don't remember.

I questioned Gerhard about two fatal airplane crashes within Denali National Park in June and July, 1981. He agreed the Kahiltna Pass crash on December 15 was the third fatal airplane crash within Park boundaries in 1981. I moved to admit nine NPS airplane crash rescue reports during Gerhard's tenure through December, 1981. Ms. Neda objected and the judge asked the relevance. "[I]t was a large part of his job to . . . plan for and execute rescues involving airplane crashes within Denali National Park." Judge Kleinfeld admitted all nine reports, ruling, "Might bear on foreseeability of circumstances."

Exhibit 1, the 84 page Kahiltna Pass incident report prepared by Gerhard, and Exhibit 2, 23 pages of handwritten notes kept by NPS employees during the rescue, were admitted into evidence. Using both, I walked Gerhard through the events of Wednesday morning, including an 8:45 a.m. call from the McGrath Flight Service Station to Gerhard reporting that a civilian pilot [Geeting] had located the crash site and a later direct call from Doug Geeting at 10:22 a.m. Gerhard read his notes of this call aloud.

A. He says that the wind is up from the Peter's
[Basin]. . . [and] I think it says not too
strong. Plane is intact. The right wing buried in
snow. And someone was waving the light.

Q. Mr. Geeting told you at 10:22 that the wind was
not too strong at the crash site?

A. That was the words I believe he used. . . .

Q. At the time you wrote this down, Mr. Geeting had
   had time to get up, take off in his aircraft,
   circle the crash site, remain there for a period
   of time, fly back to Talkeetna, land, go to his
   office, pick up the phone and call you, correct?

A. That's correct.

Q. You were still sitting in your office in Mt.
   McKinley National Park at the main headquarters,
   not in Talkeetna, waiting for the Chinooks to
   arrive from Wainwright?

A. I was still in my office when I talked to him on
   the phone.....

Continuing through the NPS notes, Gerhard explained his Thursday request that Sandy Kogl, a part-time NPS employee, drive from Park Headquarters to Talkeetna with a pickup load of NPS survival gear. Months earlier, Gerhard had taken the Talkeetna cache of survival gear to Park Headquarters for inventory. On Wednesday morning, he had two caches of survival gear available to him—the Talkeetna cache and the Headquarters cache. Despite knowing from 6:22 a.m. onward that the Chinooks were to arrive at McKinley Park airstrip at 10 a.m., he did not recall going to either cache that morning for survival gear. (He kept his personal equipment in his residence.)

Gerhard identified the handwriting of Ranger Tom Griffiths in Exhibit 2.

Q. Do you see where it says "airdrop, make up ahead
   of time, snowshoes or skis best?"

A. Yes, I see that.

Q. Do you know what [Griffiths is] referring to there?

A. I really don't know. I'm not sure what his
   notes were for. It may have been a discussion
   we had. . . .

The judge wanted to know the date of Griffiths' note. Gerhard answered Thursday, "the same day that Sandy Kogl brought the [survival] gear down."

Gerhard had recently listened to the tape recording of Doug Geeting's comments at the rescue critique. When I asked if he recalled Geeting saying the weather was good at the crash site early Wednesday morning, Ms. Neda objected (hearsay). I argued I was offering evidence that Geeting said the weather was good both for its truth (i.e., the weather was good) and to impeach Gerhard, who now claimed he could not remember Geeting saying this. Ms. Neda argued the evidence should come in only through Geeting's live testimony. Judge Kleinfeld allowed Geeting's statement at the critique into evidence only to impeach Gerhard and not to prove that the weather was, in fact, good. Although I sensed the judge wanted me to, I did not play the critique tape because my boombox was not set up and I wanted to cover one more subject before we adjourned for the day.

The handwritten NPS log for Saturday morning contained entries for the two Chinooks departing (8:56 a.m.) and Chinook 525 returning to Talkeetna with a mechanical problem (9:27 a.m.) I directed Gerhard's attention to the 10:29 a.m. log entry.

> Q. Do you see where it says "Akland helicopter in the air"?
>
> A. Yes.
>
> Q. Do you know why National Park Service personnel recorded in their log that the Akland helicopter had taken off at 10:29 a.m., Saturday?
>
> A. I have no idea. I didn't make that entry. . . .

It was 4:30 and time to adjourn. Judge Kleinfeld said he had a short criminal trial the next morning and offered the choice of standing by in court to squeeze in 30 to 60 minutes before lunch or starting at 1:15 after a shortened lunch. Ms. Neda and I chose the 1:15 start.

Chapter 17

Gerhard

Day 4 began on schedule Friday afternoon at 1:15 p.m. with Gerhard on the witness stand. For the first time, we had no spectators at all.

Gerhard acknowledged that under the Denali SAR Plan, he was to give high priority to the protection of human life, to find and provide emergency medical care, and to evacuate victims in distress using the most effective resources with the least elapsed time. He agreed a search and rescue or SAR mission had priority over every other activity and he was to provide everything necessary. The Denali SAR Plan contained a ranking system to determine the seriousness of the situation presented and listed resources to be used in specific order. For example, he was to contact commercial air taxis before involving military aircraft.

Q. . . . Did you request [an air taxi]?

A. We did utilize Doug Geeting on that morning, I believe, although he was out flying before we made a request.

Q. It is true, is it not, that on Wednesday morning, Doug Geeting voluntarily went up to look for the crash site without you requesting him to do so?

A. That's correct. . . .

Q. You didn't ask any civilian aircraft to search for the crash site, did you?

A. I don't recall if we asked civilian aircraft. We
   had the location of it. . . .

Q. . . . did you hire any civilian aircraft to fly
   to the [crash] site to try to conduct a rescue?

A. Again, I knew that there were aircraft in the air
   at the time, so I knew that there were aircraft
   there trying to do what they could.

Q. The answer to my question is no, you did not
   hire any civilian aircraft to try to fly to the
   [crash] site and to conduct a rescue, correct?

A. I did not call the civilian aircraft and say,
   could you go do that, no, I did not. . . .

Q. . . . [Y]ou didn't call Geeting or anyone else
   to say, load some climbers on board and see
   if you can land at the south side of Kahiltna
   Pass, did you? . . .

A. No, I didn't. . . .

Q. You could have just picked up the phone either
   Tuesday night, or first thing Wednesday morning,
   and asked someone to do it, and said the Park
   Service would pay for it, couldn't you? . . .

A. Yes, I think I could have done that. . . .

Q. . . . Did you call out any rescue organizations?

A. Yes, we did.

Q. When?

A. When we utilized the volunteer climbers from
   Talkeetna the next day.

Q. After you had flown to the site, failed in your
   rescue effort, and then flown to Talkeetna.

A. It was the next day, yes, after we arrived in
   Talkeetna. . . .

Q. Actually, you didn't ask for them, you were
   standing there at the Talkeetna strip, and Art
   Mannix came up to you and said, "Do you need some
   help, Bob?" Right?

A. I don't recall his exact words. He volunteered
   to assist. . . .

Q. Had it occurred to you by then to ask for any
   civilian assistance?

A. I can't recall my thoughts. . . .

Gerhard agreed the NPS documents required that "[i]f a helicopter
[evacuation] is chosen as the primary method of evacuation, a contingency
plan must be established simultaneously for ground evacuation." In other
words, if he used the Chinooks, he was required to prepare a contingency
plan for a ground rescue.

Q. [Y]ou did not do that, did you?

A. Well, I think we did.

Q. What was the contingency for a ground rescue that you
   prepared on Tuesday night or Wednesday morning? . . .

A. . . . [W]e had people on board the helicopter who
   could, if necessary, effect a ground rescue.

Q. Is that your testimony? Wednesday morning, you
   had people on the helicopter who could, if
   necessary, effect a ground rescue?

A. Yes, we could. As we discovered later, we didn't
   feel that we were adequately prepared, but we
   could have done it.

Gerhard acknowledged the NPS had previously hired Akland
Helicopters for numerous rescues within the Park. He agreed that charts in
the book "Surviving Denali" by Jonathan Waterman accurately reflected
many evacuations by Akland Helicopters, often listing the exact cost.

Q. [Y]ou could pick up the phone and hire Akland
   Helicopters to conduct rescues within the Park,
   couldn't you?

A. I could do that if they were available.

Q. Or if you wanted to?

A. Yes, if –

Q. And if you didn't want to, you simply wouldn't call Akland Helicopters.

A. I guess that's correct. I'm not sure what you're trying to –

Q. There came a time when you stopped calling Akland Helicopters?

A. I don't believe that was my decision alone to not use them.

THE COURT: I'm confused here. On the morning of the first rescue attempt, Wednesday, did you or did you not have authority such that if you chose to, you could call Akland Helicopters and ask them to attempt a rescue with the helicopter?

THE WITNESS: I did have that authority, yes. I could have called them, I think. I guess I have to backtrack a little bit, because this is not clear in my mind, and I'm sorry I can't explain it better, but it seems like for some reason we had stopped using Akland Helicopters. . . .

Q. [T]here came a time when you made up your mind to stop using Akland Helicopters, right? . . .

A. It was not my decision alone.

Q. You're the one who made the decision, whether or not you asked others to ratify it.

A. No, that's not correct.

Q. I asked you in your deposition why you made that decision [to stop using Akland] and you gave me two answers. To summarize, one of them was you weren't comfortable with Dennis Brown's flying ability, and the other one was you had had a contractual dispute with Mr. Brown. Is that an accurate summary?

A. I believe it is, yes.

Q. And then we focused on Dennis Brown's flying ability. You never flew with Dennis Brown, did you?

A. No, I don't recall that I ever did fly with him.

Q. Nor do you know anyone in the Park Service who ever flew with Dennis Brown, correct?

A. I believe that's correct.

Q. So it's correct, is it not, that you stopped using Akland Helicopters because of a contractual dispute . . . over the amount he was charging for rescues?

A. No, I don't believe that is correct.

Q. Page 38, question at line 6, "You had flown with Dennis Brown in an Akland Helicopter?" Answer: "I'm not sure that I ever did, I don't think I did." Question: Can you tell me the name of any National Park Service employee who flew with Dennis Brown in an Akland Helicopter?" Answer: "I don't remember that anyone ever did." Question: "What, then, was the basis for the lack of confidence in Dennis Brown's ability to fly a helicopter in the mountains?" Answer: "The problem stemmed, I guess, from — I believe we had contractual problems with him."

A. That's what that says. Could I take a minute to read a little bit of this?

Judge Kleinfeld smiled during this portion of Gerhard's cross-examination. When Gerhard asked "to read a little bit of this," Kleinfeld called a recess.

When we resumed, Gerhard agreed he had never utilized the Fairbanks civilian mountain rescue group headed by Doug Buchanan. He preferred to work with the AMRG in Anchorage. He acknowledged he had never had a mountain rescue group ask for money. Although he paid 5 of the 6 Mountain Maniacs (the sixth refused) as temporary NPS employees, they had not requested payment.

To this point, the focus had been on why Gerhard did not hire Dennis Brown to fly an Akland helicopter to the crash site on Wednesday morning.

It now shifted to whether an unpaid volunteer rescue flight by Brown would have been allowed at all.

> Q. Let me ask you to assume that on [Wednesday] morning, a civilian helicopter wanted to land at or near the crash site. Was permission from the National Park Service necessary for that to occur?
>
> A. No, I don't believe it was.
>
> Q. Did you feel you had the authority to deny a private helicopter permission to land at or near the crash site?
>
> A. I believe I answered in the deposition that yes, I did feel I had that authority. I've had time to think about that, and . . . if someone had offered their services, I could have said either yes, we would like you to do that, or no, we don't need your services. But I'm not sure I could deny somebody, especially if I didn't know about it, to go up there and do something. . . .
>
> Q. Can you say whether you would have granted permission to Dennis Brown flying in an Akland Helicopter, if he'd made that request on [Wednesday] morning?
>
> A. That's really hard to answer at this time. I'm not sure if I would have or not. As I said, we had reservations about his capabilities.
>
> Q. You're telling the judge today that if Dennis Brown had asked for permission [Wednesday] morning to fly to the crash site, you may have said no?
>
> A. I may have said no or I may have said yes at the time. I don't know. I really can't recreate that.

The first item in Exhibit 1, Gerhard's "after action" report, was the phone system at Park headquarters.

Q. At 11:21 [Tuesday night, the RCC] called you at
your home, and they had previously tried to call
you but had not gotten an answer. The phones at
your home didn't work properly, did they?

A. I assume not. We hadn't received any calls.

Q. You stated [at the critique] that it had happened
before, including in emergency situations, that
people had called your home about a rescue and
they would hear a ringing sound but it wasn't
ringing in your house.

A. I'm not sure if I was talking specifically
about my house. It was on the phone system for
the park, and the phones into the park did
occasionally have problems, yes.

THE COURT: . . . there's a sentence here [in Exhibit
1], "Apparently this was the fault of the
telephone system, since the night answer phone
was switched to the superintendent's residence
that evening. The superintendent was in his
residence all evening but no calls came through."
I don't understand the first of those two
sentences. Would you tell me what that is?

THE WITNESS: Yes. We don't have any staff working
through the night in the park, especially in
wintertime, but . . . the Park Service telephone
number would be forwarded to different people's
houses. You take your turn, you'd have to stay
home and be available in case a call came
through. We call that night answer. . . .

As the judge questioned Gerhard, I reviewed my transcript of the
rescue critique for statements about the phone system.

Q. You said at the critique, ". . . It's been
something that's been happening at other times,
not just in emergency situations." . . . "But
sometimes our phone system, you dial it, and
the number will ring and ring and ring

and there will be somebody at the other end,
but they won't hear it. If that happens, try
something else, I guess."

A. That sounds like what I said. . . .

I did not ask the obvious question: try what else?

The chronology in Exhibit 1 offered an opening to attack Mr. Bridgman's
claims of bad weather on Tuesday night.

Q. . . . you mentioned that the RCC notified the
Chinooks at 7:20 [Tuesday night], and then you
say "It was decided that if Chinook helicopters
were mobilized and flown to Talkeetna that
evening, they would not arrive in Talkeetna until
the early hours of Wednesday, approximately 2:00
a.m." , correct?

A. That's what it says [in Exhibit 1], yes.

Q. That's the only reason given for not flying the
Chinooks from Wainwright to Talkeetna Tuesday
night, isn't it, that they would arrive too late?
. . .

A. That's all my report says.

Q. Isn't it a fact that at the critique, there was
no mention made of any supposed bad weather
between Wainwright and Talkeetna to prevent that
flight that night? . . .

A. I don't recall any discussion like that, no. . . .

To underscore the point, I jumped forward in Exhibit 1 to Gerhard's
4 page summary of the rescue critique and read aloud the four reasons
for the delay in the Chinooks reaching the crash site. Gerhard agreed
with them, one by one. Bad weather was not one of the four reasons. He
again testified he did not recall Bridgman making any reference to bad
weather between Ft. Wainwright and Talkeetna on Tuesday night.

Gerhard did nothing Tuesday night or Wednesday morning to
plan a rescue.

Q. What did you do to prepare to take part
[Wednesday] morning?

A. Got the equipment together that I felt
we needed. . . .

Q. So you grabbed your pack, and [Griffiths] grabbed
his pack, and you were ready to get on the
Chinook? That's it, isn't it, that's all you did?

[Objection, asked and answered, overruled.]

A. That's not all I did.

Q. What else did you do?

A. I don't recall what else I did. I got prepared to
board the Chinooks the next day.

Q. The next morning, you got up, you got dressed,
you brushed your teeth, and you grabbed your
pack. What else did you do?

A. I made a number of phone calls . . . and I would
have talked with my boss . . . and we would have
been getting prepared.

Directing Gerhard to page 29 of Exhibit 1, I read aloud his wording:
"As per Tom and myself, we should have been better prepared. I'm putting
together equipment caches, food, stove, fuel, shelter, et cetera, that will
be stored in the rescue cache, and that can be quickly grabbed whenever
we participate in a helicopter rescue." Then I read aloud Tom Griffiths'
note: "We were to go along primarily as observers, but were equipped to
participate in a throw and go rescue effort. For an extended stay, we needed
food, fuel, and sleeping bags for ourselves and victims."

Q. What equipment did you bring to [airdrop]?

A. I didn't bring any equipment specifically for a
drop, because I assumed there was gear on the
helicopter that could be used for that purpose.

Q. Was there discussion that morning in the
helicopter of dropping supplies to the victims?
. . .

A. I can't recall if there was or not.

Q. At the time of your deposition, you answered, "I don't remember any."

[Objection, not impeachment because no material difference in testimony, overruled.]

Gerhard recounted the initial flight of Chinook 033 over the crash site. He was seated just behind the pilot and co-pilot. Unlike Mr. Warden, he remembered the pilot trying to hover at the same altitude as the crash site (where Clouser thought he could have hit the Chinook with a snowball).

Q. At any time, have you been told by anyone that the weather at the crash site on Wednesday morning was good enough earlier in the morning . . . for a rescue to have occurred?

A. Well, when Doug Geeting called, he told me that the wind was not too strong, and I believe I talked with him afterwards, and for a long time, I believed that the weather was good enough that morning. I'm not sure that I believe that now. Now I just really don't know for sure.

When I asked if he remembered Geeting's comments at the critique, Ms. Neda objected (relevance). The judge overruled her objection but asked that Geeting's comments be played. This time my boombox was ready.

(Tape recording played in court.)

MR. GEETING: . . . [Had the Chinooks] been in Talkeetna . . . on Wednesday morning and ready to go at first light, okay, and once the aircraft was spotted, it takes approximately 45 minutes . . . to get up to the crash site, to the 10,000 foot level. They could have landed there. It was smooth.

And they could have gotten over and gotten the people out or . . . maybe not got them out of there that night, in fact that would have been very doubtful, but they would have been able

to get somebody there to 'em, which could have
made a difference with at least one person [Pat
Scanlon]. That's the whole beef, is, you know,
there's got to be a way, that hopefully it'll
never happen again, but if it does, I can see the
same situation happening all over again, because
. . . there's too much time it takes.

(Tape recording stopped.) . . .

THE COURT: I've admitted that for purposes of
foundation for impeachment, but not for its
substantive content. . . .

Q. You, yourself, said at the critique when you
were asked if a Chinook could have landed there
safely, "Not at the time we were there. Doug was
there a few hours earlier and said it was quite
good, so it was one of those things we missed by
an hour or so."

A. Yes, I remember saying that. That's what I
believed at the time. I respected Doug's
judgment. It doesn't mean that that's true, I
don't know what the winds were at that time, and
as I say, I'm not sure now.

The judge reminded us he needed to recess early. Kleinfeld repeated
that he admitted Geeting's statement for impeachment of Gerhard and not
for its truth. "Mr. Geeting can testify himself as to whatever he believes
to be the truth under oath." After confirming trial would resume Tuesday,
not Monday, I said Tuesday was the only day Geeting could testify and
asked permission to interrupt Gerhard's testimony to accommodate
him. Ms. Neda did not oppose the request. Court recessed until 9 a.m.
Tuesday. Week one of trial was over.

Chapter 18

A Lawyer in Alaska

When trial adjourned Friday afternoon, I was very tired. With no trial on Monday, I took Saturday and Sunday off. On Friday night, my family drove from Anchorage to Girdwood, home of Alyeska Ski Resort, where we owned half of a cabin. The weather was sunny and two days of fresh air and spring skiing with my wife and two daughters recharged my brain.

How did I come to be a lawyer in Alaska? I was born in the fall of 1947 in Yakima, Washington, an agricultural community of 40,000 that called itself "Fruit Bowl of the Nation." Yakima is east of the Cascade mountains and suffers from excellent weather with daily blue sky. I grew up with a strong sense of right and wrong and an almost naïve view of life.

My father, Andrew, grew up in Seattle, graduated from the University of Washington, fought in World War II, commercial fished for a year in Alaska, and owned an orchard supply business. My mother, Phyllis, also a college graduate, was a housewife. Her father, Ed Prentice, owned a number of apple orchards and a fruit packing plant. My father and grandfather strongly influenced me.

Ever since I can remember, I wanted to be a lawyer. As a boy, I read Louis Nizer's "My Life in Court" and Irving Stone's "Clarence Darrow for the Defense." I watched "Perry Mason" on black and white television.

As a child, I attended the First Presbyterian Church in Yakima. The pastor, Rev. Koehler, was a wonderful speaker and I greatly admired his oratory.

After skipping kindergarten, I attended public school in Yakima. The students reflected all socio-economic levels. Because I was a late bloomer and a year ahead of myself, I had no chance of making the high school athletic teams. (My senior year, the two biggest high schools in Yakima dominated football and basketball statewide.) I played little league baseball, church league basketball, and neighborhood football.

I took debate for two years in high school and excelled. An incident my senior year indicated I might have the makings of a trial lawyer. My opponent was a tall blond girl from Sunnyside who was to attend Stanford. I had the affirmative and she had the negative. To argue against my position, she used a prepared chart, which I thought irrelevant. In my final turn to speak, I speculated aloud that she used one side of the chart for affirmative and one side for negative. Without having looked beforehand, I flipped the chart over, saw it supported my position, and incorporated it into my argument. My opponent was infuriated, but I won the debate.

I wanted to go east to college but was an indifferent student and never made the honor roll. A savvy guidance counselor told me leadership helped an application, so I ran for student body vice president and won. I applied to Yale, Dartmouth, the University of Pennsylvania, and the University of Washington. I applied to Penn because it sent recruiters to my high school to promote its "boondocks" program to encourage diversity in its student body. Only Penn and the U.W. accepted me.

I have always been glad I went to Penn. My father had rowed for Washington, so I went out for the heavyweight crew, which had a "no cut" policy. The freshman coach, Ted Nash, a recent Olympic gold medalist, turned us into animals. I went from doing 4 pull-ups to 24 and ran 3 miles a day. Although I was only an alternate, Penn's freshman crew was undefeated and my sophomore year Penn won the IRAs (national championships). My junior year, after I quit rowing, Penn lost the finals of the 1968 Olympic trials to Harvard by inches. Learning to train and compete at a high level was a big change for a boy who could not make a high school team. I learned more from rowing than from anything else at Penn.

In the spring of 1968, Martin Luther King, Jr. was assassinated. Robert Kennedy, whom I supported, was assassinated. I did not want to sit in class as all this happened, so I quit Penn and was a Vista Volunteer in Atlanta in 1968-69, during what would have been my senior year. I worked with Atlanta Legal Services on welfare and social security rights, taught adult education, and organized food co-ops. I lived in an apartment in northwest Atlanta adjoining Perry Homes, then the largest Black public housing project in the South.

My mother's father, Ed Prentice, died in February, 1967, shortly after my father bought one half of my grandfather's most profitable apple orchard. In the spring of 1968, a late freeze wiped out the orchard's entire crop for the first time in 50 years. The freeze cost my father his half of the orchard and his orchard supply business, which went bankrupt. Andrew developed pancreatic cancer and died in November, 1969, at age 48.[5] (His father also died at age 48.)

In the summer of 1969, I left Vista to be with my father. When I returned to Penn that fall, I learned my senior year had been mostly eliminated. The previous requirement of 40 credits to graduate (8 semesters x 5 courses) had been lowered to 32 credits (8 x 4 courses). I had 30 credits from my first three years; I took only two courses and graduated in December, 1969. My father died over Thanksgiving weekend, about a month before. I had just turned 22.

In the spring of 1970, I flew to Alaska to work on the oil pipeline. I arrived four years early. Eventually I was hired as a track laborer or "gandy dancer" on Extra Gang 4 of the Alaska Railroad. I lived in a boxcar as we repaired the northern 100 miles of track from Healy (north of Mt. McKinley National Park headquarters) to Fairbanks. I liked the job and loved Alaska.

I entered the University of Washington Law School in the fall of 1971. I liked my classmates and a few of my professors, but I did not like law school. In many respects, law school is a trade school, nothing more. There were no trial practice courses or, if there were, I did not take any. Fortunately, law studies came easily and I was a good student. I married my wife, Martha Mills, after my first year and she entered a private law school that fall, one year behind me. My second year, I was accepted for the law review and published twice. Third year, I was Comments Editor. After I graduated, one of my papers was published as a comment.

---

5. My father tried to hide his cancer, but when it became known, a close family friend, Lester Lewis, offered to fly my mother and father anywhere in the world. Lester and his wife, Carol Ann, flew my parents and a third couple (the husband was a doctor) from Yakima to Paris first class. The three couples then floated the canals of central and southern France, stopping at the headquarters of Moet &Chandon for a private tour. Andrew died about a month later.

I was completely broke in Vista and in law school. My tuition was low but my wife paid $1000 a semester. I worked for Seattle Legal Services my first and second years. We both had summer jobs. My third year, in addition to being on law review, I had two part-time jobs. We still had no money and went on food stamps.

When I graduated in June, 1974, I had the credentials to be hired by a big Seattle law firm but did not apply. Instead, I passed the Washington bar exam and worked for the Seattle Regional Office of the Department of Housing & Urban Development. When my wife graduated in December, we soon boarded the Alaska ferry and headed for Anchorage. We had agreed that if she did not like Alaska, we would leave. She liked it. That summer we both passed the Alaska bar.

In Alaska, I worked for a small law firm doing insurance defense work for a little under two years. Then I worked twelve months for a law firm doing prepaid legal work for members of Teamsters Union Local 959. My wife worked as a law clerk and then became an assistant attorney general for the State of Alaska. I started my own practice in March, 1978, one month before our first daughter was born. By then, I was playing Friday night poker with a group including Tom Scanlon.

Chapter 19

Gerhard finish

Apparently Judge Kleinfeld spent Mondays in Fairbanks. I used the day to meet with several witnesses to prepare their testimony and to finish trial notebooks for the U.S.A.'s witnesses, including Ed Hommer.

When court resumed Tuesday morning, I informed the judge that Doug Geeting could not be present at 9 a.m., but anticipated being in court at 1:30. Ranger Gerhard resumed the stand and cross-examination continued.

When Chinook 033 landed in Talkeetna shortly after noon on Wednesday, Gerhard accepted Art Mannix's offer to round up local climbers. Thursday morning, he requested the Army's HART from Ft. Greely. Thursday afternoon, he called in the AMRG from Anchorage.

> Q. You could have done that, made [any] of those requests on Tuesday night if you had chosen to, couldn't you?
>
> A. I could have made those requests. It wouldn't have made any difference in this incident.
>
> MR. GALBRAITH: I ask that the last comment be stricken. It's not responsive to my question.
>
> THE COURT: I will disregard the comment. Mr. Gerhard, this would proceed much more rapidly if you would listen to the question, answer it, and stop. . . .
>
> THE WITNESS: Yes, Your Honor, I'm sorry.

Q. [Wednesday afternoon], you still weren't putting [together] an airdrop of materials to try to drop to the victims, correct?

A. We had already tried one airdrop, and that hadn't —

Q. You hadn't tried an airdrop. You weren't on the second helicopter [525], were you?

A. No, but it's my understanding that that had been done. . . .

THE COURT: The helicopter you were in did not try an airdrop, is that right?

THE WITNESS: That's correct, we didn't feel we could.

THE COURT: When did you first talk to anyone about the subject of an airdrop?

THE WITNESS: I don't really recall. . . . I just know that we would have, and that the second helicopter did plan to try that. . . .

THE COURT: How do you know that the second helicopter was going to do that?

THE WITNESS: My recollection at this time is all from . . . [the rescue critique].

THE COURT: So the way you know that the second helicopter was going to do that is that at the critique somebody mentioned that the second helicopter was going to do that?

THE WITNESS: That's how I remember it at this time. . . .

No NPS Ranger was aboard the Thursday afternoon Chinook flight. Gerhard admitted there was less survival gear available to airdrop on that flight because of the absence of the two Rangers and their personal packs.

At Gerhard's direction, the Park Service paid Geeting $350 for a two hour flight at daybreak Wednesday morning, although Gerhard did not request the flight. Using Exhibit 1, Gerhard testified NPS costs totaled $6979 (he paid himself and other NPS staffers five days of hazard pay) and military costs totaled $111,364.

THE COURT: . . . Under military aircraft costs where
$111,364 is listed, does that mean that the
National Park Service wrote a check to the U. S.
Army for that amount?

THE WITNESS: I don't believe we did in this case, no.

THE COURT: Do they send bills?

THE WITNESS: We have been billed by the military
at other times. It's not been consistent. . . .
I'm quite certain we did not get a bill for
this one. . . .

THE COURT: Based on your past experience, what would
it have cost to hire the helicopter service in
Talkeetna? Brown, I think the man's name was?

THE WITNESS: . . . I think they're on the order . . .
of around $500 an hour. . . .

THE COURT: So that would be $2,500 a day for maximum
use? . . . If you'd had [Akland] sitting there at
your beck and call for the entire four days, [it]
would have cost you about $12,000?

THE WITNESS: Quite possibly. . . .

Bob Gerhard considered Art Mannix to be an experienced and competent
climber whose judgment he respected. When I offered the Mannix letter of
January 14, 1982 into evidence, the judge admitted the letter, but reiterated
that he wanted to hear live testimony from persons listed in Gerhard's report,
including Geeting and Mannix. So much for a 4 day trial!

At the critique, Gerhard called the Mannix letter "really good" and read
it aloud. I noticed the judge reading the letter and asked if he wanted me to
stop. He did. I stood silently at the podium until he finished.

Q. During that four day period, did you give any
thought to preparing an airdrop and attaching a
bright-colored streamer?

A. I'm quite certain we talked about airdrops. I don't
recall whether we specifically talked about adding
a streamer to it.

THE COURT: . . . you quite certainly thought of airdrops?

THE WITNESS: They were a part of our plan. We had tried right from the first day to make an airdrop, and had the helicopter been able to get overhead, . . . we certainly would have done that.

THE COURT: When did you first think of an airdrop?

THE WITNESS: It was attempted on the first time we arrived at the site with the second helicopter.

THE COURT: I didn't ask you that. I asked when you, Mr. Gerhard, first thought of an airdrop?

THE WITNESS: I can't recall at this time when that thought first came into my head. I've worked on other rescues in the past where airdrops have been used, so they would be in my thoughts at any time.

I referred Gerhard to his deposition testimony where he listed three rescue options--landing near the site, dropping people off, and doing a hoist evacuation. "You do not list [a] fourth option, performing an airdrop, correct?" A. "I must have forgotten to say that at the deposition."

The tape recording of Gerhard telling the rescue critique of the pathologist's opinions as to the cause of death of Dan Hartmann (punctured lung) and Pat Scanlon (uncertain) was played in court. Judge Kleinfeld made it clear he wanted to hear live testimony from the pathologist. The U.S.A., not plaintiffs, planned to call him.

Cross-examination ended with a list of damaging statements (or admissions) made by Gerhard at the rescue critique. I highlighted a number of these in the critique transcript and my paralegal, Donna, made a separate cassette tape and transcript of only these comments. My $70 boombox had a numerical counter and Donna referenced the starting number for each excerpt. (She did the same for all trial witnesses who spoke at the rescue critique.) In court, I would read Gerhard's comment, ask if he said that at the critique, and, if he denied it, play the tape recording of him saying those exact words. When he figured this out, Gerhard became very agreeable. Ms. Neda objected, but the judge ruled, "I will allow [counsel] to lead in this manner. He has a hostile witness."

Gerhard admitted saying "we should have been better prepared" and "I guess I kept resisting thinking that this was going to get as big as it did, and that was a mistake on my part. We should have geared up faster." Gerhard agreed with all of my checklist, item by item. The cross-examination of Ranger Gerhard lasted an hour on Thursday, three hours on Friday, and two and a half hours on Tuesday, or slightly more than a full trial day.

In her direct examination, Ms. Neda covered Gerhard's education, work experience with the NPS, and qualifications as an Emergency Medical Technician. She brought out that other federal agencies exercise law enforcement powers inside Park boundaries, including the FBI, Fish and Wildlife, the Drug Enforcement Agency, and the NTSB.

During the morning, a court clerk brought me a note to call my office. When I did, I learned Doug Geeting would not testify. As the lunch recess was called, I advised that Geeting would not appear in the afternoon.

When court resumed, Ms. Neda moved for an order requiring plaintiffs to provide the U.S.A. with a copy of the written transcript of the rescue critique. Initially, Judge Kleinfeld directed me to provide the transcript. I argued that plaintiffs had paid a court reporter to prepare the transcript, my office had edited it to identify the speakers, and the U.S.A. had always had possession of the tapes and could have prepared its own transcript. Kleinfeld reversed himself and ruled "plaintiffs' transcript need not be provided to the government."

Ms. Neda resumed direct examination. Gerhard agreed that 25 climbers [6 Mountain Maniacs, 6 AMRG, 13 HART] were not needed at Kahiltna Pass on Saturday. When she asked why Clouser walked over the Pass, Gerhard testified the Mountain Maniacs were insistent. He said a HART member [Strauss] objected strongly that Mike should have been carried, like Hommer.

Gerhard testified the Kahiltna Pass rescue was unique because it involved an airplane crash with survivors. He believed the Denali SAR Plan required a paramedic to be aboard military rescue flights. He, Griffiths, and the Air Force PJs met that requirement.

Gerhard knew Dick Hunze at the Talkeetna Flight Service Station. He did not request a notice to airmen or NOTAM to be issued restricting air space over the accident site.

Q. At any time during this rescue, whether it be Wednesday morning or any time, did you tell Mr. Richard Hunze to forbid aircraft traffic in the area of the accident site?

A. No, I did not.

Q. [I]n December '81, could private aircraft land without permission in Mt. McKinley National Park?

A. . . . [T]hey could land anywhere within the Park or Preserve boundaries.

Q. Additionally, in an emergency situation such as this, could [an air taxi] land . . . without the National Park Service's permission?

A. It's always been my understanding that in an emergency, any aircraft could land, that's correct.

When Gerhard was contacted late Tuesday night, the RCC had already requested the Chinooks. Asked if he disagreed with the RCC's rescue plan, he answered, "No, I did not. I think that was the best decision to make in this incident."

Ms. Neda touched briefly on Dennis Brown. Gerhard said Brown was difficult to deal with in a business situation. As to piloting, "I only know what I have heard from talking with other pilots and other people in the Talkeetna area, and I don't recall anybody I talked to that said he was a very good pilot."

Ms. Neda's last question was longer than most.

Q. Turning to [the rescue critique summary written by Gerhard], . . . in the center of the last paragraph, it states "The consensus of opinions of the critique was that the rescue was well organized and well run. A common theme heard many times was that the cooperation between the various agencies and groups involved in the rescue was excellent."

   I note you say consensus of opinion. How about your opinion and your assessment based on your experience of other rescue missions? . . .

A. I agree with those statements as they're written,
   yes. I think it was carried out as best it could
   be, given the conditions that we encountered and
   the resources we had, yes.

On recross-examination, I felt constrained to ask questions only on
matters raised by Ms. Neda's direct. It was time to get Gerhard off the
witness stand.

Q. It's your belief, right now, that this Kahiltna
   Pass rescue was a well organized, well run
   exercise, is that correct?

A. That's correct. . . .

Q. It wasn't [the] necessity for an EMT that kept
   you from calling either Akland Helicopters or some
   other Talkeetna based [air taxi] . . . , correct?

A. That's correct. . . .

Q. You [testified a] private aircraft could land in
   Denali National Park in December, 1981. . . . I
   want to distinguish between private aircraft and
   air taxi operators. Could air taxi operators land
   within the boundaries of Denali National Park in
   December, 1981?

A. If . . . they were operating as commercial
   operators, then they would have to have a
   commercial use license from the Park Service
   before they could do that. . . .

Q. Helicopter landings within the Park were
   prohibited in December, 1981, were they not?

A. That's correct, except in [a] search and rescue
   operation, that could be waived.

Q. As a general rule, no helicopter, private,
   commercial, or military, could land within the
   boundaries of Denali National Park in December
   1981?

A. Except in a search and rescue mission.

Q. If it was waived, to finish your answer.

A. I'm not sure that we had to waive it, or if it would be waived automatically, I just don't know. . . .

Gerhard admitted that he could have reached Talkeetna air taxi pilots at home on Tuesday night or Wednesday morning.

Q. . . . you could have reached Dennis Brown, if you'd tried to reach him Wednesday morning?

A. I'm not sure that I would have. I don't think that he was qualified to do what he wanted to do . . . based on his reputation . . . from information I had gotten and other people had gotten.

Q. Tell me now what pilot ever told you Dennis Brown was a poor helicopter pilot?

A. Probably everyone I talked to in Talkeetna.

Q. Let's have some names.

A. Doug Geeting, Jim Okonek come to mind. . . .

I asked one question too many. At my bullheaded insistence, Gerhard named two pilots who told him Brown was a poor helicopter pilot. Geeting would not testify (for me), but Okonek was to testify. What did Jim Okonek think of the piloting skills of his former boss, Dennis Brown?

After a short redirect by Ms. Neda, the judge excused Gerhard as a witness. He was free to watch the rest of the trial. He did not.

Chapter 20

Dennis Brown

When Doug Geeting failed to appear, there was no live witness standing by. Dennis Brown's testimony by video deposition fit well here; I wanted the judge to hear it before live testimony from Larry Rivers and Dick Hunze. (Brown could testify by deposition because he could not be located in Alaska.) Federal court did not provide a television or a VCR for playing the videotape, so I brought my own. As I set them up, I overheard Jim Wilson ask Tara Neda how the videotape played. "I don't know," she replied, "I have never seen it." (Ms. Neda was not the attorney for the U.S.A. when the deposition was taken in May, 1984. James Piper, who worked in the same office as Ms. Neda, attended Brown's deposition.)

Dennis Brown had about 10,000 hours in fixed wing aircraft and held multiple pilot ratings including airline transport, multi-engine, float plane, and flight instructor. He also held a rotary license that allowed him to fly helicopters.

Q. How [many hours in a helicopter]?

A. I presently have about 3,000.

Q. Do you remember about how many hours you had in a [helicopter] in December, 1981?

A. Approximately 15, 1,600 hours.

Q. Would you [briefly] describe your helicopter flying experience?

A. I started flying helicopters in 1975 in Wyoming.
   I brought the helicopters to Alaska in '77. . . .
   [I]t's all bush style flying, all in trees,
   mountains, type of flying. I have no experience
   in city flying or anything like that.

Brown started Akland (short for Alaska Land) Helicopters with one $24,000 helicopter and grew the company to 12 aircraft, 9 helicopters and 3 fixed wing. Akland's rescue policy was "[i]f ever there was a need that existed, we were to respond to that need as quickly as we could in the best manner that we could." From 1977 until February, 1984, Akland was involved in 50 to 100 rescues mostly in Denali National Park. "Sometimes, not always," Akland was paid for performing rescues. The likelihood of payment had no effect, "none," on the company's rescue policy. Brown described awards won by Akland, including Jim Okonek's award as helicopter pilot of the year for 1980 presented in Disneyland. Okonek flew Jet Bell Ranger N1086Y. When hired by the Park Service, 86 Yankee was billed at $450 to $480 an hour.

On Wednesday, Brown was awakened before dawn by two fixed wing planes taking off and heading towards Mt. McKinley. He immediately drove to work and had an employee, David Lee, remove a fixed wing Cessna 206 and Akland helicopter 86Y from their hangars. Both were started, warmed up, and fueled. Brown described the arrival of Larry Rivers, how Rivers volunteered to go along, Rivers' departure to get survival gear from his home, and his return 20 to 30 minutes later. Brown, Rivers, and David Lee then loaded 300 pounds of survival gear on the helicopter including a stove, fuel, 8 sleeping bags, bunny boots, extra parkas, and lots of food. Spruce boughs and ice axes were roped to the struts. Brown described a three part rescue plan: (1) land at the site and bring the people in, (2) land near the site and drop off Larry Rivers and survival gear, (3) airdrop survival gear.

On aircraft frequencies, Brown overheard Geeting describe the weather at the crash site, which "was basically what it was in Talkeetna, clear, no clouds that would hinder flight, and that the wind was blowing on the mountain."

Q. Did you hear an estimate of how hard the wind
   was blowing?

A. Yes, I heard 35. . . .

Q. Can a helicopter fly in 35 mile per hour winds?

A. Yes, it can.

Q. Would you explain that please?

A. 35 mph wind is not an adverse wind for a
   helicopter at all. . . . [A] helicopter becomes
   more stable in some wind, providing you keep the
   wind on the nose, and a 35 mph wind is a good
   wind to have.

After 86Y was loaded, Brown and Rivers drove to the Talkeetna
Flight Service Station (FSS) across the runway from the Akland
office. Only Dick Hunze, Larry Rivers, and Brown were present. To
the best of his recollection:

> I told Dick that we were going to go up to
> Mt. McKinley and make this rescue of these people
> and participate in [the] rescue operations up
> there. And Dick Hunze made a comment saying that
> we weren't authorized to make a landing up there;
> that the military had been called. He said that
> there was aircraft that had already departed
> Anchorage and had already departed Fairbanks.
> They were military aircraft and that they were
> going to make the rescue themselves and that I
> was to stay out of it.

Q. Do you recall anything you said in that conversation?

A. I know we talked about the fact of going up
   there and that we could make the rescue almost
   immediately. We'd be up there in 30 minutes from
   that time and I remember making the comment to him,
   something to the effect that, when is all this
   going to take place and the feeling I had is that
   it was going to happen that day but not right away.

Q. What is your best recollection about what Mr.
   Hunze told you about landing in Mt. McKinley
   National Park?

A. He said I was not authorized to make a landing in Mt. McKinley National Park.

Q. Did he say anything else along that line?

A. He told me that the aircraft from Fairbanks were stopping at [McKinley Park airstrip] and picking up [an NPS Ranger]. . . .

Q. Did he tell you, as you've testified, that you weren't authorized to make a landing?

A. That's what he told me. . . . He flat told me I was to stay out, period. . . .

Q. That morning, in that conversation, what did you understand or what did you think Mr. Hunze was telling you?

A. He was speaking for the government and he was speaking as a voice of authority and he was telling me not to get involved in any way, shape or form in this operation. . . .

Q. Did you think Mr. Hunze had authority to tell you that?

A. Yes, I did.

Q. Did you think Mr. Hunze had authority to keep you from going to the crash site in the national park?

A. Yes, I did. . . .

Q. [Did] Mr. Hunze . . . tell you you couldn't land?

A. Yes, he did.

Q. Did he tell you not to go?

A. Yes, he did.

Q. Can you state today, whether on Wednesday, you would have left Talkeetna in Akland Helicopter N1086Y to attempt the rescue if Dick Hunze hadn't told you not to go?

A. I would have left within 10 minutes after being in his office if he had not told me not to go.

Brown's notes showed the first phone call he recorded Wednesday morning was at 9:37 a.m. He testified the conversation with Dick Hunze occurred before then.

On Thursday morning, Brown offered 86Y to Jim Okonek, his former pilot, and "we both discussed the fact that we weren't happy with what was happening, and that they had lost the best day we had, and that was [Wednesday]. . . ."

> Q. Why did you offer 86 Yankee to Mr. Okonek?
>
> A. . . . [T]he basic reason that I offered it to him
>   was, one, it was a military operation . . . and
>   I was told not to hinder this operation that the
>   military was doing. Okonek was a Lt. Colonel,
>   had just retired from the Air Force a couple
>   of years before this time, and he knew most of
>   those people. And I thought if I couldn't be part
>   of this, certainly he could cut through that
>   military red tape and be part of it. The other
>   thing was that Okonek knew that mountain better
>   than anyone I could think of . . . plus he'd made
>   . . . the bulk of the rescues up there.

On Saturday morning, Brown arrived at the airport early, watched what he termed a leisurely departure by the two Chinooks, and witnessed Chinook 525 return to Talkeetna shortly after take-off. Brown then flew solo in 86 Yankee over the crash site, where he witnessed satisfactory rescue activities. Brown's business records reflected this one hour flight.

> Q. When you were up there in the helicopter Saturday
>   morning, did you think you were breaking the law?
>
> A. I did.
>
> Q. [Saturday] morning, you thought you were breaking
>   the law?
>
> A. I thought I was breaking the law. . . .
>
> Q. Given your recollection of the weather on
>   Wednesday at the crash site, or at least what
>   you'd heard about it, and what you could see,

and given your flyovers of the crash site on
Saturday, do you have an opinion as to what you
could have done for the Hudson crash victims on
Wednesday morning?

[Objection, lack of foundation, opinion, overruled.]

A. I could have landed at the [summit of Kahiltna
   Pass] above the accident Wednesday morning. I
   would have been there before 9:30. I would have
   off-loaded Larry Rivers, off-loaded the gear, and
   we would have attempted to [do] whatever possible
   to render aid or rescue these people. There's no
   doubt in my mind whatsoever, not the slightest
   shred of doubt, that I could have landed there
   that morning.

In late January, 1982, Brown loaned 86 Yankee to Okonek, who flew
a crew up to Kahiltna Pass and landed on the summit. The crew salvaged
radio gear from the Hudson wreckage.

My direct examination finished at 3:45 p.m. The U.S.A.'s cross-examination
by Mr. Piper, Ms. Neda's predecessor, lasted 90 minutes and could not be
finished this afternoon. The judge directed me to stop at 4:20 because he
had another matter at 4:30.

In cross-examination, Mr. Piper asked about Brown's aviation background,
how he kept track of flying hours, his current medical certificates, and
other technical matters. For pilot Dennis Brown, being examined under
oath by an FAA attorney was equivalent to a taxpayer enduring an IRS audit
under oath.

At the time of his deposition in May, 1984, Akland was in liquidation in
Chapter 7 bankruptcy and Brown was its "operator." Piper asked if Akland
"ever received any certificates of suspensions or violations recorded
against it by the FAA?" Brown answered, "Not while I was there." In
court, I objected that FAA violations by Akland two or three years after
the rescue were not relevant. Ms. Neda argued that FAA suspensions close
to the time of the deposition could cause Brown to be biased against
the FAA.

THE COURT: . . . It does appear that some of the
   material might be admissible for proof of bias

regarding Mr. Brown's motivations . . . and
some of the material may possibly bear on the
foundation of Mr. Gerhard's opinion that Mr.
Brown was a bad pilot at the time of the rescue
attempt, 1981. So I'm listening to those two
things as I listen to the evidence. I can also
see possible probative value on why Mr. Brown
would choose not to fly in after being told by
the FAA person at Talkeetna not to fly in, if he
felt himself to be in jeopardy of some sort of
government action.

Judge Kleinfeld adjourned court until 9 the next morning.

It was time to decide what to do about Doug Geeting. Second only to Clouser and Hommer, I believed him to be the most knowledgeable witness about the weather at the crash site early Wednesday morning. The judge wanted his live testimony. He was under subpoena but refused to appear. Should I have a U. S. Marshal go to Talkeetna, arrest him, and force him to testify?

Geeting mailed a typed letter saying he would not testify. Dated April 4, it bore an April 11 postmark and was received in my office on Monday, April 13, though I did not see it until after court on Tuesday. Full of misspellings, the letter claimed he could not get away from his business for the next two months because he was "extreamly [sic] schedualed [sic] to fly climbers" in and out of the mountains and he felt testifying in this case "was not a life or death afair [sic]." I did not take the letter at face value. Geeting could fly from Talkeetna to Anchorage, testify in court, and fly back to Talkeetna in 4 or 5 hours total. My gut feeling was he possessed personal courage as a pilot, but not as a witness. Different things cause fear in different people.

Geeting acted admirably in the rescue. On his own initiative, he located the crash site at the earliest possible time on Wednesday. He spoke bravely at the rescue critique, expressing plaintiffs' theory of the case: why didn't the Chinooks get there earlier? With Gerhard's blessing, he was the person who told Tom Scanlon of Pat's death.

I had been uneasy about Geeting ever since Tom introduced us in April, 1984. As the case developed, it became clear that Talkeetna was a company town and the National Park Service was the company. Gerhard had the ability, by himself, to make an air taxi profitable. He could call whatever air taxi operator he chose to perform whatever missions he believed necessary. Akland Helicopters went bankrupt in part because it fell from his favor. In my "rate the pilots" questions, Gerhard used the word "very" only with respect to Geeting ("very comfortable"). Being the favorite pilot of the NPS Rescue Ranger was a profitable title to hold. I now understood that Doug Geeting's testimony might put his livelihood at risk.

When Gerhard testified he no longer believed the weather was good enough to land early Wednesday morning, red flags went up. It was doubtful Gerhard would put himself out on a limb without knowing what his favorite pilot would testify. At the Pretrial Conference, Ms. Neda listed Geeting and she again named him as a witness in her opening statement. Why? If he was going to testify for the U.S.A., it would be better to cross-examine him as a hostile witness.

The analysis boiled down to one question: could plaintiffs win without Geeting's testimony? If so, I should not call him. If not, I had to. For both clients, I answered that we could win without Geeting's testimony, so I would not have him arrested and forced to testify.

Chapter 21

Mountain Maniacs

Day 6, Wednesday, April 15, started 25 minutes late. Art Mannix, leader of the Mountain Maniacs, was the first witness. Given the respect the other climbers accorded him, Art was younger, shorter, and thinner than expected. He was 26 when the rescue occurred and 32 at trial.

Mannix was given to understatement. He had been in the Alaska Range "quite a bit," had been to the summit of Mt. McKinley "a few times," and believed "I still have a lot to learn about the mountains." He was an EMT. He could not remember how he learned of the Kahiltna Pass crash. At the Talkeetna airport shortly after noon Wednesday, he went up to Rangers Bob Gerhard and Tom Griffiths "and asked them if they needed some help. They said 'Yeah, we do.' . . . [T]hey asked if I could just get some friends and . . . some gear together." He agreed one hour was about how long it took to get ready.

Using a Washburn map, Mannix showed the judge how high Chinook 033 flew on Wednesday afternoon. It reached the intersection of the east fork with the main Kahiltna Glacier, significantly closer to Kahiltna Pass than where they were dropped off the next day. The helicopter hovered at that location and "[it] seemed like we were really close . . . within fifteen or twenty feet of [landing]." The Chinook returned to Talkeetna without consulting the climbers. "[W]e sort of wished we had gotten off. . . . [W]e felt as though we could have roped up and just jumped out. . . . [I]t would have been risky," but "that's what I would have felt like doing. . . . But we're not pilots."

Mannix described Thursday morning's airdrop of a military radio from a C-130 to the Chinooks on the frozen meadow.

A. . . . They handed me a radio. Then they asked us what our radio name would be, and we gave them a radio name. . . .

Q. What was that radio name?

A. Mountain Maniacs. . . . We got let off just a little bit below where the junction of the Southeast Fork of the Kahiltna merges with the main Kahiltna. The chopper landed fully there, which is probably the more correct way to exit from a helicopter, I guess. We landed. We all jumped out. All our gear was thrown to us, we all piled on top of our gear so that it wouldn't get blown away. The helicopter took off . . . and then we all hooked up and put our packs on and started heading up. [It was between 10 and 11 a.m.]

Q. How was the going?

A. . . . [I]t wasn't that bad, it's always nice to be in the mountains. . . .

Q. How were you walking? Were you on boots, skis, snowshoes?

A. . . . I was on snowshoes. I think most of us were on snowshoes. Brian [McCullough] . . . had skis on with skins.

Using the two Washburn maps, he showed Judge Kleinfeld where they were dropped off. Mannix was pointing to the border of the old Mt. McKinley National Park. Fixed wing air taxis were not allowed to land within Park boundaries so they would land just outside, taxi to the border, and unload. Air traffic in the climbing season was so busy that this part of the Glacier was nicknamed "Kahiltna International Airport." In a whiteout, the Mountain Maniacs tried to follow the route from Kahiltna International to the entrance to the West Buttress route, about ½ mile below Kahiltna Pass. How far did they get on Thursday?

A. We couldn't tell, really, how far we got on Thursday, because we had white-out conditions

the whole time we were there [until Saturday
morning]. . . . [T]he whole time we were going by
a compass. . . . [W]e were shining our headlamps
into the compass and following the fluorescent
needle northwards. . . .

Q. . . . How [were] you able to climb in the darkness?

A. . . . We figured as long as we were roped up,
if someone fell in a hole, there were enough
people to pull him out. [We] climbed until
pretty much people got tired. We set up camp. We
weren't really sure of our location after the
first night, nor after the second night. . . . We
figured if we followed [the Glacier] north, we
would get to the Pass eventually.

Q. Did that turn out to be true?

A. Yeah. On Saturday morning, we awoke and it was
clear. . . . We ended up being about a quarter of
a mile from the Pass, pretty close to where we
wanted to be. . . .

Mannix marked a blue question mark on the Washburn map where
the Mountain Maniacs spent Thursday night. He suggested the question
mark; visibility was too poor to fix the location. On Friday, "It was
snowing, winds from the south, which was favorable for us to move
because it was to our backs, and warmer than normally at that time
of year at that altitude." Using the West Buttress photo, I asked him
to show the second night location. Art commented that the Pass was
steeper than it looked in the photo.

THE COURT: Is it steep like a rock wall, where you
get somebody up on top to drop a rope to you?

THE WITNESS: No. No, you don't have to put any
belays in or anything like that. I mean, you can
walk up it. In certain times of the year, you'd
have to put crampons on it, because it might get
glazed [and] . . . it'd be too slippery to climb
up. But it's not technically difficult, no.

Mannix reviewed Gerhard's hand-drawn sketch of the crash site in Exhibit 1, including the route the rescuers followed to reach the wreckage, and found it accurate. [Gerhard estimated the crash site to be 200' below the summit.] The rescuers crossed the summit on "a round shoulder," "a mellow shoulder," about thirty feet wide at the top. The snow cornice was to the west, away from McKinley.

> If . . . you're in a white-out or something, it's really abrupt here [to the west]. And at that time it was a wild looking cornice. When we went back and salvaged [a radio from] the aircraft a month or so later, the cornice had blown off, and it wasn't as bad as it was . . . during the rescue. . . .

Q. What happened on Saturday morning?

A. We woke up whenever the first person woke up. Keith Nyitray, George Ortman, and myself immediately started getting our gear on to move. We already had hot thermoses prepared from the night before. We took off without breakfast. The other fellows broke camp. . . .

Q. Was it still dark?

A. No. . . . It was light enough to see. [It was clear.]

Q. You took off without breakfast and –

A. We headed out immediately, and got over the Pass, and down the other side. The snow was really deep on the [north] side of the Pass where the crash was, because it all had been blown up by the southerly wind and had deposited itself on the lee side of the Pass. . . .

Q. Was it difficult going . . . from the summit of Kahiltna Pass [down] to the crash site?

A. No. We waded through snow and got down there in pretty short order. . . .

THE COURT: . . . Why did you leave before breakfast? What was the –

THE WITNESS: Well, we wanted to get there as soon as
    possible. I didn't feel like hanging out and eating
    breakfast while we were so . . . close. . . .

Q. Was that your goal throughout this climb, to get
   to the crash victims as soon as possible?

A. Yes.

Q. Were you actually attempting to reach them
   Friday night?

A. We had discussed it, and we decided that if we
   were able to get to the base of that headwall
   [leading to the summit] . . . at night, we
   wondered whether we should go up it or not. We
   decided against going up it . . . in the dark
   . . . not knowing if we were going to hit a
   cornice on the top. We decided that it wouldn't
   have been wise, we probably would have to wait
   until it cleared up, to go over the Pass.

Q. [What did you do on arrival at the crash site?]

A. . . . Ed and Mike were alive, so we tended to
   them. . . . [T]hey looked like they were in good
   shape mentally.

       I know that with frostbite you're supposed to
   keep it frozen in the field. You're not supposed
   to thaw it out in the field or else more damage
   can happen if it's refrozen. So our immediate
   concern was getting some hot sugary liquids
   in them, which is good immediate treatment of
   hypothermia – and getting them out of there was
   the main concern. . . . It was an easier first aid
   situation than I was prepared to deal with.

Yes, he would describe them as "wasted." The survivors were
"disoriented and bruised up – strong-willed, and quite in better shape than
I thought [,]" meaning there were no broken arms or broken legs. They
appeared to be hypothermic with "slowness of movement, slowness in the
way they were thinking. They weren't crisp . . . ."

Q. Do you remember either of them making any
   comments about any previous rescue attempts or
   aircraft in the area?

A. . . . I think it might have been Ed who expressed
   dismay and anger that the previous help that had
   been there wasn't more effective. That's what I
   got, eventually, from them. I guess Ed has been
   in the [military], and I think he mentioned that
   he thought that the performance . . . from that
   aircraft, or something, could have been better.
   That's what he said at the time. . . .

Q. You do recall them talking about that when you
   first reached them there at the crash site?

A. Right.

I directed him to his four page letter to the rescue critique. He had
read it recently (after I gave him a copy on the visit with Mike) and seemed
to defer to it during his testimony. Did he consider what he wrote in the
letter to be more accurate than his testimony in court? A. "I think the facts
are probably [more] accurate. Maybe some of my emotions in there have
changed a little bit since then." I did not ask how his emotions had changed.

Responding to a question about rappelling from the Chinook Wednesday
afternoon, he answered, "I don't think, even in that situation, I would have
rappelled from that helicopter. . . . With respect to the helicopter pilot not
landing there, we felt bad, and we felt bitter, but in hindsight I can't really
hold it against him. . . . That's the pilot's decision." This answer was not
helpful. I decided not to ask, hypothetically, how much sooner the Mountain
Maniacs could have reached the crash site had they exited Chinook 033 on
Wednesday afternoon.

His letter implied an airdrop would have been successful because the
snow was deep enough to hold the drop and Clouser was mobile enough
to retrieve it.

Q. You say in your last paragraph: "Ed, and Mike
   especially, were capable of retrieving any drops
   within perhaps a couple of dozen yards below the
   site and a hundred yards in any other direction."

> Is that based on your judgment of their physical
> condition when you got there Saturday morning?

A. Yeah. But that could have been wrong.

Mannix had bitten me twice in a row. Before I could form another
question, he resumed his answer.

> Mike could actually walk. We had a rope and
> helped him, but he could walk over the Pass
> with us. . . . [I]t would have been something to
> go for.

Q. I understand.

A. I've had air drops in the mountains. . . . Doug
Geeting in particular, I've had him drop stuff
from an airplane that landed from me to you
outside my tent, that close. But that was on . . .
a more favorable slope. . . .

Q. I understand. Later in your letter you say:
"Despite the slope angle, the snow was deep
enough to hold a projectile. And with the aid of
a bright colored streamer, a parcel may have been
fairly easy to recover." Do you think the snow
was deep enough on the [north] side of the pass
to hold an air drop?

A. Yeah.

Q. Is the use of a bright colored streamer fairly
common for air drops?

A. In that situation it would be. But you'd have to
ask Mike if he thought he could retrieve something
like that. I mean, it was my speculation.

He was retreating again, so I finished quickly. Cross began
immediately.

Q. Hi, I'm Tara Neda. I represent the United States
in this matter.

A. I've heard of it.

Q. Even up here. I take it you wouldn't second-guess
   the Chinook pilots. Is that what your testimony is?

A. What do you mean by that?

Q. You wouldn't second-guess their judgment as
   pilots-in-command and their concern for [the]
   safety of you and their crew?

A. No, I trust them. . . .

Q. Have you ever jumped out of a helicopter before?

A. I do it every day. No, never.

Q. You were joking when you said you do it every day?

A. That's right. . . .

Q. What was the visibility like [Friday]? Was it
   pretty poor?

A. If I remember correctly, yeah. I remember at times
   we couldn't tell whether we were in the middle of
   the glacier or too far to the west. Because there
   are some pretty good slots [crevasses] on the
   west side of the glacier, and we wanted to stay
   more to the east side, to avoid them.

Q. You couldn't see that far?

A. . . . There were times when you could see, maybe,
   the second guy in front of you on the rope, and
   then that was it.

Q. So this wasn't the visibility in which you would
   want to traverse the crest of a [pass] and rope
   down on the north side?

A. I think that during daylight hours, when you
   could see a rope sling, we would have done that.
   But not at night.

When counsel finished, Art Mannix was excused, but stayed in the
courtroom to listen to the next witness. The court called a 10 minute recess.

Brian McCullough was bigger, physically, than Art Mannix. He was
22 when the rescue occurred and 28 when he testified. He had extensive
climbing experience in Alaska.

[W]hen I was 18 years old, I came to Alaska
on an expedition to climb Mt. St. Elias [19,000
foot peak near Cordova]. . . . Then I did quite a
bit of winter skiing, back-country skiing, ski trips
sometimes over 100 miles long. My first big major
climb was Mt. Huntington, which was the fourth
ascent. . . . I got frostbite and I lost five toe-
nails . . . Since then I've climbed Moose's Tooth,
the first ascent on the south face of Mt. Hayes,
which is a 7000' face. And I did the third ascent of
Mt. Russell, which is a very technical route. . . .

Wednesday morning, McCullough got a call from Talkeetna Air Taxi asking if he would participate in a rescue. He said yes, caught a ride into town, grabbed his backpack and skis, and arrived at the airport just before Chinook 033 took off. The Chinook flew up Kahiltna Glacier to about the blue question mark on the Washburn map, where Mannix had the Mountain Maniacs camping Thursday night. "It became apparent that we were going to try a landing. . . . We hovered there for a time. . . . I think they dropped the back door so the guy could look out. . . . The lighting was very flat, couldn't see the ground. Then all of a sudden we realized we were pulling up and banking away." Brian had on rappelling equipment and wanted to rappel out. He believed Art Mannix and Mark Bloomfield, "the best team we could have," had on the same gear. If he could have thrown his backpack out with a rope tied to it to determine height, he would have jumped if they were no more than 20 feet high. "[T]he snow is usually quite resilient and you can get away with that."

McCullough knew exactly where the Chinooks received the radio air drop on the frozen meadow. His uncle's gold mine was located nearby and he worked there several summers. Judge Kleinfeld smiled during this testimony.

When the climbers were dropped off on Kahiltna Glacier Thursday morning, he estimated they were twelve miles from the crash site. Brian was the first trailbreaker. Then he and Art and Mark Bloomfield took turns breaking trail. Asked where they camped that night, he agreed with Mannix's blue question mark.

The weather Friday was "quite poor" and climbing up Kahiltna Glacier was "pretty arduous." They were roped in two parties of three, with the second party following the trail of the first. They climbed in the dark with the person in front breaking trail by headlamp. The rearmost person, using a headlamp and compass, was "doing a lot of the vocal, 'Go to the right,' 'Go to the left.'"

Q. What was the plan for Friday night?

A. . . . We were given an estimation of where the plane was by Bob Gerhard. And we thought maybe we would go down by rope and do a systematic search, going back and forth, while still being roped from above, perhaps.

Q. Go down by rope from where?

A. From the low point of Kahiltna Pass . . . anchor the rope . . . proceed down one rope length, and arching like a pendulum, perhaps locate it.

Q. You would have to be arching like a pendulum because it was dark, and there was little or no visibility?

A. Yeah. Very, very poor visibility.

The climbers decided not to do this on Friday night "[b]ecause we were quite tired from climbing up the glacier and visibility was poor."

I asked the question I backed off from asking Mannix. Could the Mountain Maniacs have reached the crash site on Thursday if they had been allowed to rappel or jump from the Chinook on Wednesday afternoon? After an objection based on speculation was overruled, he answered the climbers would have been "closer in mileage and we would have been a day earlier. Yes, we would have made better time." Q. Would they have reached the crash site Thursday afternoon or evening? A. "[W]e would have got there faster than we did. . . . I would say there was a good chance we could have made it then." He would not go further.

Jim Wilson cross-examined. No, Brian had never rappelled out of a helicopter. He agreed the weather conditions during Wednesday afternoon's Chinook flight were very poor with low clouds, turbulence, and flat light. "[T]hey were not very good for flying at all."

Q. If this had been any situation other than a
   rescue mission, you personally would not want to
   have been flying that afternoon, would you?

A. I would not fly under conditions like that. . . .

Q. You're not second-guessing the decision not to
   land Wednesday afternoon, are you?

A. Not at all. No. . . .

Q. You believe that [the Chinooks] flew as much as
   they possibly could?

A. Yes.

On Friday, he was in complete white-out conditions all day. The
temperatures were quite warm for winter, the visibility was very poor, and
the wind was blowing. "But as far as being a ski party on the glacier, it's not
abnormal to travel in those kind of conditions."

Q. You indicated that if you had gotten out of the
   aircraft on Wednesday, there was a possibility
   that you could have gotten to the accident site
   on Thursday night. But it's equally possible that
   you couldn't have gotten there until Friday,
   isn't that true?

A. Yeah. It's really hard to speculate, in the
   mountains, what the time frame would be.

When Brian McCullough was excused, he and Art Mannix left the
courtroom to drive back to Talkeetna.

Chapter 22

Griffiths

NPS Ranger Tom Griffiths, Gerhard's boss, had not been deposed or interviewed and I did not know what he would testify. This was worrisome because his comments at the rescue critique and his additions to the 84 page rescue report indicated he was smarter than Gerhard. As he took the stand at 11:37 a.m., my goal was to finish him before lunch.

Now age 46, Griffiths was still stationed at Denali National Park. He was a passenger on Chinook 033 when it overflew the crash site Wednesday noon. He was "strapped in . . . on the side in the back of the ship. There was a small window adjacent to where I was that I could see out of a little bit." He knew they "were making real tight turns, trying to get in close to the crash site. And I could see . . . the plane down there . . ., [but] we were quite a ways from it."

He remembered the Chinook hovering at the summit of Kahiltna Pass. "At one point on the top of the pass I know that we were sort of stationary for awhile, it's like we were trying to land." He could not tell how close they were to the ground "because there was a lot of blowing snow, and there was lots of wind, and it was very turbulent. And I really didn't have much depth perception, because it was pretty much a white-out. . . ."

Griffiths seemed poorly informed about decisions made during the Chinook flight. There could be only one explanation.

Q. Am I correct that you were not hooked up on the intercom with the pilots and the others [Gerhard, PJs, and flight crew]?

A. Yeah. I had a helmet on, but no communication.

Q. So you couldn't tell what they were saying?

A. No.

Q. And the helicopter was noisy?

A. Yes, very noisy.

Gerhard was in front with a good view and communication with the pilots and the PJs. Griffiths was in the rear with a poor view and no communication.

Turning to Gerhard's incident report, Exhibit 1, Griffiths acknowledged he reviewed and approved it. He also wrote parts of it, including a portion he read aloud.

> [Reading] "We were to go along primarily as observers, but we were equipped to participate in a throw-and-go rescue effort. For an extended stay, we needed food, fuel, and sleeping bags for ourselves and victims." . . .

Q. What did you mean by that?

A. Well, I meant that the basic equipment we took with us was basically adequate for survival, but that for an extended operation of any length, or if we had to travel a great distance, that we would probably need additional stuff.

Q. When you say the basic equipment you took with you was intended for survival, you mean the survival of you and the survival of Mr. Gerhard, correct?

A. Yes, that's correct. . . .

He acknowledged that before Wednesday's flight, he and Gerhard simply grabbed their personal packs for themselves. He recalled saying at the rescue critique:

> Bob and I kind of misjudged things initially. I think we probably could have gone prepared to

```
get out, but we kind of went along thinking we
were just going to be observers, and we didn't
take the things with us that would have allowed
us to have survived for, you know, a long period
of time. We could have. We could have [survived].
```

After playing the tape recording of him saying this at the critique, I was finished. Before Ms. Neda could start, the judge called a lunch recess, which lasted from 11:50 to 1:32 p.m.

When court resumed, I received permission to reopen cross-examination to cover two matters. Griffiths identified some of the handwriting in the NPS log as his. He wrote "air drop, make up ahead of time, snowshoes or skis best?" in Talkeetna after the Chinook had flown over the crash site on Wednesday noon. When I read him the NPS entry about the Akland helicopter taking off on Saturday morning, it was not his handwriting and he did not know why it was recorded in the log.

On direct, Ms. Neda reviewed Griffiths' education and NPS work experience. Unlike Gerhard, he had reached the summit of Mt. McKinley. Seven years before his May, 1981 assignment to Denali National Park, he climbed the northeast to southwest traverse, "the second time that had been done."

He remembered phone calls from Gerhard late Tuesday night and early Wednesday morning. He had understood that Gerhard would bring from the cache "a couple of pairs of snowshoes and a stove. We felt we'd share a stove between us, and some fuel." "Q. Did [Gerhard] in fact do that? A. Yes."

Griffiths testified he was dressed as he had been on his 1974 McKinley climb: wool pants and shirt, bunny boots, and expedition parka. He had an ice axe, shovel, crampons, etc. in his pack. Did he recall the weather conditions on Wednesday morning's flight?

```
A. To me, they were the most turbulent conditions
   that I'd ever flown in in a helicopter. It was my
   first time in a Chinook. . . . I thought that it
   would take a lot of wind to blow a Chinook around
   because they're a pretty big aircraft.
```

When we tried to hover on top of the pass,
at one point I was looking out the side window,
and I had the feeling that we were sliding
backwards. The Chinook was facing into the wind,
which would have been [facing] to the south. . . .
And I had the feeling that we were being pulled
over in the downdraft. I don't know whether the
pilot had control or didn't have control, but
I remember thinking that it was very dicey and
very dangerous and very scary. I have been in
helicopters a lot of times before, and that was
the worst that I've ever been in.

When Ms. Neda finished, Tom Griffiths was excused.

Chapter 23

Larry Rivers

There were only three witnesses to Wednesday morning's conversation at the Talkeetna FSS. Brown's deposition testimony had been played in court and awaited completion of cross-examination. When Hunze was deposed four years after the conversation, he had no memory of it. The testimony of Larry Rivers could be dispositive.

My first contact with Rivers had been by telephone years after the rescue. Although he was cooperative, even friendly, much of what he told me was troubling. He remembered the events "real well." It was a long summer day and it was really, really windy and that is why they did not fly up to the crash site. When I gently pointed out the day in question was December 16, so it could not have been "a long summer day," it stopped Rivers cold. Perhaps his memory was not that good, he said. He thought it was "extremely windy," but he did not recall when. Dennis Brown told him, "Let's go up in the Bell 206 helicopter and take a look." Rivers went home and got survival gear, but they didn't actually load it in the helicopter. He was apprehensive about flying; it was not a day to go near the mountain except in a life and death situation. They went to the Talkeetna FSS to file a flight plan. According to Rivers, Dennis Brown and Dick Hunze had a confrontation almost every time they were together. Hunze said a military rescue was underway and they would prefer that civilians not go into the area. According to Rivers, "because of that and because of high winds and because they were assured that the military was on the way, we didn't go." I was not the first person to contact him. He had received 4 or 5 other calls about events, but had not given a statement, written or recorded, to anyone. He had been told what Dennis Brown said in his deposition. When I offered to send him the transcript, he said he would like that. (It was not improper to let Rivers read Brown's deposition as Rivers could be questioned about whether reading it influenced him.)

I first met Larry Rivers the Monday before trial when I was in Talkeetna with Mike. He was a big man, the size of a linebacker. Rivers had driven to Anchorage two days ago to meet me to prepare his testimony. He had read Brown's deposition and while he had no disagreements with it, he had his own mind about what happened and what he remembered.

Rivers listed his occupation as "registered guide and outfitter." He was 39 at the time of trial. He remembered the event of the Kahiltna Pass crash but not the date. He was willing to assume it happened Tuesday afternoon, December 15. On Wednesday, "I remember in the morning, we had went down to Akland fairly early in the morning to talk to Dennis Brown [about a place for our youth pastor to stay]." Rivers "couldn't say what time it was."

> Dennis was taking some phone calls and he informed me that one of Hudson's airplanes had gone down and that he was going to take the helicopter, the [Bell] 206, up and take a look for it, wondered if I wanted to go along.
>
> Q. What did you say?
>
> A. Surely. Always when there's an aircraft down, we all pitch in.
>
> Q. What did you do?
>
> A. Well, I know I wanted to check the weather 'cause I was concerned about the weather and we were going to the mountain, so I went home and I picked up some equipment. I don't ever fly anywhere without a certain amount of survival gear.

He returned to Akland with a bunch of gear, some he could remember and some he suspected he brought. He was sure he got sleeping bags, pads, shovel, some climbing rope, a couple of cans of Blazo and a stove "cause I anticipated being out there." He brought his parka and bunny boots. It was highly likely he grabbed extra bunny boots because "I have probably 15 or 20 pair." As a big game guide, he kept survival gear like that on hand "all the time." He also brought "some grub, some food" and a pot or two for melting water and cooking. In all likelihood, he also brought additional climbing gear and snowshoes.

They "put it in the helicopter." Dennis loaded part and he loaded part. He put some in the inside baggage compartment, some in the back seat where he could reach it, and he tied some to the outside strut on the right side. Rivers said that normally the right side is the pilot's seat, but, for this flight, Brown was going to be flying the left seat. The plan was for Rivers "to unstrap and jettison equipment if it came to that." Then they went to the Talkeetna FSS to check on the wind. Only Brown, Rivers and Dick Hunze were present.

Q. What happened at the flight service station that morning?

A. I know in particular I was checking for what the winds were because I was concerned about them. . . . [T]he minute we were there, Dick gave me a briefing on what the weather was on the mountain, told us that the military was on the way with their helicopters to do the rescue, that they had departed. I know there was some other discussion to the effect that we were gonna go up and have a look. He stated that the military was on its way and my understanding was from Fairbanks, on the way to the Park. It seems to me that there was some mention that they had checked in at Park headquarters at McKinley, but I cannot state that for a fact. We were going to go up there and I don't remember how the statement was made, but something to the effect that they already had the rescue in progress and were not interested in our being part of it. They thought we'd be in the way. . . . There was also some discussion about if the aircraft was in the Park of having an authorization to land or not to land, but where that went I don't recall.

Q. Do you recall if Mr. Hunze said that he would prefer that civilians not go into the area?

A. I don't recall that he said civilians. I recall understanding pretty clearly that it was preferred that we didn't go in there.

Q. Was there a confrontation between Mr. Brown and Mr. Hunze that morning?

A. Oh, there's always a little bit of friction there, but open confrontation, I wouldn't say so, no.

Q. Do you know what time it was when you were in the FSS station?

A. No. In the morning. I would say mid-morning. . . .

Q. Did Mr. Hunze tell you or Mr. Brown to stay away, that the military was in control of the situation?

A. Probably was talking to Dennis. I know the conversation was back and forth between them, so I would say it was between he and Dennis.

Q. Do you recall him saying that?

A. Yes.

Q. What happened next?

A. Well, I was a little bit relieved that the military was on the way that had the bigger equipment, the more stable equipment to handle it. I wasn't particularly excited about going up in those winds, especially if there were someone else with bigger aircraft to deal with it. . . . And since it'd been called off and there was already supposedly experienced crews and aircraft on the way, we went about our day. . . .

Q. Now, I understand you were personally concerned about the risk of flight that morning?

A. I was.

Q. But you were still willing to do it?

A. Yeah. . . .

Later, when the rescue was delayed and Rivers and Brown saw the Chinook crews at the Swiss Alaska Inn "sitting down there and having coffee and lunch and chatting," Rivers said "that I thought we had made a mistake by waiting that long if that's what [they] were gonna be doing."

Ms. Neda conducted cross-examination.

> Q. You know Mr. Hunze, he's the flight service station weather briefer, is that right?
>
> A. Yes, ma'am.
>
> Q. He's not an air traffic controller, is he?
>
> A. No, ma'am.
>
> Q. Haven't you stated before that as a pilot you know Mr. Hunze is not authorized to order you not to take off or to order you not to land somewhere?
>
> A. That is correct.

"Stated before?" From my viewpoint close to the podium, I could see Ms. Neda was referring to a yellow sheet of paper that appeared to be notes from an interview with Rivers.

> Q. Also haven't you stated that you, as a pilot, would not have been dissuaded by Dick Hunze's statements because the weather was so bad that day?
>
> A. Dick Hunze's statement that the weather was so bad had nothing to do with it.
>
> Q. No, I'm sorry, not Mr. Hunze's statement about the weather. My question to you is haven't you said that you would not have been dissuaded by Dick Hunze's statements as concerning the military on its way because the weather was so dangerous? Did you say that?
>
> A. No, ma'am. I would have gone in spite of the weather. The reason we didn't go was the combination of one, the weather, but primarily because the military was on the way and we were asked to stay out. I was very concerned about the weather, yes.

Q. Do you recall saying on November 15, 1985, that if
the weather had been okay, you would have gone?

A. No, ma'am.

Listening to this, I gathered someone acting for the U.S.A. called
Rivers on November 15, 1985 and made notes of their telephone
conversation. Apparently Larry said if the weather had been okay, he and
Brown would have gone regardless of what Hunze said. Using these
notes, Ms. Neda directly challenged Rivers on the witness stand. When he
denied saying this, Ms. Neda had no way to impeach him, to prove what he
said on November 15, 1985.

Q. Is it true?

A. If the weather had been okay, we would have gone?

Q. Yes. In spite of what Mr. Hunze told you, would you
have gone if the weather was okay that morning?

A. I really didn't have any control of it 'cause I
was not flying the aircraft.

Q. Would you have gone though?

A. If Dennis would have gone, I would have gone. . . .

Ms. Neda returned to the yellow notes of the November 15,
1985 interview.

Q. Is it also true that it was fine with you that the
military was on their way because the weather was
extremely dangerous and the winds were blowing?

A. That's correct. . . .

Q. Do you know if it was late in the morning or
early in the morning?

A. It was in the morning and I would say it was mid-
morning or earlier, but I could not say for sure. . . .

Q. Now, you alluded . . . that there was always
friction between Dennis Brown and [Dick Hunze]. . . .
Do you know the basis of that friction?

A. No, ma'am, nor the extent of it.

Q. How do you know there was friction?

A. Observance.

Q. Was it true that Mr. Brown felt that the flight service station was hurting him financially by not telling pilots about his fuel tanks?

A. I have no knowledge of that whatsoever.

Q. Is it true that Mr. Brown felt that the flight service station was hurting him financially because they would accept boxes on their front porch where he was charging people to warehouse those boxes?

A. No knowledge of that whatsoever.

When Ms. Neda finished, there was no redirect. Given where Rivers started from (high winds on a long summer's day), I decided to leave well enough alone. He gave only one troublesome answer in cross-examination. It sounded like he agreed the weather was extremely bad that morning. Rivers was an important witness on the Brown—Hunze conversation, not on Wednesday morning's weather. Other witnesses could better describe the weather at the crash site.

Chapter 24
Hunze and Dennis Brown finish

As Larry Rivers left the courtroom, I asked for a recess. Judge Kleinfeld first wanted to discuss the trial schedule. Trial was taking longer than he estimated. The judge could tell counsel to speed up if the questioning dragged. Not only had he never done so, he repeatedly asked for more testimony, not less. We also had two spectators. Earlier in the day, I approached the twenty-somethings. Were they witnesses? No. Were they press? No. They were Judge Kleinfeld's law clerks. He told them to sit in the courtroom (just sit, not take notes) and watch "a real Alaska trial." I took this as a sign the pace was acceptable.

The judge asked what other witnesses the parties expected to call. After I listed plaintiffs' remaining witnesses, the judge summarized plaintiffs' case as taking the rest of today plus two more days. When Ms. Neda finished listing the U.S.A.'s witnesses (she did not list Ed Hommer), the judge summarized defendant's witnesses as taking about one day. He then informed us the workers at Anchorage's electric utility, Chugach Electric, had gone on strike and the case had landed in his court. Kleinfeld could give us the rest of today and only half a day tomorrow, Thursday. Friday and Monday he would be in Fairbanks. Next week, we could have a full trial day Tuesday, but Wednesday and Thursday would be broken up, and Friday he would be in Fairbanks. At most, we might get two full trial days next week.

Asked if I saw a problem finishing trial next week, I answered, "In all honesty, I do." The judge indicated he would look into flying to Anchorage at noon Monday to give us an extra half a day. I suggested that counsel travel to Fairbanks on Monday as plaintiffs' economist lived in Fairbanks.

The judge was intrigued. Ms. Neda added that Mr. Strauss from the NWTC at Ft. Greely could also testify in Fairbanks on Monday. Pleased, the judge said he had "an appointment to talk to Senator Murkowski at 10:00 o'clock on Monday. My guess is that will be about 20 minutes, half hour, so it'll just be a recess for you. . . . That way we'll definitely be able to finish this trial next week. . . ." These comments understated his enthusiasm for holding a trial day in Fairbanks. Court recessed from 2:45 until 3 p.m.

Dick Hunze was a natural to follow Larry Rivers. To control him, every question I asked would be word for word what I asked in his deposition.

Hunze described himself as an "air traffic control specialist" stationed at Talkeetna since February, 1976. He was 47 at the time of trial. Yes, his deposition had been taken and he was appearing under subpoena.

> Q. You have no recollection whatsoever of a
>   conversation with Dennis Brown on Wednesday
>   morning, correct?
>
> A. That's correct.
>
> Q. You also have no recollection of any conversation
>   with Bob Gerhard on Wednesday morning?
>
> A. That's correct.
>
> Q. You have no recollection of talking with Mr.
>   Brown at any time on Wednesday?
>
> A. That's correct.

This was the heart of what I needed, but I also wanted to establish that Hunze knew or had been in a position to know the information Brown and Rivers testified Hunze told them. He agreed that he had lots of experience observing rescue operations in the Park and he knew the Park Service's role in coordinating rescues within the Park. Yes, normally Bob Gerhard would call him "to coordinate and to let [him] know what's going on, so [he] would know what to expect." Hunze explained the Park Service did not have aircraft type radios and used the FAA for communication "if they had information to be passed to the rescuing aircraft."

He remembered being on duty, alone, on Wednesday. He recalled knowing "Chinook helicopters were coming down from Fairbanks to attempt to rescue the survivors." He probably got their inbound flight plan. When I directed him to the RCC log, he agreed that he learned at 9:50 a.m. Wednesday "that two Chinooks will be approximately one hour late due to maintenance problems." He had no recollection about "what the weather was like at the crash site on Wednesday morning." I had no further questions.

Ms. Neda began direct examination immediately. She asked him to describe "what a flight service station weather briefer does?"

> A flight service station provides services to pilots and provides weather information or navigation aid information, outages. We process their flight plans. We just provide advisory service for arriving and departing when there's no control tower at the airport, provide emergency services, . . . issue NOTAMs for navigation outages, if it's on our field. . . .
>
> THE COURT: What do you issue?
>
> THE WITNESS: Notices to airmen of outages that would affect their flight or advise a pilot of an outage on his route of flight. . . .

As a flight service station specialist, he did no controlling. "It's strictly an advisory service." He did not have authority to clear an aircraft to land.

> Q. Have you ever told the pilot of an aircraft that they were not authorized to land in Mt. McKinley National Park?
>
> A. No.
>
> Q. Why is that?
>
> A. I'm not authorized to tell a pilot he can or can't do anything.
>
> Q. During a rescue is there any way you could advise a pilot that air space is restricted over an accident site?

A. If there was a NOTAM issued to restrict the air space, I could advise him of the restriction. . . .

Q. With regards to restricted air space over the National Park, how would a NOTAM be issued? Would that be your initiation or someone else's?

A. No. It would have to be initiated by the Park Service.

Q. Do you know . . . if Mr. Gerhard requested of you that a NOTAM restricting air space be issued by the FAA?

A. No, he did not. . . .

THE COURT: I missed something there. Who issues the NOTAM, the FAA or the Park Service?

THE WITNESS: We would issue it on their request. In other words —

THE COURT: Who would they make the request to?

THE WITNESS: They would request it through me and I would then issue it. But I can't, on my own, decide. . . .

If a NOTAM had been issued on Wednesday, there would have been a record of it in the FAA accident package. There was no such record. Hunze was excused.

I badly wanted to finish the Dennis Brown deposition, but Ms. Neda had not cut any of Piper's long cross-examination and there was more time left on the videotape than in the trial day. The deposition restarted where Judge Kleinfeld had overruled my objection to questions about Akland Helicopters receiving post-rescue suspensions from the FAA. Mr. Piper did not bring out that Brown sold Akland and was in Mexico from August 1, 1983 until April 16, 1984 or that the FAA violations filed against Akland were for operations while Brown was in Mexico and he knew nothing about them.

While in Talkeetna, Dennis Brown personally flew about a dozen rescue flights by helicopter. Four to six of them were around 10,000 feet or higher. One was in winter.

Mr. Piper showed discomfort when Brown explained that on clear days (like Wednesday and Saturday), he could tell the winds on Mt. McKinley from the ground in Talkeetna. If snow plumes were visible, there were high winds. If not, no high winds. Brown had not seen snow plumes on Wednesday morning.

As Piper moved to contacts between Dennis Brown and Gary Fye and me, I stopped the videotape and suggested we fast forward to a summary question so we could finish the deposition before adjourning. Ms. Neda was unsure. The judge asked to look at the typed transcript to determine whether Piper's questioning was cumulative and consumed undue time. Ms. Neda offered to stipulate to admit the entire transcript into evidence as opposed to the judge viewing the videotape. Judge Kleinfeld responded "I'd just as soon see the video. . . . because I'm trying to evaluate whether I want to believe Mr. Brown and to what extent." When the judge ruled we should skip ahead, we reached the part of the videotape I had dreaded for three years.

> (Videotape played.)
>
> MR. PIPER: Let the record reflect that this morning at approximately 9:30 a.m.. . . . I received a telephone call from Mr. Galbraith. . . . At that time, I asked Mr. Galbraith if I could talk to the witness, gave him a phone number, and he told me that he would give that phone number to the witness when he came to visit with him.
>
> Q. Was that phone number given to you?
>
> A. No, it wasn't.
>
> MR. GALBRAITH: I'd like the record to reflect that this has gone on long enough. I've indulged it and if the Judge wants to hear it, that will be up to the Judge. But I certainly have no obligation to do Mr. Piper's legwork for him. Mr. Brown has been in Talkeetna, with a telephone in his house, by his testimony, for more than a month. And of course, he's been accessible since December 1981 for contact by federal investigators and other persons. There are . . . people at this deposition whose identity hasn't been stated on record, who probably could have contacted Mr. Brown at their leisure about this case.

MR. PIPER: I have nothing further.

MR. GALBRAITH: . . . I would like to identify [gesturing the camera to the people seated at the deposition table] - there's a David A. Brown, title, Evaluation Specialist, from the federal government in attendance today and an F. Christopher Bockmon, an attorney for the Department of Interior.

Q. Did you ever receive a telephone call from Mr. Piper?

A. No, I didn't, or a letter.

My redirect filled in the background Piper had skipped about Akland's FAA violations while Brown was in Mexico. My anger showed clearly on the videotape. When I finished and the attorneys were preparing to leave, Dennis Brown made a statement. He, too, was angry.

THE WITNESS: . . . You would like, for some reason I don't understand, [to] make it appear as though I'm trying to have dodged you before this morning, and that's not the case. Had you contacted me, I think that we would have been able to have some communication. Or, had someone come to see me from the government, I would have chatted with them. So I want to make it real clear that I am only here to [state] the facts, as best I can. . . . I do not know this person [gesturing to Galbraith]. I do not know Mr. Scanlon. And if you want to contact me again, I'm sure I'll do whatever I can to give you the facts as I . . . remember them.

MR. PIPER: I move that this gratuitous statement be stricken from the record. . . .

(Videotape finished.)

MS. NEDA: I move that this last statement be stricken from the record, as gratuitous, as well [as] non-solicited.

```
THE COURT: Denied. Mr. Piper asked a number of
   argumentative and inappropriate, in form,
   questions. And I think the witness had a right
   to make himself clear. And since his interests
   are somewhat different from Mr. Galbraith's, it's
   understandable that Mr. Galbraith might not bring
   it out.
```

The judge's tone of voice showed he was upset. There was nothing further. Court was adjourned.

Determining the facts at trial necessarily involves the credibility of the lawyers. When Tara Neda asserted that Larry Rivers had previously said it was too windy to fly to Kahiltna Pass on Wednesday morning and Rivers denied saying this, Ms. Neda could not contradict him and she lost credibility. Terry Bridgman testified that the reason the Chinooks did not fly from Ft. Wainwright to Talkeetna on Tuesday night was bad weather. In cross-examination, I impeached him using his statements at the rescue critique. My credibility went up as Bridgman's went down and it had stayed up throughout the trial. It was ironic that Mr. Piper's attack on my credibility was played on the same afternoon the judge accepted my suggestion that we hold some of the trial in Fairbanks. Essentially I had a gold star on my forehead that afternoon. By attacking my credibility, Mr. Piper made himself look bad. More important, he made Dennis Brown look good.

Chapter 25

Tom Scanlon

Day 7 began Thursday morning at 10:00 a.m. with Tom Scanlon on the witness stand. As the personal representative of his brother's estate and a named plaintiff, Tom had a right to attend trial and could not be excluded during any testimony. But he had not attended trial; this was his first appearance in the courtroom.

For the Scanlon family, listening to mistakes in the rescue, observing the mechanics of the American legal system, learning how Pat died — all could be sources of pain. A trial was not going to bring Pat back. When Tom asked if it was necessary to attend, my answer was no. He seemed relieved. No Scanlon family member attended trial.

Tom and Pat looked a fair amount alike. Both were "solid," as Clouser put it. Tom had black, wavy hair, medium length; Pat's had been brown. Tom was 43 at the time of trial. His life had changed since December, 1981. He now lived and worked in Anchorage, though he still owned businesses in Talkeetna.

On the day of the crash, Tom was working on the North Slope as Camp Services Supervisor for Standard Oil of Ohio. He "was responsible . . . the last five years for the Base Operations Center." When Tom called his brother Tuesday night, there was no answer. Wednesday morning he called the Fairview Inn and learned there had been a plane crash. Tom hopped the next jet to Anchorage and arrived in Talkeetna at 7 or 8 p.m.

When questioning moved to conversations with rescue participants, Mr. Wilson raised hearsay objections. Conversations during the four day rescue were admitted under the res gestae exception to the hearsay rule.

(Res gestae means in the heat of the moment.) Conversations after the rescue were barred as hearsay except for conversations with representatives of the U.S.A. (Gerhard and Major Hayes), which qualified as admissions against interest by a party opponent. All conversations during the rescue took place at the Fairview Inn.

Q. What did [Doug] Geeting tell you [Wednesday night]?

A. . . . Obviously I was upset. And my conversation with Doug was an ongoing conversation over two or three hours. . . . I talked with Ron Garrett [Mountain Maniac]. . . . Doug assured me that everything was going fine, that he had flown up there that day, I believe twice. That he had seen three people walking around on the outside of the crash. That the fuselage was intact and it appeared that they were all right. . . .

Q. Did Mr. Geeting tell you how the weather was at the crash site on Wednesday morning?

A. Yes. He said it was fine in the morning . . . [and] he had gotten relatively close to the crash site. . . .

Q. What did Mr. Garrett tell you Wednesday evening . . . ?

A. . . . Ron was very critical. . . . [H]e was the first one that brought the issue up of, in his words, "What the hell was going on?" And I think he made a comment to me at the time that we had to get somebody in charge to do something right away and that's when I went back to Doug Geeting and Geeting said "Don't worry about it. You stay out of it. We'll take care of it." . . .

Tom had multiple conversations with Chinook flight crew members on Thursday and Friday. He bought them "drinks," meaning "[e]verything from VO and water to a lot of coffee and orange juice. It was not uncommon to have half the people in the Fairview not drinking alcohol." Then the flight crews refused to let Tom buy any more drinks.

> Basically it was . . . Friday, because I had
> told my [bartenders] . . . not to accept money
> from them. I was behind the bar, tending bar
> myself, and they came in and I started to set
> them up and they said they refused to allow us to
> buy a drink for them. Basically they said, "Let's
> just wait till this is all over with before you
> buy us any more drinks. You've done enough." . . .

THE COURT: Were these men in uniform?

THE WITNESS: Yes. Two of them, three of them were.
There was no question that they were in the
flight crew. I mean there's [points to location
of flight insignia] . . . And the one made the
comment . . . they'd be lucky if I let them in
there after this whole thing was over. . . .

The Scanlon parents came to Alaska for that Christmas and arrived in Talkeetna early Friday morning. On Saturday afternoon, they were at the Talkeetna airport preparing to fly to Anchorage to meet Chinook 033 at Providence Hospital. When Doug Geeting told Tom that Pat was dead, Tom was able to reach his family before they took off. The Scanlon family spent the holidays in Anchorage and Tom did not return to Talkeetna until after Christmas. He had several conversations with Bob Gerhard in late December or early January.

Q. . . . what did Mr. Gerhard say to you?

A. He was very conciliatory. He . . . apologized for
my brother's death and at that point I guess I
got very concerned because he made the statement
that he hoped we never found out how many
mistakes were made. And it was a screw-up . . .
on his part and he said on everyone's part. And
he said "I'm sorry." . . .

Q. Do you recall anything else he said about
mistakes made at that time?

A. . . . I think he used specifically the term
"beginning to end." He said there was a lot of
mistakes made. . . .

Gerhard told Tom about the rescue critique and encouraged him to attend. Tom did not. I asked him to tell the judge why he was not attending trial. Tom turned to face Judge Kleinfeld and said in a voice raw with emotion, "I just don't want to hear about it. (Pause.) As simple as that." The judge nodded.

The next post-rescue conversation was with Air Force Major R.J. Hayes, the information officer for the rescue. Tom got to know him during the rescue, when Hayes was in Talkeetna. Eight or nine months later, in the summer of 1982, they had lunch at Elevation 92, a well-known restaurant in downtown Anchorage.

Q. What did he say to you about the rescue at that time?

A. The reason for the lunch was R.J. is a well-known photographer, journalist, writer, and he had written a poem about Mt. McKinley [which he gave to me].

Q. What do you remember about what Major Hayes said to you at that lunch?

A. He made the comment that in his 21 years with the military - he was personally embarrassed. He said it was the worst military operation he had ever been personally involved with. He made other declarative statements saying that if something isn't done, there should be criminal negligence charges against "he." I did not ascertain who "he" was.

The damages case was straightforward. The Scanlon family was based in Clarks Hill, Indiana, and operated a fifth or sixth generation farm raising corn, wheat, and soybeans. The father of Tom and Pat owned 300 acres and aunts and uncles owned another 1000 to 1200 acres. Pat was the only child in the combined families interested in farming. In addition to helping his father, he farmed his aunt's 300 acres.

Pat was a high school graduate, no college. He had farmed since he was 5. He was a good athlete in high school (football, track, golf) and was well liked socially. (He took after Tom.) Pat had worked for Conrail, successor to Penn Central, since he was 18 and had solid railroad earnings. Pat's federal income tax returns were admitted. Most of his earnings were from Conrail.

Because of its high land value, the Scanlon farm had been incorporated in the mid-70s and the five Scanlon children were given shares in the farm. Tom testified all income earned by the farm was paid to the three operators, Mr. and Mrs. Scanlon and Pat. The plan was that income from the farm would continue to be distributed to the operators and not paid as dividends to the shareholders.

Pat had driven to Alaska in November, 1981 with a goal of "[working] on the Slope for two to three, four years to get enough money to be able to go back and then take over all the farms." Tom believed he could get his brother a job on the North Slope because of his position with Sohio. "I worked with a wide range of subcontractors at Prudhoe Bay. Right, wrong or indifferent, one of the ways you get jobs up there is through personal contacts. . . . [I]t was a matter of getting him the right job."

Tom described how he got work on the North Slope for his younger sister, Eileen. "[S]he started out at approximately 65 or 60,000. After a year and a half, she was hired by Husky Oil . . . and she made, I know, $10,000 more than I did. She made approximately $79,000. . . ." Tom and Eileen arranged a similar job for his other sister, Mary Anne, but she did not like working on the Slope.

Tom had found tentative work for Pat as a roughneck. Brad Essary told Tom there would be no problem with Pat starting after January 1, 1982.

Judge Kleinfeld had another matter at 11 a.m. Court was recessed from 10:50 until 1:30 p.m.

When we resumed, Tom testified he knew his younger brother well.

    Pat was a good guy. I think he was very well
    liked. He was very social. He was famous for his
    parties at the family farm. I think he was a good
    worker. I think he had a good reputation working for
    CONRAIL. He was very industrious. . . . He also went
    out and hired a number of fellows to cut firewood
    and moonlighted by the selling of firewood during
    the winters. He had a strong work ethic and he had a
    strong desire for money and material objects. He was
    your normal, everyday guy. . . .

Pat had been engaged in high school and dated regularly, but had not married. Tom identified a number of photos, including Pat's high school prom picture. Pat lived with his parents at the family farmhouse. Sometimes he paid rent, sometimes his work covered rent and food. Pat owned shares in Conrail.

Pat's death certificate was admitted. Judge Kleinfeld declined to admit the autopsy report from Dr. Lindholm, the pathologist, reserving his final ruling until after the pathologist testified.

When Mr. Wilson cross-examined, he covered damages quickly. Yes, Pat was single at the time of his death. No, he had no children. No, he had no dependents and no one was depending on him for financial support.

When Wilson turned to liability, he had Tom read to himself his deposition testimony about conversations with Chinook flight crews. Tom agreed that in his deposition he had been unable to remember specific language used by members of the Chinook flight crews. He agreed he did not testify in his deposition that Major Hayes felt anyone was "criminally negligent" in the rescue. Tom said he remembered it only after the deposition finished.

Wilson again asked him to read certain parts of his deposition to himself. Judge Kleinfeld asked for a copy of the transcript and read the same portions. As Wilson was focusing on questions 33 pages apart, I stated my intent to bring out additional deposition testimony on redirect. The judge ruled such redirect would be allowed, but he wanted to read the context of the remarks now. When Kleinfeld finished, Wilson returned to the lunch with R.J. Hayes. The poem written by Hayes was admitted into evidence.

I considered this selective (and silent) reading of Tom's deposition to be misleading and decided to read his deposition testimony into the record to clarify its context. Plaintiffs had a right to do this and it offered an opportunity to repeat damaging testimony. As we proceeded, I read Tara Neda's deposition questions and Tom read his deposition answers.

Q. . . . "Did you have conversations with [the Chinook flight crews] relating to their conduct and their rescue attempts?" . . .

A. "I asked them how it was going. . . . I guess it must have been Thursday night we were — we

were (pause). I tried to buy them a drink and
they wouldn't take the drink." . . . "And the
short one, . . . the guy that was about 33 or 34,
. . . nothing that he said directly. He was just
(pause) he talked a little bit about the initial
rescue and some of the problems."

Q. "And what did he say to the best of your recollection?"

A. "I don't remember. But the intent was he cast
some doubts in my mind [as] to what was going on,
what had transpired up to that point."

Q. "You can't remember specifically, but in general
you had some bad feelings as a result of the
conversation?"

A. "Yes. . . . "

Setting his deposition aside, I asked Tom if he later remembered more specific instances of conversations with rescue participants.

A. I've thought about it. Yes, they had been more
specific. I guess my point was and is right now,
whatever Doug Geeting, Ron Garrett, and [the
Chinook flight crew members] said only raises a
question of what happened and that's my point.
I'm not here to say yeah or nay on anybody's
faults. I'm just saying . . . it raised a serious
question in my mind about this series of events
and that's [what] I've asked the Court to do, is
to look at the facts and let that dictate.

[Motion to strike denied.]

I asked Tom to resume reading aloud from his deposition starting just after a break in the deposition.

Q. Do you remember why we took a break [in your
deposition] at that point?

A. I cried.

Q. So this is immediately after that?

A. Yes.

Q. Can you read the answer beginning at line five?
   (Pause.) - if you need [a break], just - [Tom was
   about to cry again.]

(Pause.)

A. No, I'm fine.

   [Reads from deposition] "As I was saying,
   approximately eight to ten months after the
   accident, I had lunch with Major R.J. Hayes
   at Elevation 92. . . . And R.J. . . . [t]old me
   specifically at that time that in his 21 years
   in the military, that was the most embarrassing
   exercise he had ever witnessed and basically
   it was inexcusable. I think almost in exactly
   those terms. And that was the thrust of the
   conversation, that it was not handled well at all
   by the military."

Q. [Deposition put aside.] . . . [A]fter this
   deposition ended, you remembered the use of the
   words "criminal negligence?"

A. Yes . . .

Judge Kleinfeld addressed Tom when his testimony was finished:

THE COURT: You may be excused. Mr. Scanlon, I want
   you to know that the requirements of law put
   the lawyers for both sides in a position where
   they have to ask you some questions that seem
   cold-blooded. Everybody understands how you feel
   about what happened [to] your brother. . . . It's
   a different line of inquiry here, but everybody
   understands your human feelings.

As Tom left the courtroom, I asked for a recess.

Plaintiffs next called Major Sam Baker, Chief of the Rescue Coordination
Center at Elmendorf Air Force Base in Anchorage. Baker qualified as a
hostile witness and, in fact, seemed to resent testifying.

Q. In addition to presently being the Chief of the
   RCC, you were involved in the actual search and
   rescue for the Kahiltna Pass crash, correct? . . .

A. I flew the second C-130 mission on the first
   night or the first day. I don't know what else
   you want. I was the co-pilot.

THE COURT: When you say "first day," which day do
   you mean by first day? Tuesday?

THE WITNESS: Tuesday.

Baker confirmed that the first C-130 flight, the one that picked up the ELT signal, reported seeing flashing lights. He acknowledged that personnel on the second C-130 flight also reported seeing flashing lights, although he personally did not. This second flight launched parachute flares "to let the survivors know that there was somebody in the area looking for them and an effort was being made." He was certain that before he took off on the second C-130 flight, the ELT coordinates had been plotted on a map and it already had been established that the crash site was in the vicinity of Kahiltna Pass in Denali National Park.

Major Baker explained the organization of the RCC, how RCC mission folders were created, and what information was recorded. If possible, the mission folder was to contain a running entry of calls made as they happened. Baker considered the information in the controller's log to be reliable. He agreed the RCC folder reflected the departure of two Chinooks from Ft. Wainwright in Fairbanks at 9:50 a.m. Wednesday.

Major Baker described controller training. He identified the National SAR Manual. (The judge had his own copy.) Baker testified RCC controllers also were required to be familiar with the RCC Plan. My intent was to use both to establish the standard of conduct for this rescue.

The first example of non-compliance went back to Doug Buchanan, who travelled to Anchorage to make RCC personnel aware of the Fairbanks civilian mountain rescue group. The National SAR Manual required the gathering of such information. Baker admitted the RCC currently did not have a list of independent mountaineering groups. If he needed such a group, "I'd go to the Alaska State Troopers for it." He could not think of any instance where the RCC called on a mountaineering group for assistance.

During Gerhard's testimony, I had focused on the Ranger's passivity in planning the rescue. Now I asked why the RCC planned the rescue, not Gerhard. Baker did not think Denali National Park was exempted from RCC responsibility. Asked his understanding of whether the boundaries of national parks in Alaska were excluded from RCC coverage, Baker answered, "I would have to read very close the Alaska Air Command circle and see how it addresses that." I read aloud the provision in the Denali SAR Plan providing "the responsibility and authority for SAR operations [within the Park] is retained by the NPS."

> Q. That indicates to you, does it not, . . . [that]
>   the National Park Service retained authority and
>   responsibility for search and rescue operations
>   within Denali National Park?
>
> A. I'm not sure of your word "authority." They
>   certainly were first. . . .
>
> Q. In general, your understanding is that the
>   boundaries of the national park, specifically Denali
>   National Park, are exempted from [RCC] coverage?
>
> A. That would not be a primary consideration when I
>   was prosecuting [search and rescue].

It was 3:45. The judge said he had to adjourn and announced trial would resume in Fairbanks at 8:30 on Monday. Day 7 and week 2 of trial were over.

Chapter 26

Trial Routines

The break from Thursday afternoon until Monday morning was welcome. I spent Friday preparing for final witnesses and took Saturday off. Sunday, I flew to Fairbanks.

Trying two major civil trials in four months at the beginning of 1987 required adjustments to my law practice and personal life. Trials are stressful and disruptive: often I would be completely unavailable to my other clients. I needed an experienced law partner. A decade earlier, I had worked with Pat Owen when he was a law student. He possessed enormous common sense and did high quality work. After graduation, Pat became a successful trial lawyer and then CEO of a technology firm. He had recently laid himself off and was now practicing law out of his house. I approached Pat and offered a 50-50 partnership. He accepted. There was no equitable way to cut him in on my two contingency trials, so we delayed the start of the partnership until May 1. In the meantime, I moved to bigger office space, he moved in, I gave him my hourly work, and he kept what he billed. This arrangement kept my hourly clients happy.

Both my wife and I worked full-time as attorneys, so we divided chores. I cooked and she did the dishes. The child care of our two daughters, ages 6 and 8, was divided 50-50 using a straightforward "every other day" system where one parent did absolutely everything from morning until night while the other parent had the day completely off. When I was in trial, however, my wife did it all. We invited my wife's mother to Anchorage for the Mt. McKinley trial.

Several aspects of the Fairbanks trip bothered me. Clouser would miss Monday's testimony. He was a presence in the courtroom; the witnesses were distinctly aware of him. Mike was also an astute observer. I often asked his opinion on how things were going, how a witness struck him, how he read the judge. It was also good to be cheered on. A few years later, I represented a construction company as plaintiff in a two week jury trial. My client was liquidating and its key employees no longer lived in Alaska. After the first three days, I had no client representative sitting next to me in court. This so unnerved me that I asked Donna to sit in the back of the courtroom to lend moral support. My law partner came by the courtroom for the same reason. I could not deal with the construction case solely on a monetary basis; I needed someone to care who won. This was not a problem in the Mt. McKinley trial.

Previous experience led me to develop strict routines to attempt to sustain a uniform level of performance at trial. The Fairbanks trip would disrupt these routines and increase the risk of an "off" day. Plaintiffs could not afford a bad day at trial. Almost every witness had the potential to destroy plaintiffs' case single-handedly. For example, the U.S.A. argued Dennis Brown was not a sufficiently skilled helicopter pilot to help the victims on Wednesday morning. If even one knowledgeable witness supported this view, the judge could find Brown not to be a competent pilot and we would fail to satisfy the "worsened the victim's plight" requirement and lose the trial.

To date, I had lost two civil trials, one of which was my first. It was a small property damages case ($4000) and I learned a great deal from losing it. Eight years later I lost a small claims trial to the collection manager of a car dealer when my client did not show up for trial. After I started my own practice, I averaged one major civil trial (two weeks or longer) per year. Not counting the small claims loss (no client), I had a decade long winning streak.

In my one previous trial in federal district court in Alaska, I represented an insulated pipe supplier as plaintiff in a Miller Act (construction bond) case against a contractor. The case was to be tried without a jury before a federal district judge so formidable and coercive that I believed he would never allow any case to be tried in his court. Despite a Christmas trial date and a settlement conference before another Alaska federal district judge, the case did not settle. As soon as trial began, it was apparent that we were before a highly skilled trial judge who clearly enjoyed the long trial. My client prevailed completely. (I hoped this judge would say kind words about me to Kleinfeld at the judge's luncheons.)

My most recent trial, the "A" trial in February, was in state court. Opposing counsel was the most prominent insurance defense attorney in Anchorage. After two weeks of this legal malpractice case, the jury ruled entirely in plaintiffs' favor. Instead of appealing, defendant offered to pay almost all of the amount awarded. My elderly client accepted, payment was prompt, and I received my largest contingency fee on the eve of the Mt. McKinley trial. It was unlikely Judge Kleinfeld, in federal court in Fairbanks, heard about this Anchorage state court trial, but this recent success emboldened me to say at the Pretrial Conference, "I have tried some cases, too."

From these and other multi-week trials, I developed rigid routines that began well before the start of trial. The goal was to avoid peaks and valleys, to operate at a flat level of efficiency. First, I cut alcohol and caffeine from my life. When caffeine disappeared about ten days before trial, I discovered how tired I was. This left time to catch up on sleep so I could begin trial more or less rested. It was unavoidable that I would become more and more fatigued as trial progressed.

Second, I paid attention to my physical conditioning. A trial, like a bar exam, is partly a test of stamina and physical strength. I tried to be in shape before trial began. During trial, I began each morning with sit-ups and push-ups. I tried to run every day after trial. I made it a point to eat well. When I ate out for dinner (most nights), I chose something I wanted, regardless of cost.

Trials involve enormous stress. I discovered three ways to alleviate it— alcohol, movies, and running. The drawbacks of alcohol were poor sleep, reduced alertness, and poorer courtroom performance. Common sense convinced me not to drink during trial, but many trial lawyers are heavy drinkers. There was no time during the week, but the escape of a movie on Friday or Saturday night was part of the routine. I happened upon running by accident. In 1985, I entered a 10k "Terry Fox Run" and discovered I enjoyed running longer distances (I had never run 6 miles before). The release of endorphins was relaxing. That fall and winter, I became a runner. In mid-June, 1986, I entered the Mayor's Marathon in Anchorage and ran my first marathon in 3:31. (I recovered on the trip to Ft. Greely and Fairbanks and the deposition trip to Detroit and Indianapolis.) Later that summer, I broke 40 minutes in a 10k.

I never kept a journal during trial for lack of time and energy, but it is not difficult to reconstruct this trial's routine. Generally I would be at work by 7 a.m. Around 8:30, I would drive with Mike (he could park free at my office) to the federal courthouse, where I dropped him at the front door, saving a long walk. Exhibits and my boombox were stored in the courtroom, so I carried only that day's witness notebooks, extra copies of depositions, and the like. Federal court was in session from 9 or 9:30 until noon and from 1 or 1:30 until 4 or 4:30. I stayed in the federal building over the lunch hour and ate in the excellent cafeteria. (Even the judges ate in the cafeteria; you could view the "judge's luncheon" in a glass walled room.) With lunch over, usually I worked at a cafeteria table or, if available, our table in the courtroom. During the day, I tried to eat during recesses (outside the courtroom). I preferred fruit (a banana plus an apple or an orange) because sugar from a candy bar would yield a high followed by a crash. (Food was more important in state court, where we would continue without lunch until 1:30 and then adjourn for the day.)

When the trial day ended, I drove Mike back to my office and immediately went running. (I had a built-in shower in my office.) In the first mile, no matter how slow the pace, I would stop and throw up. This was not something I could control. (I never vomited during normal runs.) When I finished throwing up, my stress level was lower and I felt better. I finished the run with the distance (2 to 5 miles) depending upon how tired I felt. After a shower, I began preparing for the next day. By this time, all support staff had gone home. (The state court schedule was easier for running and for working with staff.) Whether my work was finished or not, I went home in time to be in bed by 11 o'clock. It was more important to sleep than to dot every "i" and cross every "t." If I had trouble falling asleep, I would increase the distance of the next day's run. (Physical fatigue helped overcome mental fatigue.) If I still had trouble sleeping, like the night before trial started, I tried to content myself that I was lying still and not expending energy.

Judge Kleinfeld's trial schedule had many more days off than usual. This was a blessing because I had not fully recovered from the "A" trial in February. It was a huge relief to have two days off the first weekend and I was happy to have one day off the second weekend. (During regular Monday to Friday trials, there are often no days off, even on weekends.) On these long weekends, I did not vary the routine of no alcohol and no caffeine. (The no alcohol rule was extended past the end of trial after the "A" trial in February. The night of that jury verdict, I walked to a neighbor's house, had a few drinks to celebrate, and said something that forever ended a friendship with my host. My judgment had its guard down.)

In a normal trial, I strove not to put any of my witnesses on the stand without having met with them first. Because of the hostility to this rescue case, I was happy to have a witness appear in court at all. Art Mannix was not prepared, Brian McCullough had some preparation, and Larry Rivers was carefully prepared. Occasionally, I interviewed a witness in the evening, after trial. Dr. Mills was "prepared" in 30 minutes after a day of cross-examining a Chinook pilot.

Trial preparation for government witnesses was totally different. There was no opportunity to go over testimony with federal employees, civilian or military, because these witnesses were represented by Ms. Neda. It was unethical for me to contact them directly, let alone meet with them. To prepare, I reviewed their deposition, if one had been taken, and highlighted the questions to ask at trial. If there was no deposition, I reviewed documents that mentioned them and highlighted a copy of the document.

For each witness, whether I had a lengthy deposition or no documents at all, I prepared an outline of questions. Using college ruled paper and skipping many lines between questions, I printed large block letters abbreviating the subject area (WHAT DO WED MORNING). Plaintiffs bore the burden of proving many facts and I did not want to fail to prove something because I forgot to ask a simple question. There is a fine line between being thorough and asking too many questions. I counted on the judge to tell me if I was getting too detailed. So far, this had not happened.

The stress of this trial surfaced in unexpected ways. On day 2, after a full afternoon of cross-examining Mr. Bridgman, I stopped for gas on my way to interview Dr. Mills at his office. Although there was still snow on the ground, I was driving my summer car, a red Porsche 928. (My wife's mother was in town to help and we gave her the Suburban.) Late that afternoon, my wife got a telephone call from the Anchorage Police Department. Anyone own a red Porsche? The police told her I filled my car with gas at a Chevron station and drove off without paying. She had until 6 p.m. to pay or criminal charges would be filed. When my wife raced to the gas station to pay (and apologize), the owner said she noticed me filling the red Porsche and "he looked like his mind was a million miles away."

Chapter 27

Economist

Dr. Richard Solie, a professor of economics at the University of Alaska, Fairbanks, had a side career as an expert witness in personal injury cases. I had never used an economist and got his name from Joe Young, then the most successful plaintiff's lawyer in Alaska. About half of Dr. Solie's clients were defense attorneys and he was well-respected.

In a typical personal injury case, a layman (a juror) can calculate lost wages. If an injured person cannot work for three months, one calculates how much in wages would have been earned, subtracts any substitute wages earned (usually zero), and the difference is lost wages. In cases involving very serious injury or death, the Ninth Circuit Court of Appeals required that an economist be used. For Pat Scanlon, Dr. Solie calculated the "lost accumulations" suffered by his estate. For Clouser, who could no longer work as an operating engineer or a mechanic, the economist calculated "lost wages" to the date of trial and "loss of earning capacity" in the future.

Knowing an economist would be expensive, I delayed hiring Solie as long as possible. This did not help. Dr. Solie's bill for both clients was over $12,000, more than all other litigation costs combined.

Court began at 8:30 a.m. The federal courthouse in Fairbanks was an old building and Judge Kleinfeld's courtroom was much smaller than in Anchorage. There were no spectators.

Dr. Solie obtained his Ph.D. in economics from the University of Tennessee in 1965. He had testified in front of Kleinfeld before. The first page of his reports for each client was a cover letter stating the economist had no interest in the case and was not being paid on a contingency basis. It was ethical for me to take this case on a contingency fee and to be paid only if successful, but it was not ethical for an expert witness to be paid that way. Win or lose, Solie would be paid the same amount.

Dr. Solie had prepared a series of transparencies to illustrate his testimony, but Judge Kleinfeld refused to view them. When I asked for guidance on how much detail he wanted from the economist, Kleinfeld said it was permissible to question in summary fashion, adding, "Obviously we've all been through this type of report many times, so it's practical to just bring out the things that are unique to the case." I did not correct the judge, but I had never called an economist to testify before.

Damages to the Scanlon estate were presented first. Dr. Solie used two different methods to calculate "lost accumulations." Under Method A, past and future lost accumulations totaled $619,685. Method B totaled $653,603. Under either method, the net loss far exceeded the amount listed in the federal tort claim filed for Pat Scanlon, which limited any award to $400,000. Had I made a mistake?

Judge Kleinfeld was skeptical of Dr. Solie's methodology (I silently shared his concerns). Normally, both sides in a lawsuit call an economist and each expert presents damage calculations. If liability is found, most fact-finders (judge or jury) find damages to be somewhere between the high number from plaintiff's economist and the low number from defendant's economist. Here, the U.S.A. had not listed an economist on its witness list and I had succeeded in preventing the U.S.A. from calling its own economist so there would be no low number.

Dr. Solie was still testifying about the Scanlon damages when we recessed for Judge Kleinfeld's 10 a.m. appointment with Senator Frank Murkowski. When court reconvened, I quickly finished my questions on Scanlon. As I turned to Clouser, the judge indicated he wanted to move faster. I tried to move more rapidly, but we did not go fast. Over half of the direct examination consisted of Judge Kleinfeld questioning Dr. Solie one on one. There was nothing I could do.

The economist calculated what Clouser might be able to earn as a computer programmer. (No one in the courtroom knew whether Mike would be employed as a computer programmer in the future.) Dr. Solie calculated two sets of figures. Under the first, Clouser could not work at any gainful employment. Under the second, Clouser worked full-time as a computer programmer for the rest of his expected work life. The loss to Mike if he could work full-time as a computer programmer versus an operating engineer was $165,434. If one assumed Mike would never work again, the loss was $951,420. After applying applicable discount rates, these numbers changed to $167,749 and $848,184, which established the range of Clouser's damages. Ultimately, the key question was whether Mike would ever work again. This was a question for the judge, not an economist.

THE COURT: Let me ask something that troubles me here. . . . What do government bonds yield now?

THE WITNESS: Today they're probably in the 7% range.

THE COURT: If a man has an eight hundred thousand dollar lump sum and invests it at 7%, he gets $56,000 a year. After taxes . . . , he winds up with about $40,000 a year, is that right?

THE WITNESS: Yes.

THE COURT: And that means he can spend forty thousand a year for the rest of his life and still have the $840,000 lump sum as far as his estate, is that right?

THE WITNESS: Yes, that's correct.

THE COURT: So why doesn't the method wind up with an amount that puts the individual in a position much better than he would have been economically if he had not been hurt?

THE WITNESS: The reason is . . . [inflation] . . .

THE COURT: So it's the anticipated future inflation that breaks it back out?

THE WITNESS: Yes, that's right. . . .

[Judge questions Dr. Solie for 6 more pages on subject.]

Direct examination finished just before lunch. Court adjourned at 11:55 a.m. to resume at 1:15 p.m.

Mr. Wilson's cross-examination brought out that while the economist deducted the federal income taxes Pat Scanlon would have paid, no deduction was made for Indiana state income taxes. He also pointed out that Dr. Solie assumed Pat would have received free board at the family farmhouse for his entire life, long after the Scanlon parents died. Similarly, a 25% deduction in food costs continued throughout Pat's entire life expectancy. Dr. Solie testified that if he had not made the assumption of free board and a 25% reduction in food costs, Pat's estimated lifetime consumption would have increased by $274,000, decreasing claimed damages by the same amount. The $400,000 listed in Pat's federal tort claim for economic loss now appeared reasonable.

Wilson also established that Dr. Solie had not deducted Clouser's employee business expenses. These were substantial when Mike worked out of state and lived in a motel. This issue and others resulted in high annual wage estimates. For example, Dr. Solie estimated the value of wages and fringe benefits Mike would have earned in 1982 at $29,904, triple the $9,623 Clouser earned in 1981.

The judge called an afternoon recess at 2:45 p.m., with Wilson still working through the economist's tables on Clouser. With adjournment scheduled for 4:30, I wondered if we would get to Mr. Strauss from the High Altitude Rescue Team today.

After the recess, Mr. Wilson moved faster. (I had long ago decided against any redirect.) When he finished, Judge Kleinfeld asked even more questions. Finally, the economist was excused.

When offered a 10 minute recess, I asked how late court would be in session. The judge responded that he was reluctant to run beyond 5:00. He added, "We also have to consider that I have to absorb all of this material and my attention may wander if we [go] too late into the evening." Court recessed at 3:19.

Dr. Solie's testimony started at 8:30 and we had already put in a full trial day. The judge was warning that he was near the limit of his ability to absorb information. In law school, I used to read old law reviews for amusement and I once read a study on what time of day serious mistakes happen at trial. A highly disproportionate percentage of reversible error occurred in the last hour. The length of a trial day was shortened in response to such studies.

Chapter 28

Strauss

It was 3:30 when Bill Strauss, still a civilian employee of the Army at Ft. Greely, took the stand for cross-examination. The late hour was troubling, as Strauss was an important liability witness. For Pat Scanlon to have survived the plane's slide on Wednesday night, it may have been necessary to secure him in a rigid stretcher inside the fuselage or to remove him from the plane wreckage entirely. The HART possessed stretchers (akiohs) and the needed manpower to accomplish either task.

When I took Strauss' deposition at Ft. Greely, he was not at all what I expected. A civilian employee of the Army, he was then 33 and cool. He became a rock climber growing up near Phoenix. When his 1972 draft lottery number was 3 (of 365), Strauss enlisted "since they had me dead to rights." His first Army duty was at Ft. Carson (Colorado Springs) on the mountain rescue team, where he participated in a half dozen rescues involving plane crashes. He transferred to Europe and attended the Army Mountain Guide Course taught by the German Army. He also became a professional ski instructor through the American and German ski instructor associations. At the end of his tour of active duty, he remained in Garmisch, Germany, working for a ski school. In summer, he worked as an Outward Bound instructor in Colorado. Strauss started work at Ft. Greely in June, 1980.

Dressed in civilian clothes, Strauss recounted his education, climbing experience, and rescue training and expertise. His Army job consisted of "training specialists in military arctic mountaineering." The Northern Warfare Training Center had 35 instructors. The High Altitude Rescue

Team consisted of 12 volunteers from these instructors. HART members received extra training and were outfitted with lighter weight and more technically useful equipment. Yes, the team has been called "the Army's leading edge" in military mountaineering. In his view, "[The team is] there for . . . responding to military-type accidents involving military personnel[,]" not civilian rescues.

Strauss had been a HART member since his arrival in June, 1980. Kahiltna Pass was the HART's only rescue, military or civilian, in his almost 7 years there. Yes, the team trained on Mt. McKinley in 1980, 1981, and 1982. The last year, "we assisted in the establishment of a medical research camp at the 14,200 foot level." Was this Dr. Mills' camp, the one he asked for assistance with at the rescue critique? Yes.

The HART trained often on Mt. McKinley in part because "[i]f something's going to happen, it's probably going to be on Denali."

Q. . . . [T]he HART might be called to assist in an
   air taxi crash on Mt. McKinley at 10,000 feet
   or above. That's what the team is there for,
   isn't it?

A. The team is not there [to respond] to accidents
   involving air taxis above 10,000 feet on Mt.
   McKinley. If such a situation ever arose, and it
   hasn't yet, where we were required, that might
   happen. But it hasn't happened.

Q. I'm sorry. Did it not happen in the Kahiltna
   Pass rescue?

A. Yes, it did.

Strauss' unexpectedly partisan attitude slowed what should have been straightforward foundation testimony about the HART's capabilities. The team was on permanent five-hour response time. Mobilization involved ten people with equipment to stay for an extended period. The team was configured to fly to altitudes above the tree line and to operate in difficult terrain. It could move as far as necessary, using skis, snowshoes, and other equipment at 10,000 feet on Mt. McKinley. Yes, the team was trained and prepared for a Kahiltna Pass type rescue.

Strauss identified Exhibit 58, his after action report. After he learned about the Kahiltna Pass rescue on Wednesday afternoon, the team mobilized itself that day. It was requested by Gerhard through the RCC about 10 a.m. Thursday. The team moved its equipment to nearby Allen Army Airfield. 7 HART members were flown in a C-130 to Talkeetna, arriving about 1:30 or 2:00 p.m., too late to load gear onto a Chinook for that afternoon's flight to the crash site. Thursday afternoon and evening, 6 more team members drove from Ft. Greely to Talkeetna, bringing HART membership to 13. At my request, Strauss read aloud from his after action report:

> "Alert Procedures. The existence of this mission became known inadvertently, indicating serious flaws in the way in which the HART is perceived by other rescue agencies ([Chinooks], RCC, etc.), lack of knowledge of HART capabilities by those agencies, and the exclusion of the HART from interagency contingency planning." . . .

Q. To put it another way, [the RCC] forgot that [the HART] has this [ground rescue] capability . . . ?

A. . . . [Y]es, they might not have had us in mind. . . .

Bad weather prevented any activity on Friday. On Saturday morning, the team took off in Chinook 525, which soon returned to Talkeetna for repairs. When these were complete, Mr. Bridgman flew the HART to the south side of Kahiltna Pass and unloaded the 13 team members and their gear at 9700 feet. Some team members set up camp, which Strauss labeled "absolutely essential," and some, including Strauss, headed to the crash site. While Mike Clouser walked out, Ed Hommer was carried on an akioh (stretcher). The HART members set up a rope system to help traverse Kahiltna Pass.

While the color photographs taken by Strauss as he climbed up the south side of Kahiltna Pass and down the north side to the crash site were already admitted into evidence, I did not think there was enough time to go through them. Portions of the south side were wind-blasted and hard walking. On the north side, there was deep snow and it was not slippery. He estimated the wreckage was several hundred yards below the summit.

The degree of slope ranged from zero at the summit to 25 degrees at the crash site.

With Saturday's perfect weather, Strauss estimated the HART could have performed the rescue by itself, with no Mountain Maniacs or AMRG climbers, in "4 to 5 hours." If the team had been contacted by the RCC on Tuesday evening, it would have taken the HART 4 hours to be ready to move. It was a two hour drive from Ft. Greely to Ft. Wainwright or a 45 minute Chinook flight. On Thursday, the C-130's flight time from Ft. Greely to Talkeetna was 45 minutes. Strauss agreed that any time the HART was to be used, it required the Chinooks to insert it.

At the January, 1982 rescue critique, Lt. Col. Leavitt, then head of the HART, strongly implied that, if dropped off by the Chinooks at Kahiltna Pass on Wednesday morning, the team would have performed wonders for the victims. I carried my black boombox to Fairbanks to play his comments. Strauss remembered Lt. Col. Leavitt speaking at the critique and identified his distinctive, deep voice.

```
[Hearsay objection overruled because admission.]

(Tape played.)

LT. COL. LEAVITT: . . . the military makes a
    fundamental choice when they alert a high
    altitude team the [Chinooks] are going. They're
    going to choose between a high altitude [ground]
    rescue team, that's us, or the paramedics [Air
    Force PJs]. If they picked the [Air Force PJs],
    they're going to do something quick and dirty,
    put a monkey on a string, grab the victims and
    put 'em back in. Okay. Pick the [HART], we're
    ready to go forever.

    Now, once you've made that choice and we're
    still sitting at Ft. Greely 300 miles away and
    they're trying to do what they could with the
    choice they'd made, which is the [Air Force PJs],
    now I'm not able to critique that decision.
    If we'd have been in the [Chinook] and they
    could have dropped us off on the south side [of
    Kahiltna Pass], we'd have been good. But . . .
```

```
[the] fundamental decision was wrong through no
one's fault.
```

(Tape stopped.)

When I finished, Ms. Neda conducted direct. She had Strauss repeat that the National Park Service had never before, or since, called the HART for a rescue on Mt. McKinley. She brought out that Strauss had objected to Clouser walking to the Chinooks on Saturday.

```
A. [I] would not have permitted him [to walk] to the
   Chinooks, no.

Q. Why is that?

A. Based upon my limited knowledge of first aid, I
   know that serious tissue damage can occur when
   you walk on frostbitten feet and I would not have
   allowed him to walk. . . .

Q. Was it the HART that, in fact, permitted Clouser
   to walk?

A. No, it was not.
```

The HART spent three or four hours mobilizing itself on Wednesday after Strauss learned the Chinooks were at Denali on a rescue mission. When the team met a C-130 Thursday noon at Allen Army Airfield, 30 minutes were required to load the gear, 45 minutes to fly to Talkeetna, and 30 minutes to unload the gear in Talkeetna. Ms. Neda asked him to describe what each individual team member carried.

```
     Each person has a rucksack consisting of
all their personal gear that weighs between 60
and 80 pounds. That's a rough estimation. And,
in addition, whatever you can't cram into your
rucksack you carry in a kit bag. It's a large
canvas parachute bag. They weigh 30, 40, possibly
50 pounds, depending upon what's being placed in
the bag. There also skis that each person
had. Skis and poles and that type of equipment.
Those are the individual items. . . .
```

Q. And other items such as akiohs, do you recall
how many you brought and how much they weigh?
A rough approximation?

A. We had two full akiohs which weighed between 200
and 400 pounds, containing team equipment, tents,
fuel, extra rations, and this sort of thing. And
there were two empty akiohs that we thought we
would probably need. . . . I guess it would be
between 3 and 4000 pounds [total], not counting
the people.

Ms. Neda handed the witness the thirty-two 8" x 10" color photos
he took during the rescue operation. (I had used several during Clouser's
testimony.) He identified several photos of the inside of Chinook 525
showing the size of the windows (12" diameter) and how passengers sat in
the rear (lengthwise, facing in, back to window). Photograph 16 was taken
from the summit of Kahiltna Pass looking north at the crash site in shade
and Peters Glacier in sunlight in the distance.

Q. Would you say the north slope [below the summit
of Kahiltna Pass on the north side] is shaded or
lit in that picture?

A. The north slope is definitely in the shade.

Q. During your stay from early Saturday afternoon
to late Sunday morning, did [the crash location
on the north side] remain in [shade] during the
daylight [hours]?

A. Yes, it did.

Q. Did it ever have direct sunlight?

A. No, it didn't.

When Ms. Neda finished, I asked for the photographs. I did not take
time to rearrange the photos and my questions followed the order they
were in.

Photo 10, taken at 9700 feet on the south side of Kahiltna Pass and
washed in sunlight, showed 5 or 6 HART members with one tent erected

and more tents going up. Photo 24 was taken from the summit of Kahiltna Pass looking south in bright sunlight down Kahiltna Glacier. Photo 11 depicted "our personnel moving up the south side of Kahiltna Pass."

Three photographs (12, 13, 15) showed the summit of Kahiltna Pass, the location where Mr. Warden achieved a hover in 033 on Wednesday noon and where Dennis Brown would have attempted to land earlier Wednesday morning. The summit looked big and flat enough to handle a Chinook or the smaller Akland helicopter. Photo 17 showed HART members descending the north side. The next photo was taken in shade from midway down the north side looking back up at the sunlit summit. Judge Kleinfeld asked, "[With] the angle of the sun at that time of year and [the] shape of the summit of the Pass, is the north side, where the crash site is, ever exposed to direct sun? Or is it always in shade?" A. "It's never exposed to the sun. It's going to be shady."

Photo 19 showed the wrecked fuselage, mostly buried in snow, from a distance of 20-30 meters with Peters Basin, far below, visible in sunlight in the background. Photograph 21 depicted Hommer being loaded on an akioh with his snow-covered socks visible. In photo 20, only Ed's mouth and nose were visible (the rest was parka hood) and one of the Mountain Maniacs held his left arm extended towards the camera with a fierce "get away from here you son-of-a-bitch" expression on his face. Several photos depicted the wrecked fuselage before the body of Pat Scanlon was removed. All the windows were missing and the tail section was completely filled by snow.

Photo 18 showed a view from the wreckage looking up the north side towards the summit while the body of Dan Hartmann was being hauled up. Photo 22 showed HART members hauling Hommer's akioh up the north side using ropes and pulleys. The final photo, 26, looked south from Kahiltna Pass summit and showed a Chinook on the snow and, slightly below, the camp erected by the HART. The Chinook looked quite close to the summit.

When I finished, Ms. Neda had no questions. Mr. Strauss was excused.

The judge announced trial would start in Anchorage at 8:30 a.m. tomorrow, Tuesday, so we could get in a full day. Wednesday he could give us an hour in the morning and perhaps as much in the afternoon. He thought we could probably finish Wednesday, the 10th day of trial. Court adjourned at 5:15 p.m.

I caught the next flight to Anchorage. As we flew south and I looked out the window at Mt. McKinley, I had misgivings about Strauss' testimony. He was more partisan than anticipated and there was less time than expected to impeach him. Mostly I felt numb.

Chapter 29

Baker end

Tuesday morning I badly needed coffee. I slept poorly in Fairbanks on Sunday night and Monday was an extra long trial day, followed by travel. I stuck with the no alcohol rule on the return flight and did not have coffee in the morning, but I was deeply tired.

Court convened at 8:34 a.m. with Major Baker, Chief of the RCC, on the stand as cross-examination resumed. The National SAR Plan, the RCC Plan, and the agreements between federal agencies meshed well, but took time to explain. The strategy was to quote requirements from SAR plans to establish the standard of conduct and then to show how the Kahiltna Pass rescue did not comply.

Major Baker was familiar with the resources available through the RCC for airdrops to persons in need of rescue. He knew that C-130s carry a sled that can be air dropped to survivors. He assumed that Chinooks had resources available for airdrops but was not familiar with such equipment.

> THE COURT: . . . You don't know the airdrop capability of the Chinook but I think you did describe the airdrop capability of [a C-130]. Could you go over that again, make sure I have it?
>
> THE WITNESS: The C-130 [Herc] is a four-engine turbo-prop aircraft and it is specifically configured for . . . rescue and we carry on that two sleds, known as "red sleds." They have a number of items for sustaining people who are in need of rescue, to include sustaining the

pararescue specialists should we put them in. It
contains stoves, sleeping bags, food, water, a
number of items. . . .

THE COURT: That material is kept packed up, ready
for drop, on the Herc?

THE WITNESS: Yes, sir.

THE COURT: Does that include an anatomic sled?

THE WITNESS: It's in a sled. The sled is a container
that looks just like a sled and it's metal,
roughly 30 inches wide by about three feet or
more long by about 15 to 18 inches deep.

THE COURT: Is it designed so that it can be dragged
across the snow?

THE WITNESS: Yes, sir, once it was dropped in.

THE COURT: Is there some tent or some sort of
shelter on it?

THE WITNESS: Yes, sir, there is a tent on there. . . .

Baker also testified there were 21 first aid kits aboard a C-130 that could be airdropped in addition to the red sled. The judge asked if there was anything specifically "for moving people with fractures?" Major Baker was not sure.

The SAR Plans required airdrops, which is why Air Force aircraft were so equipped. Baker testified the second C-130 flight Tuesday night also had two Air Force PJs aboard.

The RCC Plan included Appendix 4 covering high altitude helicopter operations (requiring use of the 242d Chinooks) and Appendix 5 covering high altitude ground operations (requiring use of the HART). Baker knew of the "existence" of the HART, but had never worked with the team or met any of its personnel. He admitted he was not familiar with the HART's capabilities.

Baker read aloud the four main assumptions of the RCC Plan, which RCC controllers were trained to assume. "(1) There are survivors. (2) Immediate assistance is needed. (3) Survivors require medical aid and/or other assistance. (4) Survivors are incapacitated." Many provisions applied word for word to the Kahiltna Pass rescue. For example, "60% of all survivors of any type accident are injured to some extent. It must also be assumed that there is not even one able-bodied, logical thinking survivor that will be able to help himself." It was enough to read a provision aloud to Baker, have him confirm the RCC controllers were so trained, and move on.

The SAR Plans outlined three rescue methods: (a) helicopter landing, (b) helicopter hoist pick-up, and (c) land party penetration/rescue. When I asked if a Chinook on a SAR mission carried a ground rescue capability, Baker answered not unless the RCC asked the Chinook to carry such a party. He believed that Air Force PJs aboard a Chinook constituted "a ground rescue capability." Asked for what length of time, he answered, "My guess would be up to 3 days . . . as a minimum. . . ." He did not know how long the HART could function if inserted on Kahiltna Glacier in December.

> Q. On Tuesday night, do you recall if it was known whether a helicopter could perform the rescue . . . ?
>
> A. We did not know. . . .
>
> Q. On Tuesday, the rescue plan for this incident should have included [a] ground rescue capability, correct? . . .
>
> A. Correct according to the SAR Plan.
>
> Q. And correct according to your judgment as present head of the RCC and as a person who trains RCC controllers on how to develop rescue plans?
>
> A. Correct.
>
> Q. [I]n your judgment, . . . it did contain a ground rescue capability because you're of the opinion that the [Air Force] PJs on board the Chinook Wednesday had a ground rescue capability, correct?
>
> A. Correct.

The questioning turned to polar SAR provisions, which required an airdrop to victims almost as soon as they were located. To Baker, "polar" meant polar ice cap. He differentiated Kahiltna Pass from a polar environment; he believed a rescue on Mt. McKinley was <u>more difficult</u> than a polar rescue.

> Q. . . . What I'm suggesting is, as a rescue planner
> . . ., which is what you are now, the rescue plan
> on Mt. McKinley should have been (1) find them,
> (2) airdrop something to them, correct? . . .
>
> A. . . . [T]he normal search plan is (1) find them,
> (2) recover them if capable, and, if not, then we
> try to get something there to sustain life.
>
> Q. In the polar situation, it's (1) find them and
> (2) airdrop something to them —
>
> A. In the polar situation you're correct.
>
> Q. In the Mt. McKinley situation, it's the same thing,
> (1) find them and (2) airdrop something to them?
>
> A. If it's feasible.

Baker agreed SAR units could bypass the RCC and communicate directly with each other, so long as the RCC was kept informed.

> Q. Specifically, the Chinooks at the 242d at
> Ft. Wainwright could communicate directly with
> the HART in Ft. Greely and coordinate between
> themselves the need for a ground rescue force so
> long as one or the other of those, either the
> Chinooks or the HART, kept the RCC advised of
> what they were doing, correct?
>
> A. I see no problem with that.
>
> THE COURT: Counsel, how much longer do you have?
>
> MR. GALBRAITH: Fifteen, twenty minutes — he says boldly.

"He says boldly" was under my breath, for my ears only. That it slipped out at all reflected how tired I was. I did not realize the trial transcript would include the comment or I would have apologized on the spot.

Judge Kleinfeld's question told me, for the first time, to speed up. I cut the remaining material drastically. At the end, I returned to the appendixes to the RCC Plan covering high altitude helicopter and high altitude ground rescue operations. Major Baker knew of no ground rescue team in the Army other than the HART and he agreed that Appendix 5 was referring to it.

> Q. This Kahiltna Pass rescue involved a high
> altitude ground SAR operation, didn't it?
>
> A. Based on the definitions of the Plan.
>
> Q. Right. And from this appendix [5] to the Plan,
> one would have expected the ground resources of
> the HART to have been employed, correct?
>
> A. I would not - I wasn't there. I don't know all
> the plan, I don't have all the factors.

I finished at 9:50 a.m. Judge Kleinfeld called a 10 minute recess.

Ms. Neda's direct examination ignored rescue planning and focused solely on Baker's C-130 flight. He testified the Hudson air taxi's ELT stopped transmitting between the first and second C-130 flights. Ms. Neda's questions implied that if not for the "lucky circumstance" of the first C-130 being near the crash location Tuesday afternoon, no one would have survived the Hudson crash.

Major Baker testified the two Air Force PJs on Tuesday's second C-130 flight were equipped to jump out of the Herc, if necessary. To Ms. Neda, this meant the C-130 had a ground rescue capacity. She asked if the second C-130 flight was able to air drop supplies to the survivors. Baker answered that they never got a visual sighting, so they did not know where to drop the supplies. Were C-130 flights on subsequent days equipped to air drop? Yes, said Baker, but they were never able to.

Recross was brief. Major Baker was excused.

Chapter 30

Okonek

As Major Baker left the courtroom, plaintiffs called Jim Okonek [awk-oh-neck], owner of K-2 Aviation in Talkeetna. Age 55, Okonek had a shock of silver hair and carried no excess weight. The father of Brian Okonek, a famous McKinley climbing guide, he appeared happy with life. His witness file contained a September 6, 1986 article from the Anchorage Daily News featuring a photograph of him standing next to a red K-2 Cessna 185 on skis (like the Hudson plane that crashed) and smiling at the camera from behind big reflective aviator sunglasses. The Daily News article reported Okonek won International Helicopter Pilot of the Year for 1980, stating, "[T]hat year he rescued nine parties on Mt. McKinley by helicopter." Okonek was quoted saying, "There are less demanding businesses with a lot less risk. You can't begin to adequately cover yourself with insurance. If you were found negligent, you would lose everything."

Okonek served as an Air Force officer from 1952 until 1973. He worked as a rescue controller at the RCC at Elmendorf for three years, flew rescues in Vietnam, and returned to Elmendorf as Director of Operations for the Helicopter Rescue Squadron until 1973. He flew jet trainers, DeHavilland Beavers, C-47 Gooney Birds, and numerous military and civilian helicopters.

He had worked for Akland Helicopters, owned by Dennis Brown, where he flew a variety of helicopters including a Jet Bell Ranger. He did not know how many helicopter rescues he flew in Mt. McKinley National Park while employed by Akland. "I flew from about '78 through '80, three different seasons, maybe some in '81, too. . . . 1980 was a banner year on

McKinley and I had I think nine different rescues that year. Just several the year before." The maximum altitude capacity of a Jet Bell Ranger was about 15,000 feet "in the cold conditions we had at McKinley."

He identified the West Buttress photograph and testified he sold similar Bradford Washburn photos to the public. As I held the photograph near the witness stand so the judge could see (Ms. Neda came forward also), he pointed out places where he had landed the Akland Jet Bell Ranger including at 14,300 feet on the West Buttress route, just below 13,000 feet behind small peaks on the mountain visible in the photo, and on a ridge coming off Kahiltna Dome. He testified about other landing sites not visible in the photograph. All were higher than Kahiltna Pass, visible in the lower left foreground. Yes, it is possible to land "a Jet Bell Ranger on the summit of Kahiltna Pass." "It would depend on conditions, but, yes." The tail number of the Jet Bell Ranger he flew for Akland Helicopters was 1086 Yankee.

In 1981, there were restrictions on the ability of air taxi operators to land within the boundaries of Denali National Park. "You couldn't land within the original boundaries of the Park unless it was authorized or an emergency, specific authorization. . . . We couldn't land in there with either an airplane or a helicopter." He explained the requirement that air taxis land outside the old park boundaries and load or unload passengers at the boundary line at what Art Mannix called "Kahiltna International." According to Okonek, "Everybody in the climbing world would know where that was. There's a good deal of traffic through there."

In the summer of 1986, Kahiltna International became inoperable. That spring, Mt. Augustine, a volcanic island south of Anchorage, erupted and spread ash on Mt. McKinley. The ash was covered by subsequent snowfalls, but the summer sun melted the snow cover, resulting in "extremely rough surface conditions." Because of the ash problem, the NPS was asked for permission to land within Park boundaries. In July, permission was granted "to land at a higher elevation practically anywhere we thought was all right, above where the snow hadn't melted off the ash yet and the conditions were favorable. We were landing at about the 9500 foot level which would have been right in here [indicating where the Chinooks landed on Saturday] just below Kahiltna Pass. . . ." There were many landings at 9500-9600 feet on Kahiltna Glacier that summer.

Q. Let me ask the obvious. Is it possible to land a
   fixed wing at 9500-9600 feet on [the south side]
   of Kahiltna [Pass]?

A. Yes.

Q. It's not difficult at all, correct?

A. Well, yes, it's difficult.

Q. Compared to other places in the glacier?

A. Yes. The altitude has some effect but it's a
   pretty good place to operate. . . .

The questioning arrived at the touchiest part of Okonek's testimony –
Dennis Brown's helicopter piloting ability.

Q. Did you ever fly with Dennis Brown in a helicopter?

A. I think he's been aboard a helicopter I was
   flying. I don't think I ever rode with him.

Q. When he was flying?

A. Yes.

Q. Do you know if Dennis Brown had "guts" as a
   helicopter pilot?

A. Well, I'd say he probably did. I've known him to
   fly helicopters from time-to-time and do some
   things with it that I thought were rather "gutsy"
   in as much as he didn't have a lot of experience.

On Tuesday, the day of the crash, Okonek was in Anchorage. When he
heard about it Wednesday morning, he immediately returned to Talkeetna,
arriving that afternoon.

Q. Can you say whether you would have been in the
   air [to attempt a rescue] if you'd been there
   [Wednesday morning]?

A. Well, I'm confident if there'd been a helicopter
   available that I could use and I thought it was

```
     feasible to go, I no doubt would have gone. . . .
     I would have wanted to go. . . .
```

```
Q. In general, are you willing to fly in marginal
   conditions if an injured climber or an aircraft
   [crash] victim may need immediate aid?
```

```
A. Yes.
```

Ms. Neda cross-examined.

```
Q. Mr. Okonek, would you say that Mr. Brown is an
   amateur pilot?
```

```
A. I consider him an amateur, yes.
```

Oops! Ms. Neda or a federal investigator must have interviewed Okonek.

```
Q. Do you feel he was competent or qualified to
   execute a high altitude rescue as a pilot in
   command of a helicopter?
```

```
MR. GALBRAITH: Objection, lack of foundation, lack
   of first-hand knowledge.
```

```
THE COURT: Overruled.
```

The basis for my objection was that Okonek had never flown with Brown while Brown was pilot of a helicopter, so how could he have an opinion on whether Brown was competent to fly a high altitude rescue? While the judge overruled it, Okonek seemed to understand the objection.

```
THE WITNESS: Would you state the question again?
```

```
MS. NEDA: Yes. Do you feel Mr. Brown was qualified
   and competent to conduct as pilot-in-command a
   high altitude rescue such as you've described
   that you performed?
```

```
MR. GALBRAITH: Object to the phraseology "high
   altitude rescue." I think it's overly vague.
```

```
THE COURT: [to Ms. Neda] Would you rephrase that in
   terms of where the crash site was?
```

When the judge sustained my objection and directed her to specify the crash site in her question, it rattled Ms. Neda. This was not lost on the witness.

MS. NEDA: Yes. Mr. Okonuck – or Okonek, I'm sorry.

A. Okonek.

Q. Yes, I know. You're aware, aren't you, that the wreckage was located approximately at the 10,000 foot level on the Kahiltna Glacier and this was in wintertime, December, '81?

A. Yes.

Q. You've expressed your opinion as to whether you feel Mr. Brown is capable of executing a rescue attempt at that location, haven't you?

(Pause.)

From the judge's last ruling, it was clear Kleinfeld wanted Okonek's opinion on whether Brown could have rendered aid at the crash site. Testimony by Okonek that Dennis Brown was not competent to land at Kahiltna Pass or to hover over the crash victims and airdrop survival gear could destroy the "worsened the victim's plight" portion of plaintiffs' case. All other evidence in the record, from warming up the Akland helicopter and loading survival gear to Hunze telling Brown he was not to fly into Denali National Park, would amount to nothing. Much as I wanted to object, Ms. Neda's question was not objectionable. It did not ask whether Brown was capable of executing this rescue, it asked if Okonek had previously expressed his opinion on this topic. But the witness did not answer.

A. (No response.)

Q. Have you expressed your opinion concerning whether you thought he was competent enough and qualified to do something like that?

A. Well, I don't know if I have or not. I don't think I have today.

Q. No, not today.

> A. No, no.

It seemed likely Okonek had told either Ms. Neda or a federal investigator that he did not think Brown was capable of performing the Kahiltna Pass rescue. I guessed the U.S.A. again had not taken a witness statement.

> Q. What is your opinion, if I could ask you that?
> . . . [D]o you feel Mr. Brown was qualified and competent to the extent that he could operate as PRC of a helicopter at that elevation, executing that rescue?
> MR. GALBRAITH: Same objection. Lack of foundation, lack of first-hand knowledge.
> THE COURT: Overruled.

I objected again because my earlier objections had an impact on the witness and on Ms. Neda. Okonek knew the importance of the question. As he considered his answers, he often looked at Clouser. The two had met in Talkeetna the day before trial. It was not possible to shake hands with Mike without noticing his amputations.

> THE WITNESS: I don't have the personal experience of flying with Dennis Brown to make a factual judgment on that. I would say and volunteer that he was not very current in the helicopter, the 206, at the time and to go to that altitude in that type of terrain would have been demanding for a proficient pilot.

Ms. Neda returned to her original question. She wanted Okonek to acknowledge in court what he had said previously to her or to a government investigator.

> Q. Have you stated that he had no competence but it would have taken luck for him to even have gotten up there?
> A. As I understand what their conditions were –

MR. GALBRAITH: Objection. This calls for hearsay.
There's no foundation on what this witness knows
about what the conditions were. . . .

THE COURT: Pursuant to [Evidence] Rule 705, I'm
going to allow Mr. Okonek to testify in terms
of opinion and give his reasons without prior
disclosure of the underlying facts or data. But
he will be required to disclose the underlying
facts or data on redirect.

In effect, the judge ruled that Okonek was an expert witness in the area of high altitude helicopter rescues. Indeed, if anyone was an expert on a Jet Bell Ranger performing high altitude rescues on Mt. McKinley, it was Jim Okonek.

Q. Do you recall the question?

A. No, I don't.

Q. I was asking you have you at one time expressed
the opinion that Mr. Brown was not competent, he
would have needed a lot of luck to have gotten up
there, meaning Kahiltna Glacier.

A. I don't have total recall and I don't know that I
did say that.

This answer was a gift. Jim Okonek was doing to Tara Neda what Larry Rivers did to her. As with Rivers, she adopted a milder approach.

Q. Do you agree with that statement?

A. From what I knew of – had heard of the conditions
at the time immediately following the accident,
it would have been difficult to get into the
area, yes.

Ms. Neda still wanted the witness to say Brown was not competent.

Q. . . . let me just say the question again. Do you
   consider Mr. Brown a qualified and competent
   helicopter pilot to execute a high altitude
   rescue as pilot-in-command?

MR. GALBRAITH: Same objections, plus asked and answered.

THE COURT: Overruled.

THE WITNESS: I don't think I would have - I wouldn't
   have considered him qualified to do it. I'd like
   to say something further, though.

MS. NEDA: Yes, sir.

THE WITNESS: It's certainly feasible that he might
   have been able to do it. No one's able to say.

Q. It's in the realm of possibility?

A. Yes.

Q. But it's not probable?

MR. GALBRAITH: Objection. Leading.

THE COURT: It's cross. Overruled.

I knew it was a permissible question. I wanted Okonek to think
about his answer.

THE WITNESS: I couldn't judge on probability.

Ms. Neda established that Okonek's high altitude rescues all occurred in
climbing season, summer, not in December. She had him acknowledge that
he could execute a rescue in the Park in an emergency without permission
from the NPS. When she finished, redirect was essential.

Q. I believe you indicated you primarily flew
   helicopters from '55 to '73. How many total hours
   in a helicopter do you have?

A. About 8 or 9000 hours.

Q. Do you know how many hours Dennis Brown had in a
   helicopter as of December, 1981?

A. I do not.

Q. Would you even hazard a guess?

MS. NEDA: Objection to guessing and speculation.

THE COURT: Overruled.

THE WITNESS: I would guess no more than 200.

Q. If Mr. Brown had 15 or 1600 hours in a helicopter as of December, 1981 [as Brown testified in his deposition], would that make a difference in your opinion as to his ability to fly helicopters?

A. Yes. . . .

Q. One more time. You never flew in a helicopter with Dennis Brown when he was piloting the helicopter?

A. No, I never did.

Q. So you have no firsthand knowledge based on your own observation and experience of how good a pilot he was, particularly in a Bell Jet Ranger?

A. I've witnessed him fly from a distance as I remember but I've not been on board the airplane with him flying.

This was not helpful. Only a fool would ask what Okonek observed about Brown's flying "from a distance."

Q. You were asked your opinion [about the weather conditions at Kahiltna Pass Wednesday morning] and you said "From what I heard, it would have been difficult." . . . [W]hen would it have been difficult to attempt a rescue at [the crash site]? What time of day [on Wednesday]?

A. I can't answer that for sure. I know that weather and winds were a constant problem in the initial period after the accident. . . .

Q. You did attend a critique January 18, 1982, in Anchorage, didn't you?

A. Yes.

[Objection, hearsay, relevance, beyond scope, overruled because seeks factual basis of expert opinions expressed during cross-examination.]

Q. Do you remember Doug Geeting saying at the critique, [quoting from critique transcript] "[. . . on Wednesday morning] . . . They could have landed there. It was smooth."

A. I heard that. I don't remember specifically hearing that at the critique but I do recall hearing that.

Q. I'll represent to you that I played a tape recording of that into evidence here at trial. Do you believe that a helicopter could have landed at or near Kahiltna Pass in constant 10 to 15 mph winds assuming adequate visibility.

[Objection, exceeds scope of cross-examination, overruled.]

A. I'd have to say it's impossible for us to know, for me to know whether or not you could or could not. . . . I don't know.

Q. That's my point. You can't really second guess whether Dennis Brown would have been able to land at Kahiltna Pass Wednesday morning, can you?

A. I – yes, I'd agree with that, I can't.

Ms. Neda had no questions. Mr. Okonek was excused.

The U.S.A. did not name Jim Okonek on its witness list. Yet Ms. Neda knew or believed he was of the opinion that Brown was not a competent helicopter pilot. (I was too tired to remember Ranger Gerhard's testimony that Okonek did not consider Brown to be a competent helicopter pilot.) I had been sandbagged. There was nothing improper about this. If I had not called Okonek as a witness, the U.S.A. could not have called him either. I had called one witness too many. It was time for plaintiffs to rest their case.

Chapter 31

Bush Pilots

As Jim Okonek left the courtroom, I informed Judge Kleinfeld plaintiffs had no more witnesses. When the judge directed the U.S.A. to call a witness, Ms. Neda called Don Lee.

It is never too late to approach a fact witness, and, during the morning break, I approached one of the bush pilots in the hall. He turned his back and walked away, refusing to talk to me. This was Don Lee. His witness file had nothing--no interview by Gary Fye, no deposition testimony, no newspaper clipping. He did not attend the rescue critique. All I knew was that he opposed the lawsuit.

Ms. Neda handled direct. Don Lee was a "line pilot" at Talkeetna Air Taxi when Doug Geeting was chief pilot. When Geeting later started his own air taxi, Lee became chief pilot. He held numerous fixed wing ratings.

Lee first heard the Hudson aircraft was missing about 4 or 5 o'clock Tuesday afternoon. "[L]ater that evening, we got a report of an ELT and where the ELT was located, we got a quad on that location. . . ."

```
THE COURT: . . . I missed something there. What was
    your capacity that night? Why were you doing
    anything at all about this?

THE WITNESS: . . . [There's a] close brotherhood
    with the pilots there. There's a competitive
    jealousy in a sense but there's also a tremendous
    bonding because we know each other and we know
    what we're up against all the time and so we're
```

always watching out for each other. . . . We know
each other's families and it's more than just
normal search and rescue. . . .

Tuesday evening Geeting and Lee prepped their aircraft and got together personal survival gear. They also prepared a separate pack for an airdrop containing sleeping bags, extra food, heating tablets, things for winter survival.

Wednesday morning, Geeting and Lee were in the office about 6 a.m. but did not get into the air until 7:30 or 8. Lee flew a Cessna 185 and Geeting a Super Cub. Both flew alone. Lee had the airdrop pack. He described the flight conditions early Wednesday morning as "a southerly flow, a smooth southerly flow, over the mountains. . . . The light was twilight by the time we got into the mountains. . . . We had probably 5 to 10 miles visibility.   . . ." "We knew where we were, no question." When the judge asked what a "southerly flow" was, Lee answered "from the south."

Using the West Buttress photograph and the Washburn maps, he explained the search pattern. Lee, at 15,000 feet, started over Peter's Basin, north of Kahiltna Pass. Geeting, at a lower altitude, searched the West Buttress of Mt. McKinley and flat areas nearby. Then Lee searched the south side of Kahiltna Pass and Geeting searched the north side. "Doug radioed that he'd seen a light on the backside of this Pass in this corner here [indicating]. . . . [I]t was the wreckage . . . [and was] nearly invisible being white and on its side with just two narrow stripes and I actually flew by there a couple times without even seeing it."

The two pilots "set up a circular pattern to analyze the situation and feel the winds." "[W]e had . . . maybe 15-20 miles an hour just smooth air." Lee considered an airdrop but was unable to perform one "because of the location of the wreckage, the angle of the wreckage, and the wind direction." He did not consider a landing on the south side of the Pass because of "the hazards involved with the Glacier, extreme crevassed area, the wind direction, . . . [and] my situation as being alone would be fruitless." Was it turbulent around 8:30 – 9:00 a.m.? "There was a downdraft immediately at the apex of the Pass. There was a downdraft maybe a thousand feet a minute, 1500 feet a minute downdraft at that point[,] . . . [where] you had no control over the vertical stability of the aircraft, only directional control."

Doug Geeting ran low on fuel and departed first. Lee circled "for maybe 45 minutes" and then flew to Talkeetna to refuel. He departed the crash site "probably 8:45 – 9:00 o'clock I would say." Lee was in communication with Talkeetna Air Taxi which, in turn, was in communication with Mike Fisher, who was flying outbound to the crash site.

In Talkeetna, Lee refueled his aircraft with full tanks (80 gallons) "and turned around and went right back up." He believed he passed Fisher inbound to Talkeetna as he was outbound to the crash site. Lee was not able to airdrop or land on this second trip either. "The velocity of the wind had increased considerably. We had clear air turbulence then. . . . [T]he velocity of the wind had stepped up 20 to 30 miles-an-hour more than previously within that hour."

Did the winds affect his decision not to airdrop on his first trip to the crash site? A. "Absolutely."

> In order to make an airdrop on the lee [north] side of that face, you had to execute a turn right over the wreckage and maybe slightly above it. . . . [T]he centrifugal force, you'd be turning and dropping at the same time. . . . [Y]ou were right in the apex of the turbulence and you didn't have the control to fly that close to the face.

Q. How did it affect your decision not to land?

A. The wind? There was no access to the site. It was either Peter's [Basin] which was [out of the question] because it was so far down [at the bottom of the cliff] and there was maybe 4000 or 5000 feet of technical climbing to get up to [the crash site]. . . . [A]nd then the [south side of Kahiltna Pass], because of the crevasses and the wrong direction of the wind, it was not possible to land.

Lee had not asked permission from the NPS to execute this rescue because "the Park Service gives us total hands-up authority to do whatever's necessary in the event of a rescue. They've never hindered any past, previous or present, they've never hindered us in any emergency action on the mountain." Lee knew Dennis Brown and was familiar with his reputation. Q. "What is his reputation as a man? In your opinion, is he a truthful man?" A. "Without malice, I would question Dennis Brown's past integrity."

When cross-examination began, Lee turned from loquacious to taciturn. He agreed Doug Geeting planned and organized Wednesday morning's flights. Did he believe Geeting to be a credible person? "Maybe not in whole." This answer was surprising, but I did not follow up. (I had my own doubts, but Geeting's critique statements helped plaintiffs, so why undermine his credibility?)

Lee acknowledged he and/or Geeting plotted the ELT coordinates on a Washburn map with a scale of 1:50,000. Yes, those coordinates showed the crash site to be on Kahiltna Glacier. When Lee took off at 7:30 to 8:00 Wednesday morning, he had only 50 gallons in his 80 gallon fuel tanks.

On direct, Lee had been precise about the weather but not about the time. On arrival, the smooth southerly flow was "15 to − 10 to 15 knots, I'd say." The goal was to keep Lee in the air over the crash site on his first trip as long as possible because the weather was good. A corollary was to keep him on the ground in Talkeetna during the refueling break as long as possible because the winds had increased 20 mph or more when he reached the crash site a second time. It took him "about 35, maybe 40 minutes" to fly from Talkeetna to the crash site.

After Geeting spotted the crash site, Lee circled on the north side of the Pass several times before he could pick out the wreckage "because a flashlight was the only thing that showed it." It took Lee about 15 minutes to be certain he had located the crash site. Informed by the RCC log of an 8:35 a.m. call to McGrath from a civilian pilot saying the crash had been located, he agreed it was Geeting who called McGrath and 8:35 a.m. sounded right.

> Q. Then you spot them and you stay there another let's say, 45 minutes?
>
> A. Uh-huh.
>
> Q. So I've got an hour and a half so far and, again, I'm not trying to trick you.
>
> A. No, no.

Q. Then you fly back to Talkeetna which might take
   you 35 minutes so you're a little over 2 hours?

A. Uh-huh.

Q. Your total flight time [with] 50 gallons was?

A. 3 hours or so.

He added, "[w]e have bladder tanks, unreliable gauges, etc. and it's
not uncommon to fly around with 20 gallons [left]." Yes, he was alone
in the Cessna 185, and, yes, he would have had to perform an airdrop
by himself.

Q. You testified it would have been futile for
   you to land on the south side of Kahiltna Pass
   because you were alone, right?

A. Uh-huh. I wasn't prepared for technical climbing or
   I wasn't prepared for what the situation needed.

Q. So you never gave any serious thought to landing
   on the south side that morning, did you?

A. Later that morning I did.

Q. Is that on your second flight out?

A. Yes.

Q. Tell me about your second flight out when you
   did give serious consideration to landing at the
   south side of Kahiltna Pass?

On his refueling break, Lee talked to Sandy Hommer, Ed's wife,
and then called Art Mannix and asked him to fly up to the crash site.
Could he have called Brian McCullough, not Mannix? A. "It could have
been Brian, yes."

Q. And you were calling Brian because you wanted to
   load him as a passenger in your 185 and go up
   there and see if you could land on the south side
   of Kahiltna Pass, correct?

A. Yes. Or anywhere for that matter. . . .

> Q. [When did you call this climber]?
>
> A. ... it must have been like maybe 10:30 or 10:00 o'clockish when I probably called him.

After spending maybe an hour on the ground in Talkeetna, he took off and flew back to the crash site alone. On this second trip he brought along "ropes and enough stuff to possibly do it myself at that point."

> Q. So this time if you'd landed up there on the south side of Kahiltna Pass, you might have gotten out and tried to climb it yourself? If you'd been able to land?
>
> A. Knowing what I knew on the second trip, had I had that [gear] on the first trip, I would have –
>
> Q. [interrupting] I don't particularly want you to speculate and guess about what you would have done in hindsight. I didn't ask you a question about that.
>
> A. Okay.
>
> Q. The question I was asking you is, on the second flight, you brought this stuff so that, if possible, you could land and go out and try to walk over [the Pass] yourself?
>
> A. Yes.

Don Lee had been about to testify that if he had had with him on the first flight the climbing gear he took with him on the second flight, he would have landed on the first flight at the south side of Kahiltna Pass, gotten out of his Cessna 185, and climbed over the Pass to help the crash victims. I interrupted because 20-20 hindsight is not admissible evidence. Had Lee finished his statement, Ms. Neda would have moved to strike his answer and her motion would have been granted. In any event, Judge Kleinfeld got the point.

When he arrived at the crash site on his second trip, the wind had "increased considerably."

Q. And the "wind was 20 to 30 knots or miles-per-hour higher."

A. "Higher." So I'd guess 50 – 40 to 50 miles an hour at that point.

Q. Or maybe 30 to 40?

A. Yes.

Lee agreed that as Wednesday wore on, the wind grew in velocity and the weather got worse.

On the second flight, he intended "to stay until the Chinooks arrived and to help them locate the wreckage because of the difficulty in spotting it." When the Chinooks arrived, "they came in from the north at the Peter's [Basin] and then they saw me circling. I had a little brief communication with the pilot there and said 'Do you have it? Do you have it?' and they said 'Roger.' I said 'I'll get out of the way.'" He continued, "You don't need more people in that very confined place. . . ." Lee circled in the area until both Chinooks departed. The weather closed in too fast to return south to Talkeetna, so, like Bridgman in Chinook 525, Don Lee retreated north towards Fairbanks.

There was an option to ask Lee what he observed as he watched the Chinooks maneuver at the crash site. Where did they hover? How close did they get? Mike's testimony about this was strong and believable, and, in my judgment, it outweighed the Chinook pilots' testimony. If Lee's testimony backed the Chinook pilots, it might tip the scales against Clouser's observations. I chose not to risk that. When I finished, Ms. Neda had minimal redirect. Don Lee was excused and left the courtroom.

It was 11:30. Judge Kleinfeld declared a lunch recess until 1:45 p.m., 2 ¼ hours later.

Court resumed late. The judge said his schedule was growing intolerable and "it just gets worse and worse as the trial goes beyond estimated time." I did not respond that I had estimated a 10 to 15 day trial (this was day 9) and that 2 ½ hour lunch breaks did not help.

Mr. Wilson asked permission for the pathologist to testify tomorrow by telephone. (Dr. Lindholm had a personal emergency.) Ultimately, plaintiffs agreed.

THE COURT: We'll go by telephonic [testimony]. . . .
    He could be important on when and why Mr. Scanlon
    died. I do want the opportunity to question
    him myself . . . so a deposition would not
    suffice. As far as him testifying telephonically
    [tomorrow], it doesn't work out nearly as well as
    live testimony because you can't see a person's
    demeanor and people are always saying I can't
    hear [but] it may be the best we can do. . . .

Ms. Neda called Michael J. Fisher. During the morning break
when Don Lee rebuffed me, I also approached Mike Fisher. He was
upset about lawyers and contingency fees and would barely talk to me.
After I explained that Congress limited my attorney fee, Fisher talked
with me for a few minutes.

On direct, Ms. Neda brought out that Fisher arrived in Talkeetna
in 1962 and worked with legendary Alaska bush pilot Don "Wager with
the Wind" Sheldon from 1962 until Sheldon's death in 1975. Fisher had
4000 hours, lots of experience in mountain flying, and was a certified
flight instructor.

He first heard about the missing Hudson plane on Tuesday evening
when Doug Geeting called him. On Wednesday morning, Fisher estimated
he took off in a Cessna 185 at 8:30 a.m. with Tony Martin, a pilot
in training, as passenger. It took 30 minutes to fly to Kahiltna Pass. He
was in radio communication with Geeting and estimated they circled the
crash site for 20 minutes before Geeting left for Talkeetna. (Fisher had
absolutely no memory of Don Lee being at the crash site early Wednesday
morning.) He did not carry a special airdrop package; any airdrop would be
his personal survival gear.

On arrival, the weather was "high thin overcast and the wind was
high and it was from the south and it was spilling over the edge of the
Pass. And when I say "spilling over," I mean there was a downdraft on
the downwind [north] side." He experienced downdrafts "far in excess
of the airplane's ability to climb" every time we got "just over the crest
of the Pass on the north side." He estimated the wind at "30 knots with
gusts up to 50 knots."

The wind conditions prevented Fisher and Martin from making an
airdrop. "[H]aving to slow down in an area of extreme descending air,

downdrafts, would have put ourselves in a position where we could have stalled the airplane out and crashed. . . ." He considered landing on the south side of the Pass and made several attempts, but "each time we made a pass it got scary. . . . [E]ach time we got in the position where we would normally start slowing down, it just was so wild that there was no inclination to slow it down, it [was] just – 'Hey, let's get out of here.' . . ." He and Tony Martin were on scene "approximately an hour and 45 minutes and that doesn't include the travel time to and from."

Fisher brought his flying log to court. The entry for Wednesday read: "12/16/81. 1047F. Look for Ed Hommer. 3.5. Bad winds. Tony Martin." None of the other 50 entries in the log made reference to "bad winds."

No, he did not need permission from the NPS to conduct a rescue inside the Park. Was he familiar with Dennis Brown's reputation as to "truthfulness?" Fisher testified Brown's reputation was "poor."

On cross-examination, Fisher agreed the weather on Mt. McKinley is volatile and changes rapidly. He had flown in the Park since 1963. 80 percent of the high altitude flying used to be by his employer. "[Don] Sheldon had a very strong sense of commitment that if he took somebody up there, then that was his client and his passenger and he was responsible for their flying and their safety." It used to be a self-help rescue method. He described the gradual shift to the Park Service. The NPS was now considered "the organizer and coordinator of rescue efforts," but air taxi operators still had a strong commitment to their clients.

Geeting gave Fisher the ELT coordinates on Tuesday night and Fisher plotted them on a government sectional chart. "They were accurate enough that if you had flown exactly to those coordinates, you would have been within easy finding or viewing range of the wreck." Fisher also learned the Chinooks "were involved."

Geeting and Fisher planned a staggered air cover over the crash site on Wednesday morning. Geeting was to go up first, Fisher thought he was to go up second, and Don Lee was to be third. There were two goals--to find the aircraft and to overfly the site. Fisher later told Geeting, "I don't intend to charge for any of that flying," and Geeting responded "he didn't intend to charge for any of his flying either." [Gerhard paid Geeting for two hours of flying Wednesday.]

Wednesday morning, Geeting [and Lee] had already taken off when Fisher got to the Talkeetna airport. Because there was no real sunrise that morning (a high, thin overcast resulted in flat light conditions), he agreed he might have gotten to the crash site at 9, 9:15, or 9:30. Asked if the winds were 20 to 30 knots on arrival at the crash site, he testified the winds were "on the order of 30 knots and above," with gusts higher. Using the West Buttress photograph, he described where he circled and how he made "north passes" and "south passes" over the wreckage.

Fisher showed the judge where he considered landing south of the Pass. He wanted to land on the fall line, which runs diagonally on the Glacier, not straight up and down. "[A pilot] would get as high as he could. The reason for that being that he would need the room below him to take off when he decided to take off." It happened that pilots made safe glacier landings but didn't leave themselves enough room to take off again. He would have had to land downhill, into the wind. He made four or five passes over the potential landing area on the south side of Kahiltna Pass, but it would have been futile to land there. "Would you and/or Mr. Martin have been able to leave the aircraft and hike up to the crash site?" A. "Under more favorable conditions, yes. Under those conditions, no." The two of them were outdoorsmen, not mountaineers. Leaving the aircraft was a huge problem because the engine would cool to the point of not restarting in 90 minutes to 2 hours. And there was no way to keep the aircraft from blowing away while they were gone.

He could not do an airdrop because his personal survival gear was too light to fall in a proper trajectory. "I specifically remember [the] thought at the time that 'My God, if we had something heavy that we could weight this with,' make a sleeping bag weigh about 40 pounds by packing iron in it, then maybe we could plant it so it would stay." Fisher owned a machine shop and had access to such pieces of iron. He described how he and Martin would have performed the air drop. A Cessna 185 has hinged windows on both sides that open outward to about 30 degrees. The limiting guides had been removed so the windows could be tilted outward until parallel to the wing (90 degrees). Martin would drop the pack out the passenger side when Fisher touched his shoulder (it was too noisy to shout). Would Don Lee, flying alone at Kahiltna Pass, have had a more difficult airdrop than what faced Fisher and his passenger? A. "Yes. . . . I prefer to have what I would call a bombardier there."

On direct, Fisher testified the winds did not increase as he circled the crash site; they were strong the whole time. On cross-examination, he agreed that he might not have noticed if the winds increased from 20 to 30 knots. Had he made a pilot report to the FAA that morning, he would have described the turbulence as "moderate."

When I finished, Ms. Neda had no questions. Mike Fisher was excused. Judge Kleinfeld called a recess from 2:55 until 3:15 p.m.

Chapter 32

Hayes and David Brown

W hen court resumed, the U.S.A. called R.J. Hayes to rebut Tom Scanlon's testimony. Until retirement on September 30, 1985, Hayes had served as Chief of Public Affairs for the RCC at Elmendorf Air Force Base in Anchorage. Ms. Neda's examination established that he considered Tom Scanlon to be a business and personal friend. After Hayes retired, Tom helped him set up two gift shops in downtown Anchorage.

Q. Do you recall having lunch with Tom Scanlon at the Elevation 92 restaurant in Anchorage on a particular afternoon?

A. I had lunch with Tom [on] several occasions and I do remember at least one occasion at the Elevation 92 restaurant, yes.

Q. Do you recall if you gave him your poem that you authored?

A. Yes. I give almost everybody that poem but I'm sure that I gave Tom a poem. As to exactly when, I don't recall that.

Q. At that time when you had lunch were you a Major in the Air Force?

A. No. I was retired. I was operating one of two gift shops in downtown Anchorage.

Hayes strongly denied he told Tom Scanlon "at any time" that he was embarrassed by the military rescue or that any government personnel acted with criminal negligence. He went to the other extreme, testifying "the military did everything in its power" and "I'm proud of my association with it." Ms. Neda was soon finished.

Testimony of this sort often is of no great importance, but there was a bigger issue. I believed that thus far no important fact established by any witness for plaintiffs had been seriously contradicted or undermined. Why permit it now?

There was no doubt Tom was telling the truth. He was deposed in January, 1986, less than four months after Major Hayes retired from the Air Force. In his deposition, Tom placed the Hayes lunch in August or September, 1982, three years before Hayes retired. Tom would not have confused a 1982 lunch with a lunch less than four months before his deposition. The likely explanation was that Hayes had forgotten what he said and when he said it.

Q. Is it your testimony that you gave [Tom] a copy of your poem "A Most Unforgiving Lady" sometime after [September 30, 1985]?

A. I don't recall the exact time in which I gave him that poem, I do remember giving it to him.

Q. The poem's dated 1982, isn't it?

A. Yes, that's correct. I wrote the poem on the airplane returning from the [rescue] flight. . . .

Q. . . . [I]f [Tom] testified that the two of you had lunch in August or September [1982], as opposed to after September, 1985, when you retired, Mr. Scanlon would not necessarily be incorrect, would he?

A. I honestly cannot remember having lunch with Tom Scanlon or even meeting Tom Scanlon as early as 1982. . . . I really don't have any recollection of having lunch with him in that timeframe. . . .

Q. Is it correct that if [the lunch at Elevation 92
   occurred] in August or September, 1982, you no
   longer have any recollection of [it]?

A. I really honestly do not have any recollection of
   that lunch in 1982 with Tom Scanlon.

Q. Or what you said at that lunch?

A. I don't have any recollection of that lunch
   whatsoever.

Ms. Neda had no questions. Mr. Hayes was excused.

When asked for her next witness, Ms. Neda said Doug Geeting was unable to make it that day. Her only other witness was David Brown, an FAA expert. When Judge Kleinfeld asked what plaintiffs had left, I answered we were submitting the deposition of Dr. Smith. Kleinfeld preferred to read it in chambers. Court was in recess.

The Smith deposition in June, 1986 substituted for live testimony at trial. Smith's deposition testimony established the treatment Mike received after returning to Indiana and the extent to which Clouser's physical limitations impaired his ability to earn a living.

Dr. Smith explained Mike's five hospital stays between November, 1982 and August, 1983. When first seen, "the raw surface of the bony stumps [of Mike's feet] were still protruding from the wound." To diminish pain, Smith performed a free muscle flap and split thickness skin graft. In laymen's terms, the doctor cut muscle from under Mike's armpits and wrapped it around Mike's foot "roughly 240 degrees" on the right and "maybe 70 or 80" degrees on the left. The skin added by the flap has no nerves and cannot sense hot or cold. These operations were so new there was no data on how many years they would last. No further procedures were possible for Mike's feet "[w]ith the technology we have right now." The doctor also testified that a long-term effect of frostbite was that Mike was much more likely to get arthritis and much more likely to get it at an earlier age.

The lack of sensitivity in the foot flaps meant Mike could not tell if he was hurting himself when he walked. Smith would not be surprised if Mike had pain on walking. Nor would he be surprised if Clouser "could not stand for a long period of time. . . . Certainly he has a very severe injury." Dr. Smith left Mike's hands alone. Clouser had a loss of hot and cold sensitivity in both hands. The most glaring abnormality "is the grip strength which is significantly below normal for a man on both the left and right side. . . ." This loss of grip effectively prevented Mike from returning to work as a mechanic. My last question: "How would you describe Mr. Clouser as a patient?" A. "Superb."

Judge Kleinfeld interrupted his reading and court resumed at 3:47 with David Brown of the FAA on the stand. He testified a flight service station "is an advisory facility to assist pilots in flight training, in accepting both VFR and IFR flight plans, and pilot weather briefing [of] pilots. Strictly an advisory facility to help to assist the pilot."

> Q. Is a flight service station [specialist] able to control traffic? That is, [to] clear traffic for landing and take-off?
>
> A. No. Never. . . .
>
> Q. What about the National Parks? Is the flight service station specialist authorized to deny an aircraft landing rights in the National Parks?
>
> A. No. . . . A flight service specialist doesn't deny landing or take-off any place whether it's in a park or an airport or where have you.
>
> Q. And in your opinion is that a generally well-known fact?
>
> A. Absolutely. . . .

These limitations applied to Dick Hunze "as flight service station specialist at [the] Talkeetna Flight Service Station."

When Ms. Neda asked about the revocation of Akland Helicopters' air taxi license, I objected to evidence concerning events after the December, 1981 rescue. She argued the fact that Dennis Brown's FAA air taxi license had been revoked about three months before his 1984 deposition made him a biased witness. Judge Kleinfeld ruled, "If your purpose is bias, I'll allow you to elicit testimony that Dennis Brown has been cited numerous times by the FAA but I won't allow you to go into the details of each citation because of the time it would take up." Ms. Neda asked the witness, "Is it your understanding that Dennis Brown has been cited numerous times for

violations by the FAA?" A. "Yes." She introduced an order of revocation
of the air taxi license of Akland Helicopters, owned by Dennis Brown.
Objection, relevance. Denied. The order of revocation was admitted. Ms.
Neda had no further questions.

Cross-examination was short. Yes, he attended the Dennis Brown
deposition.

> Q. And you recall [Brown] testifying that he was
>   in Mexico from July of 1983 until approximately
>   April of 1984, correct?
>
> A. I don't recall those specific dates. No, I don't.
>
> Q. Am I wrong or is a large part of the basis of
>   this order of revocation the fact that Mr.
>   Brown apparently operated Akland Helicopters
>   as a sole proprietorship for a period of time
>   and then he incorporated it and it became
>   "A[kland] Helicopters, Inc." and he didn't
>   formally transfer his certificates from the sole
>   proprietorship to the corporation?
>
> A. I could not speak to that. I have no expertise in
>   that area.

There was no redirect. The witness was excused. Ms. Neda was again
out of witnesses. Another recess was called.

When court resumed at 4:19, we were in "clean up" time. I asked
to go through Plaintiffs' Exhibit List to be certain what was admitted. I
offered into evidence the discovery pleadings and responses (Requests for
Admission, etc.). Ms. Neda objected. Judge Kleinfeld admitted them all.

We stipulated to sunset and sunrise times. On Tuesday, December 15,
the sun rose in Fairbanks at 9:53 a.m. and set at 1:41 p.m., yielding 3 hours
48 minutes of daylight. On the same day in Anchorage, the sun rose at 9:09
a.m. and set at 2:41 p.m., yielding 5 hours and 32 minutes of sunlight. In
Talkeetna, the sun rose at 9:23 and set at 2:28.

Tomorrow, day 10, the judge had from 9 to 10 a.m. open. His day was
then full until 3 p.m. If we could finish all testimony by 10 a.m., closing
arguments would be held from 3 to 5 p.m. (one hour per side). Judge
Kleinfeld continued, "Then I'll need some time to study and review my
notes. I have almost two full pads of notes plus I want to look over the

exhibits before I come back with findings and a decision in this case." If tomorrow's schedule held, the judge expected to announce his decision at 9:00 a.m. Thursday morning. If tomorrow's schedule slipped, a decision would wait until next week.

It was very surprising the judge might rule so soon, but there was no time to think about it. A full night of preparing and practicing closing argument lay ahead.

Chapter 33

Pathologist

At 9 a.m. Wednesday, as the court clerk was connecting by telephone with the pathologist, I asked Mike to leave the courtroom but did not tell him why. As Clouser slowly exited, Judge Kleinfeld was visibly surprised. I informed him my client would not be in the courtroom for this testimony.

The tenth day of trial convened at 9:05 a.m. Dr. George Lindholm, in Spokane, Washington, was sworn in by telephone. Mr. Wilson conducted direct. The pathologist was 42 and had a B. S. and M. S. in biological science and an M.D. degree from the University of Washington. He was board certified in anatomic pathology (solid tissues), clinical pathology (fluid tissues), and forensic pathology. He had performed around 2000 autopsies to date with work experience including 4½ years at the King County Medical Examiner's Office in Seattle and two years in Anchorage. At the time of trial, he served as the forensic pathologist for Spokane County and surrounding areas.

The pathologist performed the autopsy of Patrick Scanlon in Anchorage at 10:30 a.m. on Tuesday, December 22, 1981. He identified his 5 page autopsy report and his cover letter to the magistrate in Healy, Alaska, who had requested the autopsy. According to the autopsy report, Pat wore bunny boots and four layers of clothing. Dr. Lindholm found a broken right ankle, a 3" laceration or tear of the skin in the back of the scalp, and bruising on Pat's right and left forehead. The neck had a sublaxation, a slippage or disarticulation of the cervical bodies, "where you could freely move those bones and slide them on each other . . . at the level of the fifth and sixth" vertebral bodies, "so very low in the neck." "His cervical spinal cord had been crushed." There was no evidence of foreign materials or drugs in the blood system. The body had been frozen and thawing was required prior to the autopsy. "To emphasize the most important, Mr. Scanlon had a broken neck with a crushed spinal cord."

Before asking for medical opinions, Mr. Wilson brought out the four sources of information reviewed by the pathologist in forming his opinions. The first two were the December, 1981 interviews of Ed Hommer by Gerhard and the NTSB. The third was "portions of taped testimony of Mr. Clouser in this case." (He listened to a tape recording of Mike's trial testimony.) The fourth was a surprise.

Q. And did you also interview Mr. Ed Hommer over the telephone?

A. Yes, I did.

Q. Was he located in Michigan when you did that?

A. Yes, he was to the best of my knowledge.

Q. Are these sources of information which you as a forensic pathologist reasonably rely upon in forming your opinions and conclusions?

A. Absolutely.

MR. GALBRAITH: . . . I object to having the forensic pathologist talk on the telephone with Ed Hommer. I assume this was in the last week or so. It's obviously hearsay. Hommer did not testify at trial here. . . .

THE COURT: I understand the objection. It's overruled pursuant to [Evidence] Rule 703.

The objection was overruled because expert witnesses can base their opinions on matters not in evidence. Judge Kleinfeld had discretion to allow Dr. Lindholm to express opinions based on hearsay evidence, and the judge could give less than normal weight to the pathologist's opinions precisely because they were based on hearsay.

When I came to court this last day of trial, it never occurred to me that Ed Hommer would testify, especially in a way in which he could not be cross-examined. This was an end run by the U.S.A. Ed's testimony would come in via a telephone conversation with the pathologist, not under oath and unheard by anyone else. With no opportunity to cross-examine Hommer, it would be dangerous to ask the pathologist exactly what Ed said.

Wilson moved to the pathologist's opinions. What was Pat Scanlon's condition following the plane crash? Dr. Lindholm answered that Pat "had a cervical or neck fracture with significant neurologic compromise. In other words, loss of motor function or ability to move his extremities." This included "immobilization of his lower extremities" or "the inability for him by himself to move his lower extremities." Also, Pat had "a probable immobilization of most of his upper extremities, with the possible exception of his fingers and that is related to testimony about removal of his gloves." There was "a possibility that Mr. Scanlon still had sensation in his upper and lower extremities."

According to the pathologist, "[Pat] died because his cervical spinal cord was compressed due to a fracture of his neck, due to initial blunt impact injuries that occurred in an airplane crash. . . . I saw that fracture and I saw the disruption of his spinal cord. I believe that occurred at the initial impact. . . ."

Dr. Lindholm believed Pat's condition immediately following the plane crash "was extremely serious and that his life, if you like, was extremely tenuous. That is based on the fact that Mr. Scanlon had a very serious disruption of his neck area." He explained that if the same injury were to occur "in [an area] where a person could be quickly [moved to a hospital], we would have a very different situation. . . . He is immobilized, which makes him highly susceptible to hypothermia because he cannot move his muscles to generate body heat." The doctor guessed that Pat's extremities were frost-bitten or frozen prior to his death.

Dr. Lindholm's voice was clear and his tone warm, even compassionate. He understood the impact of his words. As he continued, the pathologist did not know if Mike Clouser and Tom Scanlon were listening.

```
[Pat was accompanied by] untrained individuals.
The slightest movement in either the aircraft
[or] by individuals there could, and, in my
opinion, we have evidence it did, eventually
cause his death. That is certainly not the
primary cause. This is an incidental thing that
they did and I wouldn't say it's unavoidable
```

but it was highly probable that this type of
thing would occur.

In sum, the pathologist thought Pat Scanlon's "survivability was
extremely tenuous based not just on his injuries, but also the place in
which those injuries occurred and . . . the position of his body following
the injury."

Asked Pat's long-term medical prognosis after the airplane crash,
Lindholm answered, "there's a high probability that it was not going to be
possible" to remove him from the mountain alive. However, allowing for
"a lot of luck," if he did make it to a hospital, there was "a high probability
that Mr. Scanlon, had he survived, would have been a quadriplegic and
by that I mean [he] would talk, breathe, but basically be immobilized for
the rest of his life." This was Pat's prognosis before the plane slid in the
windstorm Wednesday night.

At the end of direct, Wilson moved to admit the autopsy report
and cover letter. I did not object; I had tried to admit them during
plaintiffs' case.

I had long known the cause of Pat's death because I interviewed the
pathologist less than two weeks after his letter to the Healy magistrate. In
the interview, I was not an advocate, I was an attorney evaluating a potential
case. Cross-examination would be based on my notes. There could be no
quarrel with the opinions that Pat had a broken neck and that it was caused
by the airplane crash. The opinion that Pat would have been a quadriplegic,
had he lived, was disastrous. If true, the U.S.A. had no liability for lost
accumulations to the Scanlon estate. (If injuries caused solely by the plane
crash prevented Pat from ever working, lost accumulations would be zero,
not hundreds of thousands of dollars as testified by the economist.)

Q. Dr. Lindholm, I'm Peter Galbraith, the attorney
   for the Estate of Patrick Scanlon. You're there
   by telephone so you can't look at me, but do you
   recall meeting me on March 4, 1982, when I came
   to your office and interviewed you?

A. Well, Peter, it's been a long time. I obviously
   do not.

Q. You were down in the basement of what was
   then the Alaska Hospital . . . where Dr. Rogers
   still is.

A. Very good. I still do not recall specifically.

Q. You said your opinion today was based on Mr. Scanlon's
   supposed ability not to move his extremities. What's
   the foundation for your statement that Mr. Scanlon
   couldn't move his extremities?

A. The foundation is basically the description as
   rendered by Mr. Clouser. . . .

Asked if he would change his opinion if there was testimony that
Pat could move all four arms and legs, Dr. Lindholm answered, "It would
depend on the quality of that testimony and, in a sense, the skill of the
observer." When the autopsy began, Pat was fully clothed. How could
Clouser, poking Pat through four layers of clothing, be certain Pat felt the
pokes? "[S]tatements made along those lines, although to a layman, he may
feel he is doing a good job, could be extremely bogus."

Q. Unless, for example, Mr. Scanlon moved his arms
   or legs at Mr. Clouser's request? That would be
   something Mr. Clouser could view there on the
   scene, correct?

A. That is certainly correct.

Q. So in essence your opinion would change if there
   was testimony that Pat Scanlon could still move
   his extremities, correct?

A. I would have to weigh the testimony in terms
   of the injury that I saw, because I have other
   hearsay information in the discussion over the
   telephone that Mr. Scanlon was in fact incapable
   of moving his lower extremities.

Q. And that's from Ed Hommer in a telephone
   conversation none of us here in court were privy
   to, correct?

A. That is correct.

No matter what, I was not going to ask Dr. Lindholm what Hommer told him. That would emphasize, without possibility of cross-examination, whatever Ed said.

> Q. It is possible to suffer a broken neck, a C-5, C-6 sublaxation, and not have an injury to the spinal cord, correct?
>
> A. That is correct.
>
> Q. So, one could have a broken neck, be transferred to a hospital or elsewhere, have that fracture heal, and have no permanent injuries. Correct?
>
> A. That is possible.

The pathologist agreed the injury that follows from a severed or a partially crushed spinal cord, either one, depends on the level of the injury to the spinal cord. He agreed an injury lower on the spinal cord could result in a paraplegic injury (legs paralyzed), an injury higher up the spinal cord could result in a quadriplegic injury (arms and legs paralyzed), and an injury even higher up the spinal cord could result in paralysis of the lungs and immediate death.

> Q. The control here is the level on the spinal cord that's severed, not how badly crushed the spinal cord [is], right?
>
> A. The level. That is typically correct. . . .
>
> Q. If you assume that Mr. Scanlon could move his extremities, all four, and have sensation in them, that would indicate the spinal cord was not injured in the . . . plane crash. Correct?
>
> A. It's a close approximation to correct. . . . Yes.

Dr. Lindholm was familiar with the events of Wednesday night's windstorm and that Pat "ended up in a very untenable position with his head towards the tail of the aircraft at a fairly steep angle."

Q. There was testimony that Mr. Scanlon was asked to
   assist in moving himself out of that position.

A. That is correct.

Q. And I'll ask you to assume that there was
   testimony that Mr. Scanlon was able to assist.
   That he did push and that he moved about six
   inches and at the same time he let out a moan or
   gasp. Did you read that?

[Objection, misstatement of fact, not ruled upon.]

A. That material was on the tapes and I listened
   very carefully to it and I did not hear any
   definitive testimony to the effect that he did
   in fact assist. He was requested to assist but
   there was no testimony that I know of on that
   tape material that said that he actually did
   accomplish assistance.

Dr. Lindholm explained that a basis for his expert opinion was that
Pat was not able to assist in moving himself. Without a transcript of
Clouser's testimony, I could not contradict him.

Q. If there was testimony that he did accomplish
   this assistance, would that change your opinion?

A. . . . it [would] depend on how much he was able
   to assist.

Q. Do you recall the testimony about Mr. Scanlon
   letting out a gasp or moan, or groan at that time?

A. Yes, I do.

Q. And could that not be the time that the cervical
   spinal cord was severed, resulting in paralysis
   of the lungs and final expiration of air from
   the lungs . . . ?

A. It certainly could. And I have no question that
   the final insult to Mr. Scanlon's spinal cord
   occurred at that time.

On direct examination, Dr. Lindholm had been too polite, too compassionate, to say that Ed Hommer and Mike Clouser killed Pat Scanlon by severing his spinal cord when they tried to move him away from the tail. I knew this was his opinion because he told me so on March 4, 1982. (I could see no reason why Mike should be made to listen to this testimony.) I had to be blunt as to the cause of death because I needed to prove that the neurological injury Dr. Lindholm was testifying about occurred Wednesday night, after the plane slid, not in the plane crash Tuesday afternoon.

Q. Would you agree that _if_ Mr. Scanlon still had the ability to control his arms and legs after the accident, and, if [in] the course of attempting to be moved after the plane slid, his spinal cord was severed at the location you indicated in your autopsy, he died of paralysis of the lungs resulting from severing of the spinal cord at that point?

A. I would agree with that assuming that it can be proven that Mr. Scanlon had full movement of his extremities and full sensation in his extremities prior to that time.

Q. That would indicate again that we had a man who was neither a paraplegic nor a quadriplegic, who if he could have . . . [been] stabilized until he could be removed from the mountain, had every prospect of a complete recovery from this broken neck, correct?

A. That would be correct based on the assumptions given.

The pathologist testified that a spinal cord compression at the C-5, C-6 level, where Pat's neck was broken in the airplane crash, normally would not result in paralysis of the lungs. However, the spinal cord could have been injured at a higher level than C-5, C-6. "[B]ecause we can fix a nice level here [C-5, C-6] where the fracture is, it does not mean that the cord is not injured above or below this area." For paralysis of the lungs to result, it would have to occur higher up the cervical spine or at the membrane level (at the base of the brain). A sentence in the autopsy report indicated that bruising of the brain stem (membrane) may have occurred.

Q. . . . Your autopsy says that the spinal cord pulpified or [was] crushed. That could easily happen after death, correct?

A. Oh, absolutely. . . . It's been transported. It's been moved. There could be an accentuation of the injury.

Q. So by the time you were able to examine Pat Scanlon's body, you couldn't really tell whether it had initially been severed and then later crushed or just what had happened?

A. There is some latitude there. That is correct.

It was now time to cross-examine Dr. Lindholm based upon notes from an interview he did not remember. Tara Neda had twice cross-examined witnesses (Rivers and Okonek) using notes from an earlier interview and both had flatly contradicted her. What could she do then? What could I do if the pathologist disagreed with my notes?

Q. I asked you four questions on March 4, 1982, when I came to interview you. And I'll ask you those again.

A. Very good.

Q. The first one was if Pat Scanlon had flown out by helicopter on Wednesday morning, would he have lived? Do you recall your answer?

A. I do not but I would say at this time that if we take the assumption that he was properly moved, removed, you know, no complications in that and he was obviously alive at that time, I think there is a probability that he would have lived.

Q. Thank you. That was your answer then also.

A. Thank you.

Q. The second question was, can you say what permanent injuries he would have had.

The pathologist answered that "this depends upon the information fed in." Q. "[I]t depends on the input, meaning the testimony of what movement he had prior to death. Which really means you couldn't answer [the question] from the autopsy. You have to answer that from other information, correct?" A. Yes, "[t]hat's exactly the point we made at the beginning and I want to emphasize that."

Q. The third question was, if Pat Scanlon had been provided warm clothing, a tent, heat, hot liquids, could he have survived until the rescue on Saturday?

A. I would have to say that's possible.

Q. Actually I think your answer then was that if he wasn't moved around, in other words if his neck had been able to be protected so that there was not a severing of the spinal cord, yes, he could have lived.

A. Yes, I would agree to that. I mean I think I imply that in my answer.

Q. The [fourth] question was what was his prognosis if he had been able to be removed from the mountain?

A. . . . If he truly was unable to move his lower extremities and upper extremities, we've talked about the prognosis for a degree of para or quadriplegia. And if indeed he can move his extremities, is mobile, and we are fortunate enough to extract him from the plane, move him without jarring him, getting him to facilities, then his prognosis might be good.

Q. [H]e might have had a complete recovery in that circumstance?

A. That is possible.

Q. My notes [from 1982] reflect that you suspected there was initially a tear of the spinal cord resulting in death and that it was squashed later. Does that sound plausible?

A. That sounds quite plausible based on the
   information we have. If it had been crushed
   initially, I wouldn't expect Mr. Scanlon to live
   overnight [Tuesday night]. . . .

Q. . . . Finally, [in] your February 23, 1982 letter
   to the Healy magistrate, . . . don't you mean
   that you think he got a broken neck in the crash
   and he lived for 36 hours, and then in the course
   of being moved after the slide, the cervical
   spinal cord was finally severed to the point
   where it killed him?

A. That is correct. That's a very good summary of my
   opinion at this time.

When Jim Wilson conducted redirect, the pathologist agreed that
Pat's initial injury, a broken neck, without any spinal cord injury at
all, would be considered a very significant injury, "even if there is no
neurological compromise."

Q. Why is that?

A. Because Mr. Scanlon by testimony is in a
   precarious position with his head facing
   downhill. . . . Simply a shaking of that plane,
   some slippage of that plane, improper movement by
   some party present, the possibility of freezing
   the lower extremities because he cannot move them,
   all of those things make it difficult. He will
   also have to be removed from that plane. He is
   going to have to be handled very carefully in a
   precarious position in the plane. So all of those
   things make Mr. Scanlon's injuries very, very
   serious at that point. . . .

Mr. Wilson had no more questions. I had none. To my surprise,
Judge Kleinfeld had no questions.

After the clerk hung up with Dr. Lindholm, Ms. Neda asked to call
Ranger Gerhard as a rebuttal witness. I informed the judge I needed
to call Mike Clouser solely on the subject of "what Pat Scanlon could

move." The judge agreed to hear Gerhard. The attorneys for a 10:00 hearing were in the back of the courtroom, watching us. Judge Kleinfeld made them wait.

Ms. Neda left to get Gerhard from the lobby. Clouser had a right to hear this testimony, so I went to the lobby, too. As we slowly returned to the courtroom, I warned Mike he was going to be on the witness stand again.

When Ms. Neda questioned Gerhard, he denied ever telling Tom Scanlon he was embarrassed by any aspect of the rescue. I had no questions.

With Gerhard finished so quickly, the judge was willing to hear Clouser now. Mike took the stand. He repeated that he examined Pat to try "to determine what his injuries were." He observed Pat moving his arms; he folded and unfolded them over his chest "numerous times" and he worked his gloves off repeatedly. Mike squeezed Pat's right leg down to the fracture point. "When I got close to the break, he screamed." Mike did not have "a clear recollection of what I did about his left leg." He did not recall Pat moving his legs, but Mike had asked him "not to move, period, if he could keep from it." He did not have any impression one way or the other as to whether Pat was able to move his legs.

Q. Mr. Scanlon was conscious up until . . . immediately before his death, correct?

A. Yes, he was.

Q. Did you discuss with him whether he was paralyzed?

A. As far as using the word paralyzed, no. . . .

Q. Did he ever tell you, "Mike, I'm paralyzed. I can't move my legs."?

A. No, he did not.

I had never asked Mike this question, but if Pat had ever told Mike he thought he was paralyzed, Mike would have told me.

After the plane slid Wednesday night and Pat ended up "scrunched towards the tail of the airplane," Mike asked Pat to help them move him.

A. . . . I said, "Pat, you're too heavy for us to
move. So you're going to have to help." And I
said, "Push." And at the same time I pulled and
we gained about six inches.

Q. Was [it] your impression at that time that Pat
assisted in the pushing?

A. Yes, it was.

Q. Was that assist with his arms?

A. It had to have been.

Q. I know this is difficult. Was it right after that
that he let out - did he make a noise?

A. During that time, yes.

Q. Would you describe the noise?

A. He just screamed.

Ms. Neda cross-examined.

Q. Didn't you testify earlier regarding the movement
of Mr. Scanlon that you couldn't tell if he moved
at all during those six inches, whether it was
your force or his?

A. It's always been my assumption that it was a
combination of both.

Q. Do you know one way or the other?

A. Not for a 100 percent fact.

When Clouser was excused, we had arrived at the stage of trial where
the judge declares the evidence closed and after which no more evidence
will be received from either party. There were formalities to go through.
Plaintiffs rested. The U.S.A. rested. Judge Kleinfeld announced that closing
argument would be held at 3 p.m. and we would be in recess until then.
Court adjourned at 10:14.

Chapter 34

Closing Arguments

Closing argument is the time to link testimony together, to emphasize what may have seemed obscure, and to tie the facts to the law. Our table in the courtroom had a manila folder labeled "closing" into which I stuffed hastily scribbled notes as trial progressed. It bulged with matters needing explanation and emphasis. As the judge indicated he would allow 60 minutes per side (would he?), I gave a one hour practice argument Tuesday night and another during Wednesday's long mid-day break.

Court resumed at 4:18, not 3:00. Judge Kleinfeld apologized, saying, "I know how it feels when you're about to give closing argument." Plaintiffs would go first and last and the U.S.A. would speak only once, for an hour. I planned to open with 45 minutes and to save 15 minutes for rebuttal.

Liability evidence consumed most of trial and the two practice arguments showed there was a danger I would never reach damages, especially if the judge asked questions. Accordingly, I started with damages, not liability, beginning with Pat Scanlon. This allowed me to comment on the morning's testimony.

Pat Scanlon was not a quadriplegic, I argued. He moved his arms and could feel pain in his broken right leg. While there was no testimony about moving his left leg, the instinct of a person with a broken neck would be to lie still. Pat never said, "Mike, I'm paralyzed. I can't move my legs." Ed Hommer was not called as a witness by the U.S.A. I referenced his two typewritten statements in Exhibit 1. These clarified that only Mike examined Pat, tested his extremities, and tended to him. "That's natural because Pat Scanlon was Mike Clouser's friend, not Ed Hommer's friend."

The pathologist could not tell the extent of Pat's injury before the final tear of the [spinal] cord.

I argued that but for the U.S.A.'s failure to airdrop supplies and failure to extract him from the airplane, Pat would have recovered with no permanent injuries, not even frostbite. "As the pathologist testified, you can have a broken neck and heal with no long-term disability whatsoever." If Pat had no permanent injury, the economist testified the loss to the Scanlon estate would be above $600,000. Pat's federal tort claim sought only $400,000 for wrongful death and "that put[s] a ceiling on how much the court can award."

Under Alaska law, pain and suffering can be awarded for the time period immediately before death, even if only five or ten minutes. While we had no claim for pain and suffering from the plane crash itself, "[w]e're asking for pain and suffering from essentially Wednesday at noon . . . until he died, 12 to 14 or 16 hours later." "That was an awful period of time by any imaginable standard." An award of $100,000 for these hours of pain and suffering brought the total claim to $500,000.

For Clouser, past medical expenses totaled an undisputed $135,420. An award for future medical expenses "in some amount is appropriate." The evidence established that Mike was prone to skin breakdowns and infection and the operations on his feet were so new that "no one really knows what [will happen to his feet] 20 or 30 years down the road."

The parameters of loss of earning capacity were established by the economist's low number of $167,749 and high number of $848,184. The judge had to decide whether Mike would work as a computer programmer and, if so, how much he would earn. I suggested the judge come in at the mid-point of Dr. Solie's range and award $500,000 for loss of future earnings. Five years of lost earnings, 1982-86, equaled roughly $150,000. Adding loss of future earnings and loss of past earnings put the total over $600,000.

Pain and suffering was broken into subparts. Clouser should have been removed from the mountain on Wednesday morning or provided an airdrop with heat, fluids, and shelter. "He endured an additional three days in which he had the knowledge that his extremities were freezing and 'that something was happening to my body.'" Pain and suffering in Providence Hospital lasted two and a half months. He was thawed in a warm bath and then parts of his body swelled up, requiring immediate surgery. "And then he had, I have to use the word, the horrifying experience of watching his body parts turn black and mummify and harden before his eyes." He had pain [as this happened] and then pain after . . . they were cut off using a modified guillotine procedure." Pain and suffering in Indiana before his plastic surgeries lasted 8 months. "After the amputations, bone was exposed, and skin was exposed, and the nerve ends were exposed, and his feet were in pain at all times." A muscle layer was grafted around his feet so the constant pain would stop. From the Smith deposition, I counted 5 plastic surgeries and 58 days in the hospital in Indiana. Dr. Smith testified these operations hurt. Overall, Mike was in hospitals for more than five months and, as the judge brought out, on crutches for two years following the accident. For future pain and suffering, according to Dr. Smith, "There's both a higher chance that arthritis will come and that it will come at an earlier age."

Permanent injury, the amputations to Mike's feet and hands, was another category. He could walk about a quarter mile. He could stand about an hour. He could not feel heat or cold in his feet. Mike could hurt himself walking and not know it. He had lost the power grip to open a jar. He could not operate a clutch on a pickup. "To be in public with amputated fingers on both hands has to be humiliating. That word has to be used here. If he is able to attract a wife or a live-in girlfriend, it [will] be humiliating when he takes his shoes off. . . ."

Loss of enjoyment of life was the final element. Mike used to work outdoors running a paving machine. Now, if he worked, it would be indoors.

> Everything [in] his life has had to change. He has a new job – or he'll have to get a new job. He has to wake up every morning with the injuries and amputations he has. . . . He used to date once a month. Now he's essentially a social introvert and that's not really surprising. He doesn't date any more. He doesn't mix anymore. Whether he'll marry or not is open to speculation. But certainly his chances of marrying have decreased.
>
> Part of the loss here . . . is loss of hopes and dreams and of expectations. He doesn't have the normal expectations that he [had] before this accident. He's a different person every day of the remaining 40 years or so of his life.

It was time to suggest specific numbers. Past medicals were $135 thousand. Damages for future medical expenses should be "25, 50, or 100 [thousand] and there's no specific number there." Loss of past and future earnings were $500,000 to $600,000. These monetary damages totaled about $750,000. Damages for the non-monetary items, pain and suffering, permanent injury, and loss of enjoyment of life, should at least equal the monetary damages. This added up to $1.5 million, the limit established by Mike's federal tort claim.

When the argument moved to liability, I outlined four types of rescue: (1) airdrop, (2) ground rescue, (3) winch or rappel, (4) helicopter landing next to crash site. I argued (3) and (4) were not possible even in the best of conditions. While Clouser's injuries could have been prevented by an airdrop Wednesday, I conceded that "with respect to Pat Scanlon, we may need to prove that a ground rescue was possible." When the airplane slid Wednesday night with Pat in it, he was doomed.

If plaintiffs had not introduced any rescue manuals or SAR plans, an airdrop was based on common sense. "But an airdrop is also called for in the National SAR Manual." "[T]he weather Wednesday at noon when the Chinooks were there was good enough for an airdrop to have been accomplished right then. Mike Clouser testified . . . he could have hit [Chinook 033] with a snowball. That's when it was [in front of him, to the right]. . . ."

The Chinooks had inadequate survival gear on board because of planning negligence. "But even the survival gear on board, which [was] tied down because it hadn't occurred to them to untie it to do an airdrop, could have been of material assistance. . . ." I referred to Mannix's letter and other testimony about deep snow on the north side of the Pass.

"Dr. Mills answered the [legal] cause question on an airdrop. He said if they received food, fuel, heat, the first 24 hours, they would have had minimal injuries, no significant injuries." This established legal cause for Clouser. The reason they didn't airdrop survival gear?

```
Bob Gerhard just didn't think of it. He
brought his personal pack and that's all he
brought. The pilot, Mr. Warden, . . . of the
Chinook that got close, I said, "Why didn't you
do an airdrop?" He said, "To tell you the truth,
```

it never crossed my mind." Those are the words
that I remember. "It never crossed my mind." He
didn't say, "It crossed my mind. I wanted to do
an airdrop but it was too turbulent for me to do
it." And his answer was truthful.

A ground rescue was based on common sense and the Denali SAR Plan,
which stated, "If a helicopter rescue is going to be attempted, a contingency
[ground] plan must be developed." Gerhard claimed the ground rescue plan
was "Tom Griffiths and I. We were the ground plan." If you look at what
he said at the critique and his critique report, the NPS Rangers went along
as observers. They brought their personal packs for their own survival. It
was not enough for three or four days. Quoting Gerhard's report, it was "[a]
mistaken assumption . . . that the [Air Force] parajumpers could have done
an extended ground rescue."

The National SAR Plan and the RCC Plan required a ground rescue
capability. The latter had a special appendix for ground teams in high
altitude rescue missions, which required the RCC to call the Army's HART
at Ft. Greely.

The HART was well qualified to do this kind of
ground rescue. This is exactly their mission. . . .
They had akiohs that could have been used as
stretchers and they had plenty of manpower and ropes
to move Pat Scanlon out of the airplane, either into
a snow cave or a tent. . . .

As to legal cause for the Scanlon claim, "we probably have to prove that
Pat [could] have been moved . . . outside of the aircraft Wednesday" so that he
would not die when the windstorm blew the plane down the hill. To move Pat,
"we need to show only that one ground rescue person could have reached the
crash site." If Larry Rivers or Brian McCullough "or any unknown Talkeetna
brave soul had gotten there, all they needed was one more man to get Pat
somewhere safe." "[I]f the HART had been called and been there, they could
have done it easily and they would have done it easily."

Many civilian rescuers were available. The Fairbanks mountain rescue
group led by Doug Buchanan could have been on the Chinooks at Ft.

Wainwright one hour after notification on Tuesday. Larry Rivers loaded Brown's helicopter with survival gear including bunny boots, sleeping bags and pads, stoves, and fuel. Brian McCullough was available. So was the Alaska Mountain Rescue Group in Anchorage. The Talkeetna climbers got ready in one hour early Wednesday afternoon.

The NPS Rangers were another potential ground rescue team. "Gerhard and Griffiths could have and should have outfitted themselves to be able to get off the [Chinook] and render assistance. . . ." With their winter survival skills, "they could have saved Pat Scanlon's life. They should not have gone along [only] as observers."

I reviewed the maps used by the various rescuers, the RCC, Don Lee, and Mike Fisher. Only the Chinook squadron put the coordinates on a map with a scale too large to tell if the crash was at 7000' or 20,000'.

> [W]henever there is an emergency, you have to move fast. It's urgent. You should preposition resources. You should use overkill, not underkill. Bob Gerhard said [as much] at the critique. I think this really sums up his mistakes in this rescue. He said "I guess I kept resisting thinking that this was going to get as big as it did and that was a mistake on my part. We should have geared up faster."

The negligence of the National Park Service began with the telephones. The RCC could not reach Gerhard until late Tuesday night because the phones at McKinley Park Headquarters did not work. This had happened before in emergencies. When the RCC reached Gerhard late Tuesday, he did not call Doug Geeting or Jim Okonek or any air taxi pilot in Talkeetna. He called no civilian or military ground rescue personnel. Wednesday morning he did not prepare an airdrop or organize a ground rescue team. He was passive until Art Mannix offered assistance Wednesday afternoon at the Talkeetna airport. Gerhard did not request the HART until Thursday morning or the AMRG from Anchorage until Thursday afternoon.

The Air Force's negligence began with the RCC's failure to contact civilian rescue groups Tuesday afternoon and evening. The RCC's rescue plan, relying solely on Army Chinooks with Air Force PJs aboard, was inadequate because of failure to preposition the Chinooks to Talkeetna, no airdrop capability, and no ground rescue capability. The RCC did not notify the HART at Ft. Greely.

The Army's negligence included a failure to move the Chinooks to Talkeetna on Tuesday night. The only reason given by Mr. Bridgman was bad weather on the flight route from Ft. Wainwright to Talkeetna.

> There were no statements at the critique about bad weather. The first time bad weather from Wainwright to Talkeetna was mentioned was five years after the fact, at this trial. . . . Mr. Bridgman got a lot of heat at the critique about why they didn't get to Talkeetna earlier. If there had been bad weather . . . , he would have mentioned it and he didn't mention it at the critique. And we know that not only from the excerpt that I [played] into the record, but we know it from Bob Gerhard's written summary of the critique. Gerhard went out of his way to try to explain why the Chinooks didn't get to Talkeetna [Tuesday] night. I think he listed 6 or 7 reasons and not a one of them was bad weather.

When one Chinook broke down Wednesday morning at Ft. Wainwright, the second should have flown solo. The Army's negligence included a rescue plan that allowed the Chinooks only 5 minutes of flying time at the crash site before they started using the emergency fuel reserve. The Chinooks were not equipped for an airdrop and did not perform an airdrop, although close enough to do so.

On "worsened the victim's plight," Brown and Rivers loaded the Akland helicopter and were ready to fly. Their first plan was to land and carry the victims away. "Number two, they were going to leave Larry Rivers off. . . . Number three, if neither of those two would work, they would [airdrop survival] gear." To prove the Akland helicopter was capable of the flight, I pointed to Jim Okonek's higher altitude rescues on Mt. McKinley and to Dennis Brown's Saturday morning flight over the crash site.

> And we know that Dennis Brown flew up there because the National Park Service people put in their log, "Akland Helicopter lifts off." If you

```
look at that entire log, that is the only entry
of a civilian aircraft flight made. And I think
it [indicates] the relationship between Dennis
Brown and Akland Helicopters, on the one hand, and
the National Park Service, on the other. That the
National Park Service is tracking and writing down
when Mr. Brown's helicopter takes off.
```

The only witnesses to express opinions on Brown's piloting ability, not business reputation, were Larry Rivers (favorable) and Jim Okonek. Initially, Okonek said he was an amateur, but when asked if he would change his mind if Brown had 1500 hours in a helicopter, Okonek said, "Yes, that would change my opinion. I don't think he would be an amateur in that case."

Only three people were present at the Talkeetna FSS early Wednesday morning. "One of them, Dick Hunze, honestly doesn't remember what was said. Has no recollection of the conversation whatsoever. Fine. The other two, Dennis Brown and Larry Rivers, corroborate each other. Not in each detail because that's human nature. But they corroborate each other."

```
People bad-mouthed Dennis Brown's credibility.
Although Jim Okonek didn't. He wasn't asked. And Jim
Okonek worked for Dennis Brown for two years. But
nobody bad-mouthed Larry Rivers' credibility. No
one attacked Larry Rivers. He came in and testified
that, yes, he went over and listened to the
conversation between Dennis Brown, Dick Hunze, and
Larry Rivers. And he confirmed what Brown said about
that conversation.
```

To my pleasure, I was able to quote Larry Rivers' trial testimony. Ms. Neda thought his testimony so important that she ordered a rush transcript. Without my asking, R&R Court Reporters sent me a copy with a note saying, "Thought you might want this." Boy, did I! As I quoted from the Rivers' transcript, the U.S.A.'s attorneys looked at me with alarm.

```
Rivers said [reading] "and I don't remember how
the statement was made, but something to the effect
```

```
that they already had the rescue in progress and
were not interested in our being part of it. They
thought we'd be in the way. . . . And then he [was]
asked, "Did Mr. Hunze tell you or Mr. Brown to
stay away, that the military was in control of the
situation?" Answer: "Yes." [end of reading]
```

Bob Gerhard testified that he believed he had the authority to deny permission to land during a rescue inside the Park.

My remaining 10 minutes were saved to rebut the U.S.A.'s closing argument.

It is permissible (and common) to divide closing argument and I expected Ms. Neda to argue liability and Mr. Wilson to argue damages. To my surprise, Tara Neda gave the entire closing.

Ms. Neda argued the U.S.A. was under no duty to rescue plaintiffs. For 15 minutes, she discussed the law, not the facts, and referred by name to 14 cases, discussing each. She also discussed Alaska's Good Samaritan statute, which protects certain persons who render emergency care, except in the event of gross negligence or reckless or intentional misconduct. "The government entities participating in this search and rescue are immune from liability unless gross negligence can be found and, of course, no gross negligence exists. In fact, plaintiffs did not even plead gross negligence in their complaint. Nor have they amended it to do so."

Ms. Neda argued plaintiffs failed to prove even ordinary negligence. Following a chronological approach, she started with the "coincidence" of a C-130 being near Mt. McKinley when the Hudson plane was reported overdue. "Had another C-130 gone up [from Anchorage] . . ., it would never have found this ELT [because it quit soon after being heard] and we wouldn't even be standing here today [because the survivors would have died]."

No time was wasted. Air Force PJs were alerted and Army Chinook crews assembled. She ticked off the activities – weather briefings, performance planning, preflight checks, crew rest waivers, all on Tuesday night. The commanding officer,

```
Lt. Colonel Parrish, is the one who makes those
decisions and he [decided] these Chinooks weren't
going to leave that night. That they were going to
```

```
leave at first light [Wednesday]. . . . He wanted
them departing such that they would arrive at
Mt. McKinley airstrip with daylight coming. He
wanted the daylight so they could go through the
mountain passes to the wreckage with visibility. The
reasonableness of that action is just self-evident.
```

She made no mention of bad weather Tuesday night on the flight route from Ft. Wainwright to Talkeetna.

Yes, the RCC was unable to reach the NPS until late Tuesday night, but how was this negligence? "The phone company isn't owned by the federal government. It's [a private company], Matanuska [Telephone]. That's not a federal agency."

In the meantime, "it was the RCC's decision to alert the PJs and the Chinooks. . . . [I]f the RCC had sat back and done nothing all night, we'd be in here for that. Now we're in here because the RCC did act." "[T]he PJs always accompany the Chinooks. The HART did not. The PJs train with the Chinooks. The HART did not. [All] the PJs were trained emergency medical technicians. . . . It was required. . . . You don't know that with the HART." "The PJs were quick and lightweight. Not the HART." She read aloud a lengthy Air Force regulation, the gist of which was the PJs "are trained to operate in all types of terrain," including arctic. In effect, she argued this military regulation overcame testimony that the PJs were not equipped for an extended ground rescue at Kahiltna Pass.

"[The] first choice [of the Chinooks] would be to land near the site. They approached and realized this was not possible." The next choice was winching. If winching would not work,

```
then they start searching for another place to
land and that's where we have Scotty Warden before
he had to turn and leave for Talkeetna. He said
he couldn't land on the south slope of [Kahiltna
Pass] and there were landing zones. We know that
from Saturday's events. . . . And if they could
have landed a quarter to a half mile away, can
this Court honestly assume that Tom Griffiths and
Bob Gerhard, who had climbed Mt. McKinley, and
three PJs, who had jumped out of aircraft and were
```

trained for military combat, would not have gotten
out and walked that quarter mile?

Discussing the second Chinook's actions Wednesday noon, "[t]he only
thing [Bridgman] could do . . . [was] to drop supplies and they had huge
amounts of supplies. Bob Gerhard said he knew that. The Chinook pilot
said he had it." When Chinook 525 got nearest to the site, approximately
1000 feet, "they opened their side panel . . . and that's when Mr. Clouser
perhaps sees a crew chief at the door trying to decide if they could get close
enough to make an airdrop."

Mike and I looked at each other. He did not testify about a Chinook
crew member at an open door.

The decisions of whether to land and to discharge personnel and
whether to airdrop were for the Army pilots-in-command, Warden and
Bridgman, not Gerhard. She quoted more Air Force regulations regarding
flight operations.

When Chinook 033 arrived in Talkeetna, Gerhard "finally could
begin his role as coordinator. Up until that point it was a military
operation." All decisions about inserting the Talkeetna climbers on the
Kahiltna Glacier Wednesday afternoon and Thursday were piloting
decisions, she argued.

Both Larry Rivers and Dennis Brown testified "the weather was bad.
The winds were blowing Wednesday in the morning." Waving a transcript,
Ms. Neda continued, "More than five times in only 20 or 21 pages of [his
trial transcript], Larry Rivers said how concerned he was of the weather, how
bad the weather was. . . ." She referenced Brown's deposition testimony
that he heard Geeting say the winds were blowing 35 miles an hour.

According to Rivers' testimony, Dennis Brown was on the telephone
when Larry first arrived. Yet the first telephone call in Brown's log was
at 9:37 a.m. How could Brown and Rivers have been at the Talkeetna FSS
at 8:30 a.m.?

Dennis Brown was biased against the FAA because his "testimony
was taken just a few short months after the FAA shut down his
commercial operations and also after a long history of FAA violations."
Brown had a poor reputation for truthfulness according to Mike
Fisher and Don Lee. Brown was characterized as an unqualified and
amateur pilot who could not have provided assistance Wednesday

morning. She pointed to all the [fixed wing] pilots over the crash site that morning. "Mike Fisher and Tony Martin, Don Lee, Doug Geeting, and they weren't unqualified amateurs. . . . [T]he winds prevented them from airdropping supplies. Don Lee didn't even bother to drop his pack that he had purposely packed to drop. That was the first trip very early in the morning at first light."

Ms. Neda asserted the Army's HART took seven hours to mobilize, four when it self-mobilized on Wednesday and three on Thursday after Gerhard requested it. She visualized the scene if the HART had been called on Tuesday night.

> Can you see them? Can you see them at 10:00, or 11:00 or 12:00 at night on Tuesday, gathering together after a full day's work, packing up, and after the end of four hours, one or two in the morning now, getting ready to load 3000 pounds of gear onto a C-130? Fly down for 45 minutes to Talkeetna. Arrive at 2:00 in the morning. Unload for 30 more minutes and set up camp to sleep for two hours and then get up and go for an extended expedition . . . in the dead of winter [on] Mt. McKinley.

With less than 10 minutes left, Ms. Neda moved to damages. The economist failed to factor in the actual earnings of Clouser and Scanlon. Clouser's actual earnings in 1981? $9600. "Dr. Solie's projection for 1982, the very next year, has [Mike] earning $24,497." In 1981, Pat Scanlon earned $8325. "What did [the economist project] for Mr. Scanlon's earnings in 1981? $25,995. Three times more than Mr. Scanlon really earned in 1981."

She continued with arguments undoubtedly provided by Jim Wilson. Dr. Solie assumed each plaintiff would work year around, but neither ever had. The economist did not deduct Indiana state income taxes for either plaintiff. He made questionable assumptions about decreased personal consumption by Pat Scanlon. No housing expenses for the rest of his life? A 25% reduction in food costs for the rest of his life? There was no evidence in the record that Pat Scanlon had ever grown his own food or that his parents had grown food for him. Absent these two assumptions,

Pat's expected lifetime consumption increased by $365,666, reducing the economist's calculation of loss from $619,685 to $264,029.

Clouser could work as a computer programmer in the future. "One firing does not equate to lifetime unemployment. As a matter of fact, working as a computer programmer, [he] would be earning more than he had as an operating engineer."

Ms. Neda referenced Dr. Mills' testimony that there were several ways the injuries to Clouser's feet could have occurred.

```
[O]ne of those probable ways was walking
on frozen feet, and this is because of tissue
damage, and of the probability of severe [blood]
vessel damage. This is permanent injury. . . . And
Mr. Clouser did walk. In fact, he climbed. The
Mountain Maniacs let him do it, over the protest
of the HART [Strauss]. He climbed up that steep
north slope on those ice stairs. He climbed down
the south side and then he walked that quarter to
a half mile [to the Chinook].
```

As her time was running out, she focused on the tape recording of the rescue critique. Dr. Mills' opinion at the critique was that any delays in the rescue had no effect whatsoever on the injuries to Clouser and Scanlon. At trial, the doctor's testimony was "quite different." Dr. Mills was now in a somber and serious atmosphere, he needed to be accurate, and he needed to say what he knew, not what he thought others needed to hear. Testimony in court differs greatly from the informal setting of a rescue critique where free discussion pervades. The U.S.A. would not

```
[hold] Dr. Mills, though it helps our case,
. . . to [his] statement in the critique. There
were people [at the critique who] needed to be
appeased. . . . Emotions were high. Four days of
life-threatening search and rescue operations had
just been completed. . . .

    [T]his one example shows so clearly the lack
of probative value that this tape [recorded]
critique has in this case. . . . And it is
upon this taped critique, made so ironically
```

```
in a good faith effort [by] the National Park
Service, it is upon this taped critique, a free
exchange of ideas, of wondering aloud, thinking
aloud, of appeasing one another, it's this
critique upon which plaintiffs rely so heavily
to prove their case. So heavily.
```

In summation, "There's been no fact witness . . . that's testified against this government in actuality." Look at the RCC log, look at the NPS log. "There's no objective facts in this record that indicate anything but utmost concern and effort. There's nothing in the objective facts to support plaintiffs' case." "It cannot be shown that any government act or omission was more likely than not a substantial factor in exacerbating the injuries incurred by [plaintiffs]. This action should be dismissed."

In rebuttal, I asserted a duty to rescue was a false issue. Under federal case law, there may not be a duty to rescue, but once a rescue is undertaken by the government, the law imposes a duty to complete the rescue in a non-negligent fashion. Within Denali National Park, the NPS was analogous to the Alaska State Troopers outside the Park. Applying the reasoning of <u>Lee v. State</u> [State Trooper, little girl, lion], I argued "[t]he Park Service is [not any] more likely to rescue people within Denali National Park because of [protection afforded by] an Alaska statute." The U.S.A. is "not entitled to the protection of the Good Samaritan Statute and gross negligence does not apply here."

I responded to as many of defendant's factual arguments as time allowed. The HART does not train with the Chinooks? Strauss testified the Chinooks flew the team to Mt. McKinley for their exercises in 1980, 81, and 82. Ms. Neda gave the wrong reason for Mr. Warden's departure from Kahiltna Pass. It was low fuel, not the weather. Clouser did not testify about a crew member at an open door of a Chinook.

Yes, Rivers testified that Brown was taking calls when Rivers first came in, but Brown was in a hurry and did not write them down. I quoted Rivers (from the trial transcript) saying, "I was up and about early that time of the year." I also pointed to Thursday morning, where Brown's telephone log established that he offered Okonek the Akland helicopter, saying, "Jim, do you want to use the helicopter? You were in the Air Force. Maybe you can get them to let you go up there in my helicopter."

Brown was not shut down by the FAA; he was shut down by the bankruptcy court. The FAA suspension was entered while Brown was in Mexico and he knew nothing about it.

> On Dr. Mills, apparently [the U.S.A. is] now claiming that the frozen feet are Mike's fault. Again, if he'd been provided aid, he wouldn't have had frozen feet and it would not matter what his feet were like as he walked over [Kahiltna Pass].

> [Is] the critique reliable? Of course it is. It was a candid discussion one month after the fact by all of the parties involved. In 12 years of practice, it's the best piece of evidence I've ever come across and I suggest it is of substantial value to the Court.

Judge Kleinfeld thanked counsel and announced this case would recess until 9:00 a.m. Court adjourned at 6:12 p.m.

The judge paid close attention but asked no questions. Would we have a decision at 9 a.m. tomorrow morning?

Chapter 35

Decision

Early Thursday morning, Donna received a message that the 9 a.m. decision time was cancelled. Later, we were told to be in court at 4 p.m.

Court convened on time. Tom and Mike sat with me at counsel table. Ms. Neda and Mr. Wilson were at the other table. My wife and several others were in the spectator section. I had no experience with an oral decision from the bench, but it promised to be as dramatic as the reading of a jury verdict.

As he recited oral findings of fact and conclusions of law, Judge Kleinfeld appeared to be speaking from typed notes. His early factual findings confirmed the uncontested events of the crash and rescue. Plaintiffs Clouser and Scanlon, visitors from Indiana, were passengers on a commercial air taxi operated out of Talkeetna. The Cessna aircraft "crashed in the early afternoon of Tuesday, December 15, 1981 on Kahiltna Glacier on approximately the 10,000 foot level at Mt. McKinley within the boundaries of Denali National Park." The court had jurisdiction. As tourists, the passengers had "no particular reason to outfit themselves with survival gear or [to] be aware of the risks they were taking on the flight."

Tuesday afternoon and evening, Talkeetna residents became aware the air taxi was missing. The U. S. Air Force Rescue Coordination Center [RCC] diverted a C-130 already in the air and it picked up an ELT signal and sighted lights on the ground. "The lights were . . . the flashing of a flashlight by Mr. Clouser."

Although ELT signals can bounce in a mountainous area, "the ELT information was precise" and two different individuals or groups located the crash site on Kahiltna Glacier by plotting the ELT coordinates on a map. A third group, the 242d Chinooks, "did not plot the crash site to within such narrow limits and did not know that the crash site was on the Kahiltna Glacier, but that was through their own failure to provide themselves with an adequate map, which failure was a failure to exercise reasonable care."[6]

Also Tuesday night, a second C-130 flight saw Clouser's blinking flashlight and dropped flares to tell the victims of the search effort. "At this point the U.S.A. knew there were live victims capable of flashing a light on the slope of Kahiltna Glacier." By 7:20 p.m. Tuesday night, possibly earlier, the RCC notified the Army helicopter unit at Ft. Wainwright. The Army had a large number of Chinooks available for this type of rescue mission.

> It is the regular practice of the Army to fly Chinooks on such rescue missions. The United States has undertaken to perform search and rescue operations in similar circumstances in a national plan . . . and in a local plan. And in particular, [it] is the practice of the Army to participate in rescue attempts within the boundaries of the Denali National Park. Regardless of whether the U.S.A. would have such a duty independently, the United States has undertaken such a duty to perform rescues.[7]

Chinooks were configured for rescue missions like this and had hoisting capabilities and hatches to "facilitate drops of supplies." The judge referenced the numerous and extensive SAR plans and agreements.

Tuesday night, "[t]he Army delayed . . . until approximately midnight before making a decision whether to take off" for Talkeetna, "the usual staging area for park rescues because of its location and its accessibility to Mt. McKinley." The Army's decision was to wait until first light on Wednesday morning. "[T]he delay until the next morning was based upon a decision made at a higher level of command, but . . . the decision was based upon the recommendation of Mr. Bridgman."

---

6. A failure to exercise reasonable care is negligence.
7. The judge adopted plaintiffs' position regarding duty to rescue.

In the testimony, Mr. Bridgman explained that
his reason for that was the difficulty with
weather in flying to Talkeetna on Tuesday night.
I found this testimony not to be credible. The
difficulty with the weather was not mentioned as
the reason at earlier times closer to the accident
when one would ordinarily have expected it to
be mentioned if it was the truth. No reasonable
explanation was offered for the failure to fly to
Talkeetna on Tuesday night.

This was "an extremely serious delay. It was inconsistent with the
Army's own regulations and plans with regard to rapid deployment of
assistance to help victims believed to be alive, suffering, and in need
of immediate help."

The consequences of the delay were grave. It
meant that much of the daylight on the following
day would necessarily be lost to the rescue
attempt. . . . The Chinooks did not leave for
Talkeetna until approximately . . . 9:30 a.m. on
Wednesday. The only excuse was a certain equipment
problem [which did not] justify the failure to
take off in a helicopter that did not have the
equipment problem.[8]

The Chinook pilots, the RCC personnel, Ranger Gerhard, and all
the bush pilots understood and it was common knowledge "that the
weather on Mt. McKinley is extremely changeable and extremely local
and unpredictable." Thus, "any reasonable individual would recognize the
importance of being able to approach a crash site during all daylight hours.
The Army failed to exercise reasonable care in wasting so much of the
daylight hours on the critical day, Wednesday." The Chinooks did not arrive
at the crash site until 11:35 a.m. Wednesday.

The delay in arrival was compounded by an
imprudent plan which no reasonable person would

---

8. The Army's "fly in pairs" policy was not justified.

have adopted. The imprudent plan was that instead of
flying to Talkeetna, refueling, and then leaving from
Talkeetna at first light [on Wednesday] . . ., the
Army flew fairly late in the morning to Mt. McKinley
airstrip, which is a considerable distance from the
location of the crash site, . . . and then flew from
the Mt. McKinley airstrip to the crash site leaving
them with inadequate fuel to remain at the crash site
for more than a very short time. . . . Mr. Bridgman,
in coordination with Mr. Gerhard and the RCC, did
not allow the Chinooks adequate daylight hours at
the crash site to have a reasonable opportunity to
accomplish a useful mission.

As the days were extremely short in mid-December and the weather
was extremely changeable at Mt. McKinley, "it [was] highly imprudent
to delay so long and leave so little opportunity to perform any rescue
attempt at the crash site." "Had the Army arrived earlier, it would have
been much more capable of performing some assistance to the victims of
the crash. It arrived late because of negligence."

At the crash site, "[t]here was wind in the morning. The weather was
clear. As the morning went on, the wind grew worse." Clouds came up so
quickly that the second Chinook was not able to fly to Talkeetna. The judge
found the rescue plan's inadequacy to be "graphically demonstrated by the
need of [Chinook 525] . . . to land at Nenana" instead of flying back to Ft.
Wainwright, only 65 road miles distant.

Local Talkeetna pilots flying small fixed wing aircraft flew to the crash
site in staggered shifts from before 8:00 a.m. Wednesday. Doug Geeting
spotted the crash location no later than 8:35 a.m. This information was
transmitted to the RCC and "the RCC transmitted the information to
the Chinooks." The local bush pilots intended to provide direction and
assistance to the Chinooks, "which they had been told and believed to be on
their way to effect the rescue. In addition, the fixed wing aircraft . . . [were]
prepared to make a drop . . . of emergency supplies." The judge described
in detail the difficulties faced by a fixed wing aircraft pilot trying to make an
airdrop over the crash site.

Local mountaineering experts in Talkeetna, the
community consisting in significant part of climbers
and bush pilots, became aware of the . . . crash and
were available and willing to leave immediately for
rescue efforts [early Wednesday morning.] However,
no request was made for aid to the local pilots or
the local mountaineers at Talkeetna or anywhere else,
although mountaineers who were experts at rescues
and experienced on Mt. McKinley were available in
Anchorage and Fairbanks and had . . . made their
availability clear in the past to the RCC.

But the RCC in Anchorage made no calls. Nor
did the National Park Service. . . . It was from a
failure to think of it or to direct their attention
to it. This was in violation of the search and
rescue plans adopted by the United States, which
specifically required the U.S.A. to coordinate its
efforts with such civilian groups.

Turning to "worsening the victim's plight," the judge found that Dennis
Brown, a local helicopter pilot, accompanied by Larry Rivers, "an expert
mountaineer and guide with emergency supplies," planned to fly to the
crash site early Wednesday morning to attempt a rescue or, failing that, to
drop survival equipment.

[Brown's] plan was frustrated by advice from
an employee of the F.A.A. which was based upon a
communication from the NPS or the RCC that the
Chinooks would be soon arriving. The F.A.A. employee
advised [Brown and Rivers] that their efforts were
not requested or desired and that they should not go
into the area of the crash site.

It may be, and probably is the case, that this
F.A.A. employee did not have the authority to ban
the pilot from the crash site. However, there was
bad blood between the pilot and the National Park
Service and other government officials. The pilot
could reasonably be expected not to fly to the
crash site in the face of the specific directions
that he had been given not to, regardless of the

technicalities of the authority of the F.A.A.
official who told them not to.

Whether the pilot could have accomplished the
rescue will never be known. The NPS officials
evidently questioned his business integrity. Their
questioning of his flying ability did not have a
foundation and appeared to be no more than a quarrel
with regard to his business integrity. . . .
[C]onsidering the lighter winds earlier in the
morning and the outfitting of the Brown helicopter
for a drop, I think it is more likely than not that
a drop of supplies would have been made by the Brown
helicopter had the United States not specifically
told Brown and Rivers to stay out. The plight of the
victims was sealed at that point.[9]

[W]hile it is more probable than not that the
Brown helicopter would have made a drop of supplies,
I do not think it is more probable than not that
Brown and Rivers would have been able to land and
safely extract Mr. Scanlon from the wrecked airplane
on the side of the mountain. The number of people
and the ability and the equipment they had combined
with the odds against . . . a successful landing
at the location and the weather make it less than
probable that they would have been able to remove
a man with a broken neck from the fuselage without
damaging his spinal cord. But they nevertheless
could have dropped supplies and would have had they
not been told to stay out.

On Wednesday noon, one Chinook landed on Peter's Basin and watched.

The other Chinook made no effort to use hoists
to reach the victims, did not put any PJs on the
ground, and most important, most striking to me, did
not drop any survival gear.

---

9. This finding satisfied the "worsened the victims plight" requirement.

I just cannot imagine how human beings in the safety and warmth of the helicopter, a large heavy Army Chinook, flying over these people, realizing that the weather was picking up and they probably could not land, how they could fly over and not so much as drop a knapsack to these people.

Mr. Clouser, Mr. Scanlon were out there on the mountain, tourists from Indiana, with virtually nothing to sustain life, not so much as a thermos of hot coffee. Not a tent. Mr. Clouser had no sleeping bag because he had been attempting to save the life of his friend with sleeping bags.

Chinook 033 was "full of equipment," but "[n]one had been prepared through negligence, most strikingly of Mr. Gerhard, and also of Mr. Bridgman. No drop had been prepared." The judge ruled there should have been a red sled on the Chinooks. The terrain and the snow condition on the north side of the Pass was such "that a drop more probably than not could have been safely made, would have stuck." Mike was in good enough condition "that he could have hiked to the drop and retrieved the equipment. That is proved quite persuasively by the fact that Mr. Clouser walked over the Pass days later."

The helicopter commanded by Mr. Warden got very close to the victims. It came within a couple of hundred feet. It's very difficult to place the location exactly. The victim on the ground, Mr. Clouser, thought it was within a snowball's throw. The testimony of Mr. Warden would put it slightly farther away than a snowball's throw but probably within a football field of distance, which would be partly horizontal and partly vertical. A drop at that distance could have been made, and more probably than not would have been successful.

Because the north side of the Pass was always in shadow and the light was flat, Judge Kleinfeld found "the ability of the people in the Chinook to perceive distance was lower than the ability of Mr. Clouser on the ground."

Incredibly, the Chinook flew not equipped for a drop. The only rescue that the Chinook was equipped to do was one where they could fly in without any maneuvering necessary because of the inadequacy of the fuel, land exactly at the site or extremely close to it, pick up the victims with the parajumpers . . . , who were not equipped for a long stay, . . . put the victims on the [Chinook] and leave.

[T]his was an imprudent plan. Any sensible person planning this rescue would have foreseen the possibility that the weather and the terrain, since this was the highest mountain in North America and a very complex mountain, would not permit such an easy rescue. Any sensible prudent person would have been equipped and prepared for alternatives. Most obviously, and as is required by the search and rescue plans applicable to this mission, a drop of emergency supplies.

The failure to prepare was entirely unexcused and entirely due to negligence. This negligence in the circumstances amounted to gross negligence. It was inexcusable.

The finding of "gross negligence" sent a shock through the courtroom.

There were no burdens involved with preparing such a drop. There were no financial limitations. The equipment was on the ground, ready for use. The red sleds were packed in Anchorage. Red sleds could have been available in Fairbanks when the Chinooks took off.

The burden was so slight of preparing a drop. The foreseeability, the likelihood of the need for a drop was so great because of the terrain and the weather. And the value, the importance, of a drop was so great because of the difficulty in sustaining human life on the slopes of Mt. McKinley in December that it was gross negligence not to foresee and prepare for the necessity for a drop of rescue supplies.

When the Chinooks approached the crash site, no
drop was made. Mr. Gerhard, who had the ultimate
responsibility and authority with regard to this
rescue, could have saved Mr. Clouser's hands and
feet by dropping his own pack out the hatch. He did
not do so. He had no excuse.

Mr. Warden testified, and I believe he was
telling the truth, that he did not command a drop
be made because the thought never crossed his mind.
It was not his responsibility to have the ultimate
planning authority for this rescue. That was Mr.
Gerhard's responsibility.

The judge did not believe an airdrop was discussed. All hovering was
for the purpose of locating "a suitable landing spot." Gerhard discussed
only whether they "were adequately supplied to spend several days on
a mountain, whether they should get out of the helicopter." "No genuine
decision was ever made with regard to a drop by Mr. Gerhard or by the crew
of [Chinook 033] because a drop was not thought of."

I do not fault the PJs or Mr. Gerhard or Mr.
Griffith for not getting out of the helicopter.
To get out of the helicopter on the slopes of Mt.
McKinley in December, to climb Mt. McKinley in
December, is not what can be required [by] law of
an ordinary and reasonable person. It is heroic.

There were heroic individuals involved in
this rescue. They were the Mountain Maniacs of
Talkeetna. It is appropriate to erect statues
in public places of heroic individuals like the
Mountain Maniacs, but it is not appropriate for
the law to require of ordinary people that they
act heroically.

I do understand the law to require them to
exercise reasonable care in such circumstances where
without the necessity for any heroics, at very
slight burden to themselves and with tremendous
benefit to the victims . . . , they could have made
an airdrop.

Judge Kleinfeld listed "many other failures of preparation which tend to show a lack of serious planning effort." The Chinooks should have carried horizon markers or boughs of spruce trees or other objects to drop so locations on the ground could be put in perspective. "That does not affect the responsibility to make a drop, but it tends to show a lack of planning for the mission."

From the Chinooks' departure on Wednesday noon until after daylight hours on Friday, no close approaches were possible because of bad weather. It was "normal and entirely foreseeable that in December on Mt. McKinley there would be several days of inaccessibility," which was why it was so essential that a rescue attempt be made promptly. "It is not possible to operate such a mission in normal business hours."

Wednesday afternoon, civilian mountain climbers from Talkeetna, the Mountain Maniacs, volunteered their services to assist in the rescue. "It was Mr. Gerhard's responsibility to contact them, and he should have contacted [civilian mountain rescue groups] much earlier, Tuesday night or Wednesday morning. He did not do so."

The Mountain Maniacs were landed on the Glacier Thursday morning. "They hiked up the mountain through the blizzards and the dark, endangering their own lives . . . to accomplish this rescue." It was "striking" that even with the military's tremendous advantage in equipment, money, facilities, and training, the Mountain Maniacs reached the site first and rescued the survivors. This showed "the seriousness with which they took their task."

Judge Kleinfeld contrasted the civilian climbers with the HART. Both civilian mountain rescue groups, Fairbanks and Talkeetna, were able to be outfitted and on their way within one hour. It took the military four hours.

One would think that since the individuals in the military don't have to call their superiors at work and ask for a day off, they don't have to rearrange their affairs, they don't have to worry about supporting their families during the time that they are performing the rescue mission, that the military could be ready much sooner. In addition, there are no financial limitations on their ability to keep a backpack of spare equipment ready. Yet the civilians were able to be prepared in [one quarter] the time

for a rescue mission. They arrived first. It tends to
show what could be done just as the preparation of
the drop on the Brown helicopter shows what could be
done had Mr. Gerhard and Mr. Bridgman thought of it.

As to the faulty emergency telephone service in Denali Park,
Judge Kleinfeld found "[t]he NPS knew [the phones] didn't work
properly and there was no evidence to show that any . . . efforts had
been made to get it fixed."

The National Park Service had the final
responsibility for coordinating the rescue attempt
and the individual within the NPS whose job it
was to exercise that responsibility and authority
was Mr. Gerhard. [He] did nothing but prepare his
personal supplies and call his superior to advise
him what was going on on Tuesday night. He did
not exercise his responsibility to plan and take
authority and command this rescue until it was
already too late, after mid-day on Wednesday.

The judge moved to plaintiffs' injuries. Clouser "banged his head and
had a temporary loss of consciousness. He broke a tooth and he suffered
cuts and bruises, [but had] no serious or long-term injuries." Pat Scanlon

suffered a broken neck in the airplane crash in
the C-5, C-6 area of the neck. [His] spinal cord,
however, was not severed or crushed when his neck
was broken. He was able to move his arms and he had
sensation in his legs. He repeatedly crossed and
uncrossed his arms, thus working his gloves off,
showing that his spinal cord had not been severed
or crushed in the C-5, C-6 area where the . . . the
vertebrae were broken.

Mr. Clouser made the reasonable decision that it
was safest for Mr. Scanlon to remain lying on his
back in the [passenger area] of the airplane and
to attempt to keep him quiet and warm. Mr. Clouser
sacrificed the sleeping bag which would have kept

him warm in order to assist his friend. Clouser's
decision in this regard was reasonable in the
circumstances and the sacrifice of his sleeping bag
goes beyond the reasonable and approaches the heroic
in the circumstances of being without supplies on
the slopes of Mt. McKinley in December.

Although it was warm for 10,000 feet on Mt. McKinley in mid-December, "it was nevertheless life threatening." The temperature was slightly above zero, possibly dropping below zero on Tuesday night with winds. Temperatures continued in the same range on Wednesday with increasing winds causing a substantial wind chill. "In such circumstances, human beings either suffer injury or die quickly from exposure to the elements."

Had an adequate number of individuals adequately
trained in emergency medicine been able to land at
the site on Wednesday during the daylight hours, and
had they been adequately equipped with emergency
medical equipment, they could have saved the life
of Mr. Scanlon and he would have survived in all
probability with some permanent injuries, probably
no paraplegia or quadriplegia. However, as I have
indicated, I cannot find that it is more probable
than not that such a landing of adequately equipped
rescue personnel [in] adequate numbers could have
been made on Wednesday, even if the United States
had exercised reasonable care.

When Wednesday came and went without such a
landing [of numerous adequately equipped rescue
personnel], which was not due to the failure to
exercise reasonable care, Mr. Scanlon's fate was
unfortunately sealed. . . . [10]

Judge Kleinfeld focused on the cause of Pat's death. The high winds Wednesday night violently moved the plane back and forth and down

---

10. Even though the U.S.A. was both negligent and grossly negligent with respect to an air drop, that conduct was not a legal cause of Pat Scanlon's death. The judge ruled against the Scanlon estate on liability for wrongful death.

the mountainside. "[The] movement of the airplane . . . probably itself
worked substantial damage to Mr. Scanlon's spinal cord. . . ." The
rocking rolled Pat onto his stomach, a dangerous position, and pushed
him towards the tail cone, where Hommer was huddled. Scanlon's head
and shoulders went through a small door into the luggage compartment
towards the rear of the Cessna. Clouser believed Pat would die if left
there. Enlisting Pat's help, Hommer tried to push and Clouser tried to pull
Pat back up into the center of the airplane.

> In the course of the attempt, Mr. Clouser lost
> his gloves. His loss of his gloves was due to his
> attempt to save his friend's life. It cost Mr.
> Clouser approximately half of his fingers and most
> of the use of his hands.[11]

> Up until the point where he lost his gloves,
> Mr. Clouser had been able to keep his hands warm.
> Once he lost his gloves, since no supplies had been
> dropped, it was impossible to keep his hands warm.

> The weather grew worse and worse. Wednesday
> night, Thursday and Friday there were blizzard
> conditions. During this period of worsening weather,
> Mr. Clouser's hands froze and his feet froze. He was
> unable to protect himself from the elements because
> the pilot [Hommer] . . . had not brought adequate
> emergency supplies and because the military and the
> Park Service had not planned the rescue adequately
> and had not thought to drop supplies. . . . [A]t
> some time between Wednesday night and Saturday, Mr.
> Clouser's feet and hands froze.

> Had survival gear been dropped to the victims on
> Wednesday morning, either by the Brown helicopter
> . . . [or Chinook 033], Mr. Clouser would most
> probably have retrieved the supplies and would
> not have lost . . . approximately half of his
> fingers and much of both feet. . . . As a result of
> the failure to drop supplies, it was eventually

---

11. To her credit, Tara Neda never argued that Mike negligently lost his gloves and, had he not done
so, would not have lost his fingers. The judge rejected such an argument anyway.

```
necessary to amputate parts of approximately 5 of
Mr. Clouser's 10 fingers and substantial portions of
each foot.¹²
```

On the applicable law and a duty to rescue, the judge declared himself "largely persuaded by the discussion in the Plaintiffs' Trial Brief. And I find the arguments to be well-taken. . . ." Judge Kleinfeld read aloud the language of the Alaska Good Samaritan statute and held the statute "is probably not applicable to this case under the decision in the Lee case [lion] of the Alaska Supreme Court. . . ." The judge noted the Alaska Good Samaritan statute did not preclude liability for civil damages as a result of gross negligence or reckless or intentional conduct. "And I have found gross negligence for the failure to make a drop of supplies. I just can't imagine people flying over these victims with a helicopter full of supplies and not saying, my God, we have to drop something to these people."

With liability completed, Judge Kleinfeld turned to the Scanlon Estate's damages. "Because of the findings I have made, the Scanlon estate, although negligence has been established and damages have been established, does not establish legal cause. And therefore as to the wrongful death, the Scanlon estate cannot recover damages."

The judge turned to the claim for pain and suffering before Pat's death.

```
    Mr. Scanlon's pain and suffering were exacerbated,
however, from approximately noon on Wednesday until
Thursday morning when he died. . . . Because of the
failure to make a supply drop, his hopelessness, his
pain, his freezing were all greatly exacerbated. He
lived through a period of horror and his horror was
not alleviated as it should have been by at least
some warmth and the knowledge that someone was trying
to do something for him.
```

Judge Kleinfeld found this exacerbation resulted in Pat suffering "extraordinary horror" in the final hours before death. Observing it was "very difficult to put a number to this kind of mental distress and pain

---

12. The negligent and grossly negligent failure to airdrop supplies was the legal cause of Mike Clouser's injuries.

and suffering," the judge found "an appropriate award for Mr. Scanlon's exacerbation of pain and suffering because of the failure to make a supply drop was $36,000." This number was determined by "rough justice" and represented "approximately 18 hours and approximately $2000 an hour."

Tom Scanlon and I had different reactions to this award, but there was no time to discuss it. As the judge moved to Clouser's damages, Mike leaned forward at the table.

After clarifying the U.S.A. had no liability for injuries caused solely by the plane crash (broken tooth, cuts and bruises), Judge Kleinfeld found Mike's other injuries "were legally caused by the failure to make [an airdrop]." Clouser was entitled to the following damages, "which I find to be legally caused by the [negligence] and gross negligence of the U.S.A. . . . ."

> Past medical expenses, $135,420.
>
> Future medical expenses. Mr. Clouser is certain to have future medical expenses because he is certain to have the need for treatment of arthritis and is more probably than not going to need further treatment for the skin area around his amputations. However, the evidence did not support any particular number for the future medical expenses so far as I was able to discern in going through my notes and in listening to it as it came in. Therefore the award for future medical expenses is zero.

Zero? In closing, I had asked for 25, 50, or $100,000 for medical expenses to be incurred in the distant future, 10 or 20 years from now. How could the doctors estimate those expenses now? But zero?

The judge described wage loss as "a very problematic area." He believed Dr. Solie's testimony was based on numerous questionable assumptions and he lamented that it was necessary to strike the U.S.A.'s economist shortly before trial so "we do not have countervailing evidence. We do have the excellent cross-examination that Mr. Wilson performed of Dr. Solie which assists me in evaluating evidence."

> Mr. Clouser is a 37 year old man. He cannot walk more than a few hundred yards. He has lost most of his fingers. He lived through a period of many months

with the most intense pain, as well as the horror
of watching pieces of his body blacken until they
had to be cut off with what is called a modified
guillotine. Because of the medical necessities of
treatment of this type of frostbite injury, there was
no way of protecting Mr. Clouser from the horror . . .
of watching his fingers and his feet die. There was
also no way to avoid the tremendous pain during that
process and during the subsequent period when his
bones were exposed and his nerves were exposed.

I'm impressed with the mental stability of Mr.
Clouser. I believe many individuals would not have
retained their sanity or their ability to function
as human beings after living through this. . . .

Clouser had been retrained but had not found work as a computer
programmer. "So far he's had one job and he got fired because he
wasn't fast enough. He is never going to be as fast as someone who had
all the parts of his body. . . . Mr. Clouser is severely limited in his ability
to type because of the loss of fingers." Moreover, "in the performance
of any sort of work, one has to walk. Even in the most sedentary work
I can imagine, which is my own, I have to walk up and down the
halls of this building, carrying files. Mr. Clouser would be severely
impaired in his ability to do that."

He's 37. Most computer programmers would have
been at it for 10 years or 15 years and he's
brand new. This may make him look inadequate to
employers. . . . I do not believe his earnings
experience is going to be the same as a 37 year old
computer programmer.

I also do not believe, however, that Mr.
Clouser is totally disabled. Because of his
extraordinary emotional stability, he has managed
to hold himself together and [has been] able to
perform his training, learn how to be a computer
programmer, and obtain a job. I think he has some
earning capacity.

Would Mike's mental toughness be used against him? After a zero award for future medical expenses, would an award for lost earnings be anywhere near the suggested numbers?

The judge did not accept either of Dr. Solie's two assumptions, total disability or earnings as a computer programmer from age 37 to the end of normal work life expectancy. "The correct assumption is somewhere in between." Kleinfeld detoured into a long discussion of Dr. Solie's report. It did not square with common sense. The inflation period used was too short. Dr. Solie's technique of calculating future wages for Clouser, when projected backwards, resulted in numbers that were too high.

> Considering an appropriate reduction in projected wage loss because of what could have been expected had Mr. Clouser not been injured and what I believe he can earn in alternative occupations, I believe that an appropriate damage award for loss of wages for the time from the accident to the end of the work life expectancy is $600,000.

Mike and I sat back in our chairs. Without pause, the judge moved to pain and suffering.

> . . . I've already spoken to most of the elements of pain and suffering. In addition, the kinds of injuries that Mr. Clouser has separate him from other human beings, at least from his own point of view, in a way that most injuries do not. Anyone with children has had the experience of having their children look with fear or fascination at someone whose limbs are not normal. And one trains children not to do that because it will make the people feel bad if they're looked at with horror or fascination or disgust. A well-trained child is then inclined to look with pity.
>
> The victim of a horribly disabling injury would naturally sense the way other people look at him and would not be happy with any of these responses, no more the pity than the others. A person wants to be looked at as a normal man and that's an expectation

that everybody has . . . and that Mr. Clouser was
entitled to have fulfilled. . . .

This is all in addition to the pain which he has
experienced and will experience in the future, the
arthritis he will experience in the future, the
complications which are going to be inevitable, the
re-injuries which are more probable than not because
of loss of sensation in the feet, the inability even
to live in a cold climate such as Alaska. . . .

It is very hard to put a number on pain and
suffering. For similar injuries in Alaska cases,
. . . the [Alaska] Supreme Court has damages all
over the board. I know of one case sustained as not
excessive by the Alaska Supreme Court . . . where
for a less severe injury, the Alaska Supreme Court
sustained $5,000,000.

Had I asked for too little in Clouser's federal tort claim, which limited
all damages to $1.5 million?

. . . In this case, because of the need to put
some number to the experience, I find that the pain
and suffering experienced by Mr. Clouser from the
time of the accident to the end of his normal life
expectancy, which is not impaired by the accident,
is $600,000.

From his reaction, this amount agreed with Mike. I quickly did the
math. Judge Kleinfeld had awarded the Scanlon estate $36,000 and Mike
Clouser $1,335,420.

When court was adjourned, we had to clear the courtroom quickly so
the judge could hear another matter. Opposing counsel did not speak to
each other. Sometimes lawyers congratulate an opponent on the outcome.
Not in this case.

Chapter 36

Resolution

Mike Clouser was deeply gratified by the decision. While his award was subject to an offset for the insurance settlement ($130,675), the balance exceeded $1.2 million. I told Mike the gross negligence finding would be extremely helpful on appeal. He left immediately to drive back to Indiana.

I did not sugarcoat the result for Tom Scanlon. The $36,000 award likely would be offset by the $105,675 insurance settlement, so the U.S.A. would owe nothing. Tom was gracious as always; the trial answered his questions and he was happy Mike won.

When the transcript of the oral decision was finished, I had witnesses to thank. Dennis Brown was first on the list, but there was no way to contact him. In late April and early May, thank you letters enclosing the transcript were mailed to Doug Buchanan, Art Mannix, Brian McCullough, Larry Rivers, Dr. Mills, Jim Okonek, and Mike Fisher.

On Friday, May 8, I received a telephone call from Marilee Enge, a reporter for the Anchorage Daily News. She had just read the decision. Her first question was whether Bob Gerhard had been fired; she did not see how he could not be fired. I suggested she ask the NPS. When she posed another question, I refused to discuss it further. Unable to hide my emotion, I told her the Anchorage Daily News had singled out the case as the stupidest lawsuit of the year in its 1984 Soapy Smith awards. She had not known this. Soon the reporter called back. She had discussed the case with Howard Weaver, the paper's editor. I do not recall if she said Howard was sorry. Probably not, because we did not discuss it further.

On Saturday, May 16, the Anchorage Daily News ran a front page story titled **"Judge rules U. S. negligent on rescue attempt"** by Marilee Enge. Continued at length on an inside page, the story accurately described the crash and rescue, briefly described the law, and quoted some of Judge Kleinfeld's oral decision. The story noted that a judgment for Clouser for over $1.2 million was to be entered "in the next several weeks." For the first time, I was named as attorney for plaintiffs. The only government person named was "[NPS] Ranger Robert Gerhard, who was coordinating the rescue, [and] was ultimately responsible for not arranging a drop." Dennis Brown was named, though not Larry Rivers. Brown "completely outfitted a helicopter with survival and rescue gear," but an FAA employee (not named) "told Brown that the Army helicopters would be handling the rescue and denied him permission to land within Denali Park."

That Saturday, my family and I were taking the Alaska Railroad from Anchorage to Whittier. Copies of the morning paper were scattered throughout the train. I overheard two men across the aisle discussing the Mt. McKinley case. One was extremely upset. The second noticed my eavesdropping and they fell silent. The first man's fury was so tangible that I moved to another railroad car.

The next day, Sunday, the Anchorage Times ran a story on page B-5 titled **"Judge amazed at incompetence of rescue try."** The article listed only Robert Gerhard and Dennis Brown by name and incorrectly reported the judge "has not decided whether Scanlon's estate also should be awarded damages for wrongful death."

There was no more press coverage. I did not read the letters to the editor in either newspaper.

The parties had 30 days to submit additional findings of fact and conclusions of law. Ms. Neda filed the U.S.A.'s proposed findings and conclusions on May 15, a week early. The one and a half page pleading listed 13 proposed findings without citation to any evidence. The U.S.A. proposed full offsets for the insurance settlements against the Scanlon estate and against Clouser. Under Alaska law, these offsets were proper.

On May 22, plaintiffs filed five pleadings. The first divided the oral decision into 156 separate findings and conclusions and listed evidence in the record supporting each. The second proposed 23 new findings and conclusions utilizing evidence to which the judge made no reference. (An appellate court can uphold a decision based on any evidence in the record, not just the evidence relied upon by the lower court.) The third sought money for Clouser's future medical expenses and argued it was necessary to prove to a reasonable certainty only the necessity, not the amount, of future medical expenses. The fourth argued that, despite the insurance offset, the Scanlon estate was the "prevailing party" and entitled to recover its costs from the U.S.A. The fifth was a 14 page brief urging reconsideration of the holding of no liability for the wrongful death of Pat Scanlon.

On May 29, I filed two proposed judgments in favor of Mike Clouser and the Scanlon estate. A judgment is the goal of a lawsuit; it gives the winning party the right to collect money from the losing party. The time period for appeal runs from the date a judgment is signed. Costs cannot be awarded until a judgment is entered. In an FTCA lawsuit, interest does not begin to accrue until a judgment is signed and an appeal is filed.

Ms. Neda filed no opposition to the pleadings or the proposed judgments.

June passed with no decision. When I checked the court file on July 2, I learned the U.S.A. had ordered a trial transcript, which was complete. Plaintiffs could buy a copy for $1000. This was a client cost and I did not yet need a transcript, so I asked Mike to tell me if he wanted to buy one. I warned that the Scanlon estate probably would not share the cost because I doubted Tom would appeal. I also wrote Mike: "I had expected the judge to rule by the end of June. Now I expect him to rule by the end of July. As you know, his habit is to be very prompt."

Nothing happened in July. On August 6, Judge Kleinfeld entered an Order requiring the U.S.A. to file a brief on whether the Scanlon estate was the prevailing party. Ms. Neda filed a short brief on August 20 and I filed a reply before the end of August. The case was now ripe for decision and entry of judgments.

Nothing happened for the rest of 1987. Nor was there a decision in January, 1988. Or February. Or March. Or April. Or May. Or June. Or July. Or August. Or September. Or October. Or November. Or December. 1988 passed with no action by Judge Kleinfeld.

In February, 1988, Mike decided a trial transcript was worth $1000. On June 3, he wrote of reading the transcript, "There are some places where the reading is somewhat difficult. (Just as I expected there would be.)" On July 8, I wrote that I wanted to wait to take action until August, twelve months after the last brief was filed because I was worried Kleinfeld "will be offended if our inquiry is not handled very carefully. I cannot bring myself to bite the hand that feeds us." On July 18, Mike responded, "I have no wish to bite the hand that feeds us either. Maybe he'll come through and take the pressure off." Of reading the trial transcript, he wrote: "Several times while I was reading it, I got pretty mad and just quit for a while. It is extremely difficult for me not to be bitter. As hard as I try not to, at times I feel like I am losing that battle."

In the fall of 1988, Tom Scanlon visited Mike in Indiana. They agreed it was time to do something. I could not argue. Clouser's only income was $700 a month in Social Security disability. I did my best to minimize litigation costs during discovery and trial but all of the interest earned from the 1982 insurance settlement and some of the principal went to pay costs. Mike also spent some principal for his living expenses so less than half the insurance money remained. On October 17, Mike called. He was at a loss. He never complained about living on $700 a month, but his life was in limbo.

Over Thanksgiving weekend, I reviewed the post-trial pleadings and drafted a motion, which was filed on December 14. After noting that fifteen months had passed since the briefing was complete, it reminded the judge that there is no pre-judgment interest in FTCA actions and post-judgment interest cannot begin to accrue until after a judgment is signed. If judgment had been entered in November, 1987 for the amount awarded, "Clouser would have been entitled to substantial interest [$84,332 per year at 7%], . . . [far] more than the dollar amounts at issue in [all] outstanding [matters concerning] Clouser." The U.S.A. filed no opposition.

Nothing happened in January, 1989. Nothing in February. Nothing in March. Nothing in April. It had been two years since trial.

When a lawyer misses a deadline in litigation, there are serious consequences. When the U.S.A. failed to list an economist on defendant's witness list, Judge Kleinfeld barred the U.S.A. from calling an economist at trial. In other cases of lawyer delay or neglect, a judge will dismiss a plaintiff's case or enter judgment against a defendant. What happens when there is judicial neglect?

My wife's first job in Alaska was as law clerk to a state superior court judge. She soon learned Alaska had an administrative rule that if a case had been ripe for decision for six months and no decision had been made, the judge's pay was suspended. No exceptions. As soon as the judge decided the matter, the withheld paycheck was released. A list of cases awaiting decision more than six months, including the assigned judge, was posted in the courthouse, available to the public. Federal court had no similar rule.

In mid-March, I wrote Mike that I had finished a long jury trial (my first since his) and was going on vacation with my family to Sun Valley. (On the return flight, I saw the *Exxon Valdez* surrounded by a huge oil slick outside Valdez.) I intended to take action "to extract a decision" in mid-April. Mike replied, "I am still not in a panic," and told me to do what I thought best.

On April 19, I called Tara Neda to propose a joint telephone call to Judge Kleinfeld. I reached Jim Wilson instead. He said Ms. Neda had transferred to New Mexico at the end of 1988 and he had replaced her on the case.

Talking with Kleinfeld or the presiding federal district judge in Alaska was touchy and I was reluctant to do it. Another approach, seeking a writ of mandamus, or order, from the Ninth Circuit to require Judge Kleinfeld to rule was adversarial and was likely to anger the judge. What to do?

I decided to talk to a woman in the federal clerk's office who had always been helpful. Standing at the public counter, I outlined the case, the outcome of trial, and the problem with Kleinfeld. She nodded. I mentioned a mandamus action in the Ninth Circuit. She strongly recommended against it. I brought up a private conversation with the presiding judge. She recommended against this, too. She suggested I write a letter to the case management clerk outlining the procedural history and the pending matters.

On May 4, I wrote the suggested letter and outlined the post-trial history. The letter ended: "This case seems to have fallen through the cracks. Anything you can do to check on the status of this case will be appreciated by all parties to this action." I sent a copy to Jim Wilson. On May 15, the mail brought a letter from Judge Kleinfeld, copied to Wilson. It read: "Thank you very much for your letter of May 4, 1989. As you surmised, the 'case seems to have fallen through the cracks.' I appreciate being advised of the status so that I can provide the necessary decisions and judgment."

The judge did nothing in May. Or June. Or July. Or August. The post-trial briefing had been complete for more than two years with no decision.

On September 13, 1989, Judge Kleinfeld entered Final Determinations of Findings of Fact, an Order Relating to Credits for Settlements, and two judgments. The judge adopted the first four findings proposed by Ms. Neda and rejected the rest. The U.S.A. was entitled to full offsets for the insurance settlements. Kleinfeld declared the U.S.A. to be the "prevailing party" against the Scanlon estate.

The judge improved Clouser's position on appeal. Kleinfeld increased the U.S.A.'s duty to rescue and explicitly ruled the case "analogous to Lee v. State" [lion]. Within Denali National Park, personnel of the NPS, Army, and Air Force were analogous to Alaska State Troopers outside park boundaries. Also, "[a] special duty was created by the government's control of Mt. McKinley and its exclusion of other rescuers." Judge Kleinfeld also added a new finding of gross negligence: "The accumulation of instances of ordinary negligence throughout the rescue was, independently of the failure to make a drop, gross negligence as defined by Alaska law." In other words, the government was negligent in so many different ways that the whole of the defendant's conduct amounted to gross negligence.

Going further, Judge Kleinfeld now found the U.S.A.'s conduct to be reckless: "Even considering the emergency, the repeated accumulation of violations of federal regulations and policies regarding such a rescue and failures to exercise reasonable care throughout . . . the rescue amounted to reckless disregard of the consequences. . . ." The judge added an explicit finding that the failure to make an emergency airdrop was reckless. These new findings went far beyond anything proposed by plaintiffs. Another finding rescinded the award of zero damages for future medical expenses and replaced it with an award of $15,000. The judge also rewrote the finding awarding $600,000 in total lost earnings to clarify that the court had "deduct[ed] the taxes which would have been paid on the additional earnings." This eliminated any argument on appeal that Indiana state income taxes had not been deducted.

A Judgment signed September 13 awarded Clouser $1,350,420 plus costs to be determined by the clerk. (The judge forgot to subtract the insurance offset of $130,675, so a revised judgment was soon entered for $1,219,745.) A separate Judgment awarded the Scanlon estate nothing, dismissed all claims, and awarded the U.S.A. costs to be determined by the clerk.

While Judge Kleinfeld procrastinated, the summer of the *Exxon Valdez* had taken its toll on my law office. A client owned a fish processing plant on Kodiak Island and the oil spill eliminated the entire Kodiak fishing season, putting extreme financial pressure on the client. Realizing it could bankrupt an entire fishing industry, Exxon began paying claims for lost revenue. As I did emergency claim preparation work under high pressure, I tried to shield my staff, but it was too much for Donna, my legal secretary/paralegal for twelve years. She quit at the end of the summer, prior to Judge Kleinfeld's ruling.

Before leaving, Donna prepared a cost bill for Clouser. On the first possible day, Clouser's Bill of Costs was filed seeking $7364.49. All costs were backed up with a receipt, a cancelled check, or both. Under the local rules, costs allowed often were much less than actual costs. For example, Dr. Solie's expert witness fees for Clouser alone totaled over $6000, but we could claim only $300 for the two hours Dr. Solie testified in court (for Clouser, not Scanlon). Moreover, Clouser sought only 50% of many costs, like the $60 filing fee, because they had been split with the Scanlon estate.

A hearing on Clouser's Bill of Costs was held on September 29. I appeared for Clouser. No one appeared for the U.S.A. On October 2, the Deputy Clerk awarded $3257.66 in costs. The final amount of the Judgment in favor of Clouser against the United States was $1,223,002.66.

The U.S.A. did not file a cost bill against the Scanlon estate, so no costs were awarded. The amount of the judgment against the Scanlon estate was zero.

The Department of Justice had 60 days from September 13 to appeal to the Ninth Circuit Court of Appeals in San Francisco. Would the U.S.A. appeal?

The standard of review on appeal from a decision on a matter of law is not high because judges can differ on how legal questions should be answered. An appeal from adverse findings of fact is much more difficult because higher courts give great deference to the facts determined in the lower court. In the late 1980s, many appellate judges had previously served as trial court judges. They knew first-hand that a witness's demeanor could be more important than what the witness testified. Judge Kleinfeld's detailed factual findings presented a major obstacle to a successful appeal.

The U.S.A. filed a Notice of Appeal early, mailing it on November 7. On November 14, I sent a copy of Clouser's Judgment to the Comptroller General's Office. From date of receipt until the day before a favorable ruling by the Ninth Circuit, Mike would earn post-judgment interest. The Comptroller General's Office soon informed me the post-judgment interest rate was 8.19%. If Clouser won the appeal, he would receive $274.42 per day or $100,164 per year in interest. (Judge Kleinfeld's two year delay cost over $200,000 in interest.)

On November 15, I called Mr. Wilson and asked if the U.S.A. had made a formal decision to appeal or whether it filed a Notice of Appeal to keep its options open. Nothing required him to answer. Indeed, if he told me a decision had been made not to appeal, Clouser would be paid the full amount shortly. (There would be no post-judgment interest if the appeal was dropped.) I wrote my clients: "Wilson said he thought it was the latter [keep options open]. However, . . . his recommendation is that the case be appealed and he expects to receive authorization to appeal." This was discouraging.

With post-judgment interest accruing at more than $8000 per month, the passage of time now had a different feel. In mid-December, I filed the Scanlon estate's cross-appeal to keep its options open. It had been 8 years since the Mt. McKinley rescue.

In early February, 1990, Tom decided to drop the Scanlon estate from any appeal. Wilson and I agreed to a dismissal with each side to bear its own costs and attorney's fees. In the same conversation, we set the briefing schedule for Clouser. The U.S.A.'s opening brief would be due April 19, three years after trial.

The mail brought notice of a February 23 "pre-briefing conference" to be held by telephone with a Ninth Circuit court attorney. I had participated in several Ninth Circuit appeals, but could not remember such a conference. I read the court rules, made myself available by telephone, and wondered what I was in for.

Meg Gerrity conducted the pre-briefing conference. Jim Wilson represented the U.S.A. Ms. Gerrity said we were to accomplish three things: (1) clarify basis for appellate jurisdiction, (2) explore settlement, and (3) set briefing deadlines. There were no problems with (1) and (3).

She asked Mr. Wilson to go first on settlement. He said that as an individual U. S. Attorney, he had no settlement authority at all. He believed settlement was unlikely. It was being discussed within the DOJ and he doubted it would occur, but he would not say the chance of settlement was zero. When she asked Clouser's position, I said little. Wilson had no settlement authority. Why negotiate with someone who cannot give you what you want?

Ms. Gerrity asked to talk to Wilson alone. I hung up. It was some time before she called back, alone. She asked Clouser's settlement posture. Instead of answering, I asked her impressions of the case. Surprised to be asked her personal opinion, Ms. Gerrity paused and then said the facts were "killers" and by the time one read the lower court's factual findings, one was very sympathetic to plaintiffs. She quickly added that the Ninth Circuit would display no sympathy to either party. This was the reaction I had hoped for. I said we had a very good case on appeal and explained why. Ms. Gerrity asked if Clouser was willing to compromise the judgment (take less money). I answered I had an ethical obligation to pass on any settlement offer received. She said Wilson told her he would talk to the DOJ people to see if the government would make an offer of compromise (offer less than 100% as full payment). I repeated that we would listen to any offer. Ms. Gerrity suggested postponing the briefing on appeal in order to explore settlement. I said no. The rescue happened more than 8 years ago and trial was almost three years ago. Although Clouser had a judgment for $1.23 million, he was living on $726 a month in Social Security disability. It was time to resolve the case.

Ms. Gerrity added Mr. Wilson to the conversation. She said he would confer with his superiors to see if a settlement offer was to be made. If so, Wilson was to talk directly to me unless the parties wanted the Ninth Circuit's assistance. The pre-briefing conference ended.

Mike's reaction? "There's no point in panicking now." He was happy the case was finally moving. A seven week wait for the first brief was nothing. And if the government decided not to appeal, we would know in less than seven weeks.

In early March, Mr. Wilson and I finalized the dismissal of the Scanlon estate. I now represented only Mike Clouser.

On March 12, Mike wrote that the farm where he lived had been sold. The new owners planned to tear down his rented house to farm the land beneath it. He had to move by August and he was considering Montana, where he had a sister.

On March 16, I had two calls from Jim Wilson, who was working on the U.S.A.'s opening brief. I asked if a formal decision to appeal had been made. Wilson said no and he would let me know immediately if a decision was made not to appeal.

On Friday, April 6, Wilson called and said he was faxing a substantial offer containing a structured settlement. He encouraged us to take a day or two to contemplate the offer. I thanked him for the call. Then I stood by the fax machine.

His faxed letter arrived at 1:40 p.m. The U.S.A. offered: (1) $525,000 in cash, (2) a monthly payment starting at $2100 per month, increasing at 3% per year (compounded annually) for Mike's natural life with a guarantee of 20 years, and (3) a series of lump sum payments every three years starting at $15,000, increasing every three years, and ending 24 years later with a payment of $100,000, even if Mike died first. The U.S.A. would purchase annuities to cover (2) and (3); all payments, cash and annuity, would be free from income tax. The guaranteed minimum payments totaled $1,557,133. If Mike lived to his statistical life expectancy, the total would be $2,403,644. The letter stated, "The cost to the Government of this package exceeds $1.03 million."

I called Mike and arranged to fax the offer to him. It was good we had the weekend for things to sink in. By Monday, I was convinced the settlement offer was not Wilson's final authority. What do you do when you receive a settlement offer so large it will change your client's life forever, but you are certain there is more money available? When I brought up settlement to Tara Neda before trial, I was authorized to accept $200,000 because that amount would have improved the rest of Clouser's life. The U.S.A. was now offering five times as much. I did not know if I had it in me to turn the offer down.

Mike called at 11 a.m. His first inkling was to reject the offer, but he also said he had a big grin on his face. I told him I wanted to learn Wilson's final authority and my task would be easier with no settlement authority from him. No acceptance, no rejection, no counteroffer. I would call Jim Wilson and go fishing. Mike agreed.

I called Wilson and said it was rare that an opponent puts its top offer on the table to start. Was there room to maneuver? Mr. Wilson said he would not say there wasn't room to maneuver. I was not making a counteroffer, but my client had questions. Did the government care whether my client took all cash or a combination of cash plus an annuity? Wilson said this was his first structured settlement negotiation and he would get back to me.

My client was considering two changes to the offer. First, the monthly income would begin at $2500 a month, not $2100. Wilson responded, "Why don't you just go ahead and submit a counter-proposal?" I told Wilson I had tried this case against him, I trusted him, and he had said he would tell me when a decision not to appeal had been made. I implied that absent an assertion that an affirmative decision to appeal had been made, I would assume the decision had been made <u>not</u> to appeal and the government would soon have to pay the full $1.23 million in cash. Wilson was uncomfortable.

He asked for a clarification of our numbers. After repeating this was not a formal counteroffer, I said we wanted the monthly annuity raised from $2100 to $2500 a month to start. We also needed a little more cash. How much? I said raise the lump sum cash from $525,000 to $600,000. He asked if the total additional money my client might seek was around $100,000? I said a little more. No response. Wilson asked the timeframe for settling the case. I said if it settled, it should be in the next few days, certainly by the end of this week.

I recounted the conversation to Mike. We had not rejected the initial offer and Wilson would get back to me tomorrow.

As I drove to work Tuesday morning, I felt that increasing the annuity to $2500 a month and adding $75,000 in cash was too much. After thinking on it, I now believed we might get an increase to $2500 a month and an increase of $25,000 in cash, tops. On arrival at the office, I was greeted by a faxed letter from Gary Allen, Wilson's boss. I hesitated to read it, fearing bad news. I was wrong. The government increased its offer to (1) $525,000 in cash (same), (2) $2500 a month to start (up from $2100), and (3) the same lump sum payments every three years. The letter also contained the sentence: "This is our final offer in settlement in this matter."

The new offer was an instance of the U.S.A. negotiating against itself. Jim Wilson knew the situation. Mike Clouser was grievously injured and his life would be forever improved by accepting the first offer. My obligation, however, was to get him all the money available. Recognizing the predicament, Wilson persuaded his boss, and Mr. Allen let himself be persuaded, to increase the government's offer and to say "take it or leave it." It was an honorable thing to do.

Mr. Allen's letter also stated that intra-DOJ approval would take a week to 10 days and checks would then issue in 4 to 8 weeks. The government would pay a cash only settlement, but it would be for less: "The cost to the Government of this [structured] settlement would be just under $1.1 million; should you wish a cash payment, we would recommend $1,025,000."

I called Mike and read him the letter, word for word. He had three options: (1) accept the cash and increased annuities with a total value of $1.1 million, (2) take the cash only offer at $1.025 million, (3) reject the offer. Mike immediately said he was not going to reject the offer. He had been thinking about the first offer and felt it would be foolish to reject it.

Mike was pleased by the increase in monthly payments ($2100 to $2500) but did not understand why the cash only offer was $75,000 lower. He had some resistance to an annuity, which would provide an income stream until his death. He did not like someone else managing his money. I told him the government's offer sought a prompt response, though it had no formal expiration. Mike asked if it would be possible to tell Mr. Allen he accepted the government's offer but had not made up his mind whether to take cash and annuities or cash only. I thought that could be done. We left it that we would both think about it and Mike would call me back.

I wrote a formal opinion letter recommending the case settle on the terms offered. Mike had asked what I would do "if you were Mike Clouser," so I recommended cash plus annuities. My fee, 25% of the total recovery, would be higher on $1.1 million, as we both knew. Leaving aside the fee, the structured settlement was still the better choice.

Mike called back the same day. He had decided to accept the offer and decide later which option he preferred. I faxed Mr. Allen a letter saying as much. This allowed Jim Wilson to stop work on the appeal brief. Clouser had the name of an accountant at a Big Seven firm in Indianapolis. I faxed her the settlement letters and valuations. Mike met with the accountant and described her as "a pretty smart lady." She told him if it were her, she would take the annuities in a minute. Mike agreed. On Friday, April 13, I faxed a letter to Mr. Wilson saying Clouser accepted the cash and annuities option.

It was a relief that Mike chose the annuities. He would be financially secure for the rest of his life. And he would get a pile of cash up front to start a new life wherever he chose. I was pleased for Mike and I was pleased for me.

Mike had to sign a lengthy release in favor of the government. I drafted pleadings to dismiss everything pending in federal district court and the Ninth Circuit. Jim Wilson chose this moment to ask if I was aware the FTCA placed a statutory limit on contingency fees? I told him I had found the statute when drafting the complaint and had conformed my contingency fee agreements years ago. Ever the gentleman, Wilson did not pursue it further.

On April 30, Mike and I agreed on the mechanics of payment. The U.S.A. valued everything at $1.1 million and we used that figure to compute my attorney's fee, which came to $275,000 (25% of $1.1 million). The check for $525,000 would be payable to both attorney and client (standard operating procedure to be certain the attorney is paid) and Mike would give me a limited power of attorney to endorse and deposit the check in my trust account. When the check cleared, Mike's $250,000 would be wired wherever he directed.

On June 5, Wilson called to say he had the settlement checks. The annuity check for $575,000 was sent to the annuity agent the same day. The U. S. Treasury check for $525,000 arrived in my office on June 8 and was deposited in my law firm trust account. I sent all signed settlement paperwork to Mr. Wilson. The annuity agent soon wrote that the first monthly annuity payment would be made on July 7 and the 3% annual increase would occur each year on June 7.

When the $525,000 check cleared, my bank wire transferred $250,000 to Indiana, where Mike was standing by in person. My attorney's fee was also paid.

On July 5, Clouser wrote that the first monthly annuity payment of $2500 was deposited on July 2. He added, "I think I'm gonna like this."

On June 26, the Ninth Circuit dismissed the Clouser appeal. The Order was filed in Alaska on July 2. I filed a satisfaction of judgment in federal district court stating the judgment had been paid in full. The case was over.

Epilogue

Within a month of payment, Mike bought a new truck and moved to Montana. At first, he rented a place. When he decided to stay, he bought a house. Clouser has lived in Montana since 1990.

From the attorney's fee, I made a gift of $5000 to Donna Chertkow, my former secretary/paralegal, whose work, especially with the critique tapes, was instrumental in winning the case. My wife and I used the remainder of the Clouser fee (less taxes) to pay off our mortgage.

On September 28, 1990, I sent a letter to Judge Kleinfeld describing the settlement and thanking him for the time he devoted to the case. The judge wrote back promptly. He appreciated learning how the case was resolved and was especially pleased it was a structured settlement. Kleinfeld believed injured plaintiffs were much better off with an income stream than with a lump sum cash award.

On May 23, 1991, Judge Andrew J. Kleinfeld was nominated for the Ninth Circuit Court of Appeals. He was confirmed by the Senate on September 12 and took his seat on September 16, where he has served since.[13]

---

13. While on the Ninth Circuit, Kleinfeld was closely involved with the Exxon Valdez litigation. The jury trial in that case resulted in a $5 billion punitive damages verdict. On appeal to the Ninth Circuit, the case was argued and submitted for decision on May 3, 1999. With thousands of fishermen in Alaska waiting eagerly, Kleinfeld's decision for the Ninth Circuit was not issued until November 7, 2001, two years and six months later. The Ninth Circuit reversed the $5 billion award and remanded the case to the trial court. Eventually, in 2008, the Supreme Court lowered the award to slightly over $500 million.

Mike and I stayed in touch. In the spring of 1992, I drove my youngest daughter, Ellen, to watch a World Cup ski race in Canada. We stayed with Mike on the way up and back. When I drove my family around the U. S. in the summer of 1992, we visited him in Montana.

During a sabbatical year away from Alaska from August, 1991, to August, 1992, I began writing about the case. After I retired from law in May, 1993, I started writing this book. When we exchanged Christmas greetings in 1993, Mike was upset that I was writing a book. Unsettled by his hard feelings, I hired a Los Angeles entertainment lawyer to draw up a contract to govern rights. The lawyer was helpful in bringing out the disparity in our positions. I abandoned the project, preferring to maintain good relations with a former client and friend than to write a book over his objections.

In the mid-1990s, a high school classmate who worked at Elmendorf Air Force Base in Anchorage invited me to speak to the RCC controllers. My classmate said Judge Kleinfeld's decision was required reading at the RCC. While I was pleased to hear this, I declined the invitation, explaining that I was a lawyer representing two clients, not a rescue expert.

In 1998, my family moved from Alaska. That spring, I got a telephone call from a producer for NBC's "*Dateline*" television news magazine. *Dateline* was doing a story on Ed Hommer's attempt to climb Mt. McKinley. Had I sued Ed Hommer? Why? I did not want to talk to the NBC producer, but I was no fan of Hommer. I explained the airplane crash was his fault. How so? It was a clear day and there was no mechanical failure. The crash occurred because Ed Hommer approached Kahiltna Pass at too low an altitude. It was pilot error, plain and simple. Had I contacted the NTSB to get the official findings on the crash? No, I had not. Why not? There was no conclusion possible except that the crash was Hommer's fault. A few days later, the producer called to talk about the rescue lawsuit. He said NBC's research indicated this case was the only time the National Park Service had ever been held liable for a search and rescue. Did I know if this was true? No, I did not. When I called Mike about *Dateline*, I learned he had been contacted, and, surprisingly, had agreed to an on-camera interview.

Some months later the *Dateline* piece aired nationally. It focused on Hommer's attempt to climb Mt. McKinley on artificial feet. Ed failed to reach the summit but intended to try again. NBC reported the NTSB found Hommer to be at fault for the crash. The *Dateline* reporter, John

Larson, portrayed this finding as something it took Ed a long time to get over. Larson mentioned the Mt. McKinley rescue case and said it was the only negligent search and rescue lawsuit ever to succeed against the National Park Service.

John Larson interviewed Clouser on camera. He asked if Mike received $50,000 a year for life from the lawsuit. Mike answered "close enough" and said he would trade the money for his fingers and toes in an instant. It was clear Clouser harbored no warm feelings for Ed. When Larson asked what he thought of Hommer's attempt to climb Mt. McKinley, Mike said Ed was nuts. The television portrayal of Clouser, while fair, was unflattering. He came across as bitter and disillusioned. In a shot of Mike smoking, his hand shook visibly. When I called him immediately after the broadcast, he was not happy.

Watching *Dateline* led me to contrast Clouser's later life with Hommer's. Mike received a significant financial recovery; Ed had similar injuries and got nothing. Despite double amputations above the ankle, he became a commuter airline pilot and earned a good living. He and his wife, Sandy, Dan Hartmann's sister, had two more children. Television viewers probably concluded that Ed had a happier life than Mike, which brought home the limits of the American judicial system.

I could have represented Hommer in the Mt. McKinley rescue lawsuit. The fact that the crash was Ed's fault would not have prevented his recovery. In proving the liability case for Clouser, I also proved it for Hommer. Ed's damages would have been substantial, perhaps higher than Mike's, because Ed was married, a father, and a pilot. When both feet were amputated, few would have imagined he would later work as an airline pilot. Yet if Ed had asked me to represent him, which he did not, I would have refused. Hommer was the bad guy. He caused the airplane crash and he behaved poorly afterward.

About one year after the first *Dateline* segment aired, Hommer reached the summit of Mt. McKinley on his second attempt. NBC edited the original piece, added tape of Ed at the summit, and aired it again several times in 1999 and 2000. The long, unflattering interview with Clouser remained in the telecast. Hommer set his sights on climbing Mt. Everest but died in a May, 2002 climbing accident on Mt. Rainier.

In 2003, I considered a return to the practice of law. As I was moving into a high rise office in downtown Seattle, I came across the transcript of

Judge Kleinfeld's oral decision. As I read it after a decade's interval, the desire to write a book returned. Fortunately, I had saved the 11 boxes of case files and transcripts.

In the fall of 2003, I wrote to Mike about writing this book. That December was the first year I did not receive a Christmas card from him. I continued writing anyway. In 2004, I contacted him again. This time Mike's reaction was positive. (Tom Scanlon had always encouraged a book.)

In 2006, I drove to Whitefish, Montana to see Mike for the first time in more than a decade. I needed to tell him, in person, something I discovered reading the case files and to ask for a consent and waiver of the attorney client privilege. Before I could start, Mike interrupted and apologized for "flying off the handle" twelve years earlier. He said he had no problem with me writing a book and would wait to read it until it was published. Mike (and Tom) signed consents and waivers without reading this book. I remain grateful for their trust.

As the writing progressed, I began to develop sympathy for Ed Hommer. At some level, he must have known he caused the plane crash. He was closely involved in the death of Dan Hartmann, who died as Ed was holding him, and of Pat Scanlon. Surely the many warnings in the National SAR Manual that victims should be assumed to be in a state of shock and not capable of caring for themselves applied to Hommer at Kahiltna Pass, even if Clouser operated at heightened proficiency. After rescue, Ed watched his feet mummify. Dr. Mills testified a frostbite victim who experienced this "recovery" often required psychiatric help as a normal part of treatment. (Again, Mike was unusual.)

In the fall of 2006, I happened upon an episode of the Weather Channel's "*Storm Stories*" based on the Kahiltna Pass crash. Filmed after Hommer reached the summit of Mt. McKinley and before his 2002 death on Mt. Rainier, the television show was odd in many ways. The fifteen minute segment included on camera interviews with Ed Hommer saying things that were demonstrably false.

With the help of a coauthor, Hommer had written a book called "The Hill: A True Story of Tragedy, Recovery, and Redemption on North America's Highest Peak." It was published in hardcover in October, 2001. I had always avoided the book, but after seeing "*Storm Stories*," I decided to read it.

Hommer's version of events in the book is sad and disturbing. Immediately after the rescue, he gave a long interview to the Anchorage

Times (which ran on the front page on Christmas Day, 1981) and witness statements to Gerhard and the NTSB. The book's account of what happened contradicts not only the sworn testimony of witnesses at trial, but also Ed's recollection of events immediately after the rescue.

According to "The Hill," at the time of the crash, Ed had less than one year's experience in McKinley flying. The book starts with the crash. "We were moving along at an altitude of 12,000 feet, so we had a good 1500 foot clearance." (p. 4) The photos taken by Clouser on the sightseeing flight show the Hudson plane was far below the 10,300' summit of Kahiltna Pass, visible in the distance, as it began flying up Kahiltna Glacier. In the press interview, Hommer said he gave no warning of the impending crash. (Clouser testified to the same at trial.) The book's version? "'We're gonna hit!' I shouted at my passengers. 'We're gonna hit.'" (p. 6)

Hommer fictionalizes his conduct after the crash and reverses key events to cast himself as hero at the expense of Mike Clouser. In the press interview and statements, when Ed slowly regained consciousness after the crash, Mike was already working with Dan Hartmann, trying to get him into a sleeping bag. In the book, Ed goes to Dan first, then returns to the fuselage (where Mike "was still kind of out of it" (p. 34)), grabs a sleeping bag, and stumbles back to Dan, trying to open it. "But then, it was the most terrifying thing, a giant gust of wind came swirling . . . [and] ripped that bag out of my hand like it was a piece of notepaper." Ed writes that he then retrieved a second bag and "got Dan zipped into it." (p. 35) Clouser testified it took both of them to get Dan into the first sleeping bag and the second blew away as Hommer tried to get into it himself, after Hartmann's death.

Ed writes that on Tuesday evening, the night of the crash, he shined a flashlight at Doug Geeting's Super Cub (p. 54), instead of Clouser flashing signals at the C-130 flights. Hommer's account has Geeting seeing Ed's light, turning on the Super Cub's landing lights to indicate they had been spotted, and radioing the exact crash location on Tuesday night. (p. 57)

Hommer's narrative backtracks to events immediately after the crash and he acknowledges, "After Dan died, I just collapsed for a while." Then he rouses himself, goes to the fuselage, knocks out the rear bulkhead, manually flips the ELT switch to ON, and adjusts the antenna. (p. 86) Of the two sleeping bags left (Dan has died in one and Ed let another blow away), he writes: "[We] got Pat tucked into one of them. Mike took the other, and I satisfied myself with an extra down parka as we all settled in for the night." (p. 87) For the remainder of the book, Ed has Clouser in a sleeping bag and himself going without. Unlike his press interview, Ed does not put Mike outside the fuselage the first night, calling to Pat and Ed to keep them awake so they do not freeze to death. Instead, he puts all three men inside the fuselage, with Pat and Mike in sleeping bags. (p. 87)

Ed's descriptions of Wednesday's rescue efforts are wildly inaccurate. He has Jim Okonek flying "the Bell 206" [from Akland Helicopters] up Kahiltna Glacier on Wednesday afternoon. He has the Chinooks not departing Fairbanks until 10:30 a.m. and then has the Army's HART aboard one Chinook and NPS Rangers aboard the lead Chinook. (pp. 91-92) How close did the lead Chinook get? "I could see the crew chief standing in the forward right door. I could see his flight suit, his helmet, his gloves. He was waving down at me, and I was waving back." [Is this what Tara Neda referenced in her closing argument?] "It was like we could reach right out and touch the friggin' bird. . . ." (p. 92)

After Sandy divorced him a decade later, Hommer hatched the idea of climbing Mt. McKinley. His ex-wife's reaction was the same as Clouser's. "Sandy told me she thought it was ridiculous. Just dismissed it out of hand." (p. 222) On the unsuccessful first attempt to climb McKinley, Hommer planted a brass plaque in honor of Dan and Pat. He writes that this act changed him. "I felt strangely transformed by it. Completed. Validated. Renewed." He adds, "I had never blamed myself for the crash, but I'd constantly blamed myself for surviving." (p. 263)

Hommer's version of Pat Scanlon's death is the opposite of his press interview and witness statements and of Clouser's trial testimony. According to Hommer, after the plane slid down the mountain in Wednesday night's windstorm, Pat "was all pretzeled-up in what looked to be a really painful position." (p. 104) In Ed's version, Pat's legs are downhill (towards the tail) and his head is uphill. Ed then "snaked back through the main cabin to where I was almost straddling [Pat], and from there I managed to slither my legs back into the tail cone of the airplane." Ed has Mike, still in the front, "reach underneath Pat's shoulders from the top and get some sort of leverage going underneath his back. I reached under [Pat's] thighs and butt and we moved him, an inch or so at a time." Ed reverses Pat's body position so that Ed can only reach Pat's legs, while Mike works near Pat's head. Later, when "we had Pat settled in a more manageable spot," they wedged part of the rear bench seat under Pat's legs "to keep him as level as we could. . . ." (p. 104) During a break shortly after, Pat died.

Ed's false description of Pat's death is also contradicted by a long forgotten witness interview. While reviewing the 11 boxes of files, I came across my notes from my conversation with Gary Fye after he interviewed Hommer in Talkeetna in March, 1982. Ed told Fye that when the plane stopped sliding on Wednesday night, Ed was in the tail cone and was working with Pat's head and shoulders. Hommer told Fye he was holding Pat's head in his hands like a cantaloupe at the moment of Pat's death.

I drove to Whitefish, Montana in 2006 to tell Clouser in person about these notes. Mike was relieved to learn what Hommer told Fye in the interview; Mike told me he had always blamed himself for Pat's death. In June, 2008, I flew to Anchorage and told Tom what Hommer told Fye in the witness interview. Tom appreciated learning the truth.

I hope Mike Clouser and Tom Scanlon never read "The Hill." Hommer's fabrications support Judge Kleinfeld's observation that "many individuals would not have retained their sanity or their ability to function as human beings after living through this."

Tom Scanlon still lives in Anchorage and is happy with his family and his life. Tom told me his adopted son, Patrick, looked just like a young Pat Scanlon.

Mike Clouser has managed his money well. Mike does not have arthritis and gets around on his own. Life in Montana has agreed with him, though he considers a return to Indiana. Mike looks forward to the future.

Appendix I

For brevity, clarity, and reading pleasure, many shortcuts are taken with the trial transcript. The elaborate courtesies of trial are ignored and the words and expressions "thank you," "excuse me," "you may proceed," "sir" (except for a few witnesses, mostly military), and "Your Honor" are usually deleted. Unconscious verbal tics of lawyers, witnesses, and the judge, such as beginning a question with "Right" or "Okay" or a witness saying "you know" repeatedly, are deleted. Inconsequential stammering and incoherence are edited out unless the words of a witness, lawyer or the judge reflect uncertainty about a vital matter. Where a speaker makes a false start and then restarts and speaks clearly, the false start is removed entirely. Where an obvious error is made, the correct information is inserted in brackets. Testimony from witnesses, questions from lawyers, and rulings from the judge are shortened using ellipses. Deleted questions and answers are not reflected by ellipses. Objections are skipped entirely or abbreviated. The form of some questions, answers, and rulings is improved without use of brackets or identifying marks. Preservation of the integrity of the testimony is paramount. A fictitious example of the long and short version of testimony follows:

> Q. All right. Mr. Clouser, you took these top two photos as the aircraft was flying up Kahiltna Pass [sic, Glacier] as depicted in the last photo of the -
>
> A. Right.
>
> Q. Previous roll?
>
> A. Right.
>
> MS. NEDA: Objection, Your Honor. Counsel is leading the witness and this is irrelevant.

THE COURT: Overruled under Rule XYZ (a,b,c). You
    may proceed.

MR. GALBRAITH: Thank you, Your Honor.

Q. Okay. Do you know whether or not these pictures
    accurately reflect the weather that day?

A. Ah, you mean — yes, sir. To the best of my
    knowledge, they do.

This testimony changes to:

Q. You took these top two photos as the aircraft was
    flying up Kahiltna [Glacier] as depicted in the
    last photo of the previous roll?

A. Right.

Q. Do these pictures accurately reflect the weather
    that day?

A. Yes. To the best of my knowledge, they do.

Where transcript editing might color the reader's perception of a
witness's truthfulness on a key matter, the original version is used.

The events of the plane crash and rescue took place between Tuesday,
December 15, and Saturday, December 19, 1981. During trial, days are
identified by day of week (Wednesday morning), not by date (the morning
of December 16th). Exhibit numbers are often deleted and a description of
the exhibit's content is substituted.

References to equipment are standardized (Army CH-47 helicopter
becomes Chinook, Air Force C-130 Hercules aircraft becomes C-130).
Use of military and other acronyms at trial was unavoidable and these are
arbitrarily shortened for ease of reading. The location of important military
units and civilian rescue groups is shown on the front illustration.

Appendix II

Ranger Bob Gerhard interviewed Ed Hommer in Providence Hospital on December 23, 1981. According to the Ranger's handwritten and typed notes, when Ed came to on Tuesday afternoon, Dan Hartmann was outside by the tail and Mike Clouser was helping him into a sleeping bag. Ed slipped in and out of consciousness six to eight times. Dan died two to three hours after the crash. The first night Pat and Ed slept in the aircraft and Clouser stayed outside. Of Scanlon, Hommer said: "Pat injured internally. Too beat up to move. Multiple fractures—compound. Raspy breathing. Lived through first night." Gerhard's notes continued: "Next morning, heard Doug [Geeting] with [Cessna] 185. Mike signaled with flashlight. . . . Mike and Ed outside plane when Chinooks came over." Ed described the windstorm Wednesday night and Thursday morning. "Mike and Ed tried to get [Pat] out of tail section but he died then." Gerhard spent little time with Mike. "I only talked to Clouser for about five minutes to get his name and date of birth."

John Osgood of the National Transportation Safety Board (NTSB) interviewed Hommer on December 28. Hommer described Pat Scanlon's condition after the crash:

> I went back in the aircraft shortly after [Dan died] and Mike had secured Pat as best he could. Pat was lying in the aircraft with his head facing toward the tail section of the airplane. The airplane was . . . tilted 10 to 15 degrees downhill. . . . We didn't attempt to move Pat or change his position. We would have liked to [move him] so that his head was uphill but according to Mike he appeared to have . . . at least two compound fractures on his legs. . . . [Pat] was in a lot of pain. Because of his discomfort we suspected that he might have had some internal injuries. We stabilized him the best we could in a sleeping bag and engine cover. It was dark by this time. I crawled back in the aircraft and spent the night in there holed up in the aft section of the cabin. Mike spent the night outside walking around and

just calling our names every hour or so to make sure that we didn't get
too restful and freeze to death in our sleep. . . .

Although not requested to by the NTSB interviewer, Hommer
described the windstorm and Pat's death:

[Wednesday] night the three of us were in the aircraft. There were
no windows or anything left in it at all. . . . [W]e started to get some
really high winds that night with gusts up to sixty, maybe in excess
of sixty miles per hour. One particular gust caught the aircraft and
[rolled] it on its belly and we slid approximately fifty feet down the
slope. We all thought that it was over with at this point. We thought we
were going for the long ride down the hill. . . . [W]hen we stopped, the
aircraft was [resting] at about a thirty-five degree angle downhill, and
Pat was still facing head down in the aircraft but now he was much
farther back into the aft fuselage section. . . . This really increased his
pain and discomfort.

Mike and I . . . worked on him for over an hour. I was working on
his shoulders. I was way back in the aft fuselage . . . tail cone section
pushing up on Pat and Mike was grabbing [Pat] by the pants, trying
to pull him back up. I was trying to stuff the sleeping bag under his
head to keep his head up. . . . [We told him] he had to help us help
him. . . . He said I'll try. We gained maybe an inch or two and then
we had to rest and we'd try again. We'd gain an inch or two [per] try,
then rest, and it was during this rest that Pat died. . . .

Made in the USA
San Bernardino, CA
07 August 2018